PEPYS ON THE RESTORATION STAGE

Mens cujusque is est Quisque.

SAM: PEPYS CAR: ET IAC: ANGL: REGIB:
A SECRETIS ADMIRALIÆ.

R.W. sculp

Pepys on the Restoration Stage

By

HELEN McAFEE

Benjamin Blom
New York

792.0942
P 39 p
58395
July 1967

First published 1916 by Yale University Press.
Published by Benjamin Blom, Inc., New York 52.
L. C. Catalog Card No.: 63-23195

Printed in U.S.A. by
NOBLE OFFSET PRINTERS, INC.
NEW YORK 3, N. Y.

FOREWORD

One would scarcely have the temerity to add to
the already copious literature inspired by the immor-
tal *Diary of Samuel Pepys* were it not that a sepa-
rate presentation of the highly valuable and interesting passages relating to the Restoration stage
would seem to serve a useful purpose. These passages, it is true, have been widely cited by literary
historians from Genest down, and many of them
have been commented upon by the several editors
and critics of the *Diary*. Different writers have,
however, used different, and in many cases incomplete editions—Genest, for example, basing his conclusions on that of Lord Braybrooke, first published
in 1825. Moreover, since the appearance of the last
and fullest edition by Henry B. Wheatley, 1893-
1899, works elucidating many of Pepys's statements
have been brought out. Now, therefore, that we have
a version of the *Diary* in which we may be sure no
detail of importance has been omitted, the time would
seem to be ripe for a complete selection of all passages relating to the theatre and the drama in the
decade Pepys covers—one of the most decisive in the
history of the English stage—and for a re-annotation
of this material in the light of recent researches as
well as seventeenth-century sources. Since the latter
are more or less difficult of access, the plan has been

to include in the notes the accounts of such writers
as Downes, Langbaine, and John Evelyn, where they
parallel Pepys. With these ends in view, and in the
interest of both the student reader and the lover of
the stage, this volume is presented.

Originally undertaken in partial fulfillment of the
requirements for the degree of Master of Arts at
Smith College, the work has been somewhat enlarged in size and in scope for purposes of publication. The author desires to acknowledge here indebt-
edness to Professor George Henry Nettleton of
Yale University and others who have by their criticism and interest generously assisted in its prepara-
tion. It is also a pleasure to thank Mr. Robert Gould
Shaw for his courtesy in permitting the reproduction of a quaint print of a Restoration actor from the
invaluable Theatre Collection in the Harvard University Library.

HELEN MCAFEE.

TABLE OF CONTENTS

LIST OF ILLUSTRATIONS

INTRODUCTION

I

THE CRITICS AND PEPYS'S MATERIAL ON THE STAGE

I

THE CRITICS AND PEPYS'S MATERIAL ON THE STAGE

In his Preface to the first edition of the *Memoirs of Samuel Pepys, Esq.* (1825), Lord Braybrooke endeavored to forestall objections to the number of theatrical "notices" which the work contained. For including so many of them, he offered the twofold excuse that little was previously known "from authentic sources of the History of the Stage about the period of the Restoration," and that many of the incidents recorded by Pepys were "not to be met with elsewhere." He therefore thought himself justified, he says, "in retaining them, at the risk of fatiguing those readers who have no taste for the concerns of the Drama." In view of its subsequent reception, Lord Braybrooke's solicitude for the theatrical intelligence in the *Diary* was unnecessary. Few readers have appeared to find Pepys's accounts of his visits to the playhouse fatiguing. And from the very beginning, critics delighted to honor the information which the Diarist gives us about the Restoration stage. Unlike so many famous works, Pepys's journal, after being hidden away for a century and a half, acceded immediately on its appearance to a place in the minds and affections of the reading public. And the entries relating to the stage were welcomed with especial warmth.

Ample evidence of this may be found in the reviews of the Braybrooke edition of the *Memoirs,* which continued to appear in the literary magazines[1] all through the latter part of 1825 and the early part of 1826. With few exceptions, contemporary reviewers were quick to acknowledge both the value and the interest of the references to the stage. Nearly a century has elapsed since these critics wrote; but in the main their verdicts have stood the test of time. In the long line of commentators who have succeeded them, are many distinguished names—Sir Walter Scott, Francis Jeffrey, Robert Louis Stevenson, William Archer, R. W. Lowe, Henry B. Wheatley, and Sir Sidney Lee,[2] to mention only a few. Their impressions, as well as the criticisms of certain anonymous writers, are well worth reviewing not only for their intrinsic interest but also for the light they throw on the attitude taken from time to time towards Pepys's material on the stage. Hence, by way of introduction to the present work, a brief account of the more significant of these will be presented.

The unfavorable comments, because of their extreme rarity, should perhaps be considered first. Such comments, of sufficient bulk and import to warrant notice, appeared in reviews of the *Memoirs* in

[1] A list of British periodicals in which the more important reviews discussing this aspect of the *Memoirs* appeared, will be found on pp. 327-328 of the *Bibliography.*

[2] See under these names in the *Bibliography* for titles.

three periodicals of the year 1825. All were obviously written by men who had "no taste for the concerns of the Drama" in the concrete form in which Pepys recorded them. Of these three criticisms the most impatient is that of an anonymous contributor to the July issue of *The Eclectic Review* published when the *Diary* had not yet been out a month. He dismisses thus curtly Pepys's "insipid and wearisome notices relating to the theatrical performances" in order to devote the remaining thirteen pages of his essay to other sides of the *Memoirs* that, frankly, engage him more. In the same vein writes another anonymous author of a lengthy notice, which has first place in the contents of *The Monthly Repository of Theology and General Literature* for August, 1825. "Few," he confidently asserts, "besides those that have studied the history of the drama will take any interest in his [Pepys's] descriptions of the numberless performances that he witnessed." As might be expected from the somewhat special nature of his medium, this reviewer finds the Diarist's accounts of sermons more interesting than his records of plays.

Of a different order, though like these notices in unfavorable tone, is Francis Jeffrey's trenchant criticism which appeared, also in 1825, in the November number of *The Edinburgh Review*. After a relentlessly severe examination of Pepys's character—his "ignoble taste for dress," his "want of manliness," his "penuriousness," and his many other frailties—the critic proceeds to the dramatic comment in the *Diary*; and one cannot help feeling that Lord Jeffrey's disapproval of the man unduly colored his view of the informal chronicler of the early Restoration stage. His concern for the moral throughout the theatrical material seems invariably to encroach upon his estimate of the value of the evidence. Of his general method the handling of the following passage is typical. In an entry of October 5, 1667, Pepys had noted in connection with a certain performance that it was "pretty" to see how Nell Gwyn "cursed for having so few people in the pit." "Now, whether it was *strange* or not," remarks Jeffrey, "it was certainly very wrong in Nell to curse so unmercifully, even at a thin house"; and he chastises Pepys roundly for seeming to approve. Hence the spirit of the whole criticism must be taken into account in approaching its final conclusions. "There is," declares Jeffrey at the end of the essay, "no *literary* intelligence of any value to be gained from this work. Play collectors will probably find the names of many lost pieces—but of our classical authors there are no notices worth naming."

Over against Lord Jeffrey's arraignment, it is instructive to set Sir Walter Scott's appreciation in *The Quarterly Review* for March, 1826, in an article on *Pepys's Memoirs,* about which he wrote to Lockhart, "The subject is like a good sirloin, which requires only to be basted with its own drippings." Scott is in agreement with the critic of the *Edinburgh* on one important point, the lack of literary taste displayed by Pepys in his comments on Shakespeare. In most other matters, the two reviewers differ—in nothing more widely than in general temper. Scott cannot mention the name of Nell Gwyn without be-

traying his greater humanity. "Pepys," writes the
novelist, "in his love of wit and admiration of beauty
finds room to love and admire Nell Gwynn, whose
name still carries an odd fascination with it after so
many generations." The *Diary* Scott regards as rich
"in every species of information concerning the
author's century." In short, he believes that it contains annotations "for a new edition of the Roscius
Anglicanus,"[3] and he concludes that "if the curious
affect dramatic antiquities, no book published in our
time has thrown so much light upon plays, playwrights, and playactors." Thus highly does the past
master of the art of the novel rate the past master of
the unpremeditated art of the diary.

But before Scott's estimate appeared, anonymous
reviewers had already emphasized over and over again
in the current periodicals the importance of Pepys's
picture of the Restoration stage. Perhaps the most
interesting of the favorable comments are those in
The Gentleman's Magazine (September and October, 1825), *The New Monthly Magazine and Literary Journal* (Part II, 1825), and *The London
Literary Gazette* (June 18-August 13, 1825). Although the reviewer for *The Gentleman's Magazine*
does not wax enthusiastic over the *Diary* as a whole,
he readily grants that Pepys "has thrown light on
the dramatic history of his age." *The New Monthly
Magazine* is more outspoken in its praise. "Those
who are well read in the dramatic works of Shakespeare, Ben Jonson, Dryden, Killigrew, Sedley,

[3] *Roscius Anglicanus, or An Historical Review of the Stage
. . . from 1660 to 1706.* [By John Downes.] 1708.

Beaumont and Fletcher, &c.," writes its critic, "will receive great pleasure from the frequent notices of the reception their works met with from the polite audiences of King Charles's day." He then proceeds to remark that the names of the famous players of the period occur in the *Diary* "as frequently as those of the heads of the treasury and exchequer, and this passion of our author has perhaps thrown more light upon the history of the stage, than is to be obtained even in Cibber's Apology, or any other contemporary work on the subject."

No writer of that day, however, made more of the *Diary,* or, indeed, of the theatrical material it contains, than the anonymous author of the nine extended notices which appeared between June 18 and August 13, 1825, in "the most influential of the purely literary weeklies"—*The London Literary Gazette,* edited by William Jerdan. In the second of these notices, the reviewer prefaces a long series of quotations dealing with the stage, with the following prophecy: "Mr. Pepys was a great playgoer, and his remarks on the first nights of plays, which now constitute our ancient drama, will be read with much interest; they also incidentally serve happily to illustrate the manners of the times." That the readers of this weekly took an even livelier interest in the material in question than the reviewer anticipated, may be inferred from the frequency with which he recurs to this theme in succeeding notices. In the *Gazette* of July 2 he is ready to "resume upon the generally pleasing topic of the drama and stage" with another copious selection of quotations. Again, in the next issue, he thinks it

worth while "to follow our last week's discourse, and
set out with the drama." Indeed, not until the eighth
installment, does he at length "beg leave to resume
and wind up the notices connected with the Drama
and state of dramatic representations in the time of
Pepys." In so doing, he manages to quote about
forty more passages, which added to the number of
those previously cited, bring the sum total of excerpts
touching the stage to over a hundred. As they are
confessedly heaped up in proportion to popular relish
for them, there is here eloquent testimony to the
appreciation they received from the readers of 1825.
As for the reviewer, it appears that he was con-
sciously attempting to do in *The London Literary
Gazette,* in an informal way, what the author of this
work has attempted to do formally in the present volume. "With this we close our dramatic extracts,"
he comments after his final group, "which being put
together, make in our opinion, a very valuable addition to the history of the stage."

Thus exploited, the dramatic and theatrical materials contained in the *Diary* pass out of the hands of
the reviewer of new books into the hands of the literary historian and biographer, whose permanent pos-
session they have long since become. Among the literary chroniclers, John Genest was the first to make
use of them, on a large scale, in that landmark in
the history of our drama, *Some Account of the English Stage,* published in 1832. For this reason, rather
than because of what is added to the discussion, it
may be of interest to recall his terse remarks: "The
theatrical intelligence contained in two large 4to.

Vols. is not very great in quantity, but it is highly valuable, on account of dates—and because Pepys mentions the revival of several old plays not noticed by Downes or Langbaine as having been revived."[4] From Genest to *The Cambridge History of English Literature,* which asserts that "the Diary contains a mine of information respecting the theatres," comment on the subject is so frequent and so widely scattered as to make further quotation from the histories and biographies impracticable. Suffice it to say that from 1825 down, no important work bearing upon the stage of this period has failed to testify to the value of Pepys's journal as documentary evidence. It "remains," says Sir A. W. Ward, "of course the standard authority as to the history of the Restoration stage." But even more striking than such acknowledgments is the silent tribute that has been paid to it by Continental as well as by English and American writers in innumerable citations from its pages.

Special mention, however, may well be made of certain studies, impetus to which has in part been given by the fuller editions of the *Diary* by Rev. Mynors Bright (1875-1879) and Mr. Henry B. Wheatley (1893-1899). It was the Bright edition that called forth Robert Louis Stevenson's characteristic paper on *Samuel Pepys,* now included in *Familiar Studies of Men and Books.* Stevenson did not hesitate to affirm that Pepys both "warmly loved and understood" the stage, or to defend the Diarist in his

[4] *Some Account of the English Stage* . . . , Bath, 1882, I, 39.

fine, spirited way against some of the aspersions that
have been cast upon Pepys's attitude towards Shakespeare.   In further discussion of the Diarist's entries
relating to this topic, has appeared still more recently
Sir Sidney Lee's notable study of *Pepys and Shakespeare.*[5]

But to Henry B. Wheatley belongs the honor in
our day of having added most to our knowledge and
potential appreciation of the parts of Pepys's *Diary*
dealing with the stage.   The results of his scholarly
researches are incorporated not only in the excellent
notes to his edition, but also in a chapter on the theatre
in *Samuel Pepys and the World He Lived In* (1880)
and in the sections in his *Pepysiana* (1899) on *Actors
and Actresses* and *The Stage*.   Mr. Wheatley's significant conclusions are too numerous and too detailed
to admit of quotation here.   They will, however, frequently be cited in the notes on the material from
Pepys contained in this book, which follows the text
of the admirable and now, at last, practically complete version of the *Diary* that we owe to its latest
editor.

The two following introductory chapters will take
up more specifically the chief facts in Pepys's account
of the drama and the theatre of his day.

[5] Included in *Shakespeare and the Modern Stage, with other
Essays,* New York, 1906.

II

PEPYS AS A DRAMATIC HISTORIAN

II

PEPYS AS A DRAMATIC HISTORIAN

If, as has been said, Pepys's *Diary* is "a mine of information respecting the history of the stage," no one can complain that it has been indifferently worked. Ever since its first appearance in the incomplete edition of 1825, specialists in Elizabethan plays and in Restoration plays, students of the theatre—of its music and its manners, of the art of staging and the art of acting—have ransacked its pages, each for his particular purpose. As a result, the Diarist's name is today inseparably linked with the names of the actors, the managers, and the dramatists of his time. His casual comments have become a part of the *traditio* of the English stage.

To be specific, what Pepys has given us is a body of closely dated, firsthand evidence as to the history of the theatre in the first decade of Charles the Second's reign. Its value is enhanced by the critical importance of the time it covers. For two reasons the early years of the Restoration period are of especial interest to the student of the stage: first, because with the reopening of the playhouses after the Puritan interregnum, during which they had remained officially closed, the drama and theatre entered upon a new life; and, secondly, because during the decade of 1660-1670, as so seldom has happened, the two arts developed side by side. Fortunately for us, our informal historian was interested in both aspects of the contemporary stage, in the production of plays as well as in the plays themselves. Thus we find in his journal accounts not only of the rise of rhymed heroic tragedy and the new "society comedy," but also of the innovations in the employment of actresses and movable scenery. He contributes alike to our knowledge of the continued popularity of pre-Restoration plays, the contemporary attitude towards Shakespeare, the minor as well as the major dramatists of the period, the vogue of French and Spanish plays in translation; and to our information about the reopening of the theatres, the personalities of the well-known people in the theatrical world—many of whom he knew intimately—and the manners and customs of the Restoration playhouses. Especially important are his accounts of the years from 1660 to 1663, of which there is elsewhere scant reliable record.

Yet certain objections have been raised from time to time to Pepys as a dramatic historian. There is, first of all, the question, Is he accurate? It cannot, of course, be shown that he invariably is. Besides, it would be too much to expect from the *Diary* scrupulous exactness in all things, for in this, no less than in other matters, standards have changed since Charles the Second's reign. Occasionally, there is a disconcerting divergence between the account of an event recorded by Pepys and that recorded by some other supposedly good authority. Thus, in referring to the opening of the Duke of York's playhouse in Lincoln's Inn Fields as having taken place late in June,

1661, the Diarist conflicts seriously with John Downes, who states that it occurred in the spring of 1662—and who had reason to know since he was prompter at this theatre. Again, Pepys twice refers to May 7, 1663, as the date of the first performance at the new King's theatre in Drury Lane, whereas according to this same Downes and a playbill—which R. W. Lowe terms "a not very astute forgery"—this performance took place on April 8. In both these cases, it looks as if either Pepys or Downes must have been misinformed, though facts may yet be brought to light which will reconcile the conflicting statements. Moreover, as rumor did not travel rapidly in an age when there were no daily newspapers, it would be strange if Pepys's information were not at times stale. We know this to be the case, for instance, with his report of Abraham Cowley's death, which he first enters under August 10, 1667, when, as a matter of fact, the poet had been dead thirteen days.

But in how many instances the Diarist's dates are actually wrong, the investigator may well-nigh despair of determining; the difficulty is that nearly all the clues, in the external evidence at least, lead in a circle and so eventually back to Pepys. This is the case with many of the statements about the early Restoration performances made by Genest. Downes and Langbaine cover the same period, it is true, but their material is rarely closely dated. Some slight basis for comparison is, however, afforded by the *Diary* of John Evelyn and a list found among the papers of Sir Henry Herbert—then Master of the Revels—of plays acted by Killigrew's company. In

several instances statements in them corroborate
Pepys, and in no case do they definitely conflict with
him. Pepys saw five performances at the King's
theatre which are also mentioned under the same
dates in the list just referred to, and records two performances of plays which are also recorded by Evelyn. It is interesting to find both the diarists giving
accounts of the presentations of Tuke's *The Adventures of Five Hours,* on January 8, 1663, and of
Dryden's *An Evening's Love, or The Mock Astrologer,* on June 19, 1668; and it is instructive to compare their respective comments. Few as they are,
these corroborations cannot but confirm the student in
the tendency to accept the dates of Pepys's journal,
in the main, without question.

Another charge that has been brought against the
Diarist as a dramatic historian is that he does not
always give names and titles correctly—even allow-
ing for the laxity of the age in matters of spelling.
There is a reference, for example, on September 14,
1667, to a play which he calls *The Northern Castle.*
No such play is known, and it seems probable that
the title as Pepys gives it may have been a slip for
The Northern Lass, a comedy by Richard Brome.
Possibly, too, in certain instances, the Diarist ascribes
plays to the wrong authors. He mentions on September 15, 1668, a play translated "out of French by
Dryden called 'The Ladys à la Mode,' "—which may
have been a mistake for Richard Flecknoe's *Damoi-
selles à la Mode;* and in his entry under December 10,
1663, he refers to Shakespeare's *Henry VIII*—before he has seen it, to be sure—as Sir William

D'Avenant's "story of Henry the Eighth with all his wives." But anyone who examines into the matter, will soon discover that inaccuracies such as these are, so far as can be judged, the exception.

The unique value of Pepys's comment on the Restoration stage lies, as has been said, as much in the kind as in the mere bulk of material he presents. His was indeed a many-sided interest. In intellectual and moral tolerance, where the theatre is concerned, he stands in striking contrast to his fellow-diarist Evelyn, who speaks of "very seldom going to the publiq theaters for many reasons," his chief complaint being against the "foule and undecent women now (and never till now) permitted to appear and act." Evelyn flattered himself on one occasion that he was "far from Puritanisme"; but he was not so far from it that moral scruples did not stand between him and a whole-hearted appreciation of what the contemporary theatre had to offer. As for Pepys, he could enjoy without let or hindrance everything about it, from Betterton's Hamlet to the orange-girls. "It is in virtue of his own desires and curiosities," says Stevenson, "that any man . . . is charmed by the look of things and people." Thus it was with Pepys at the playhouse. His curiosity was unbounded here as elsewhere. He liked to read plays on his trips to and from Deptford on Admiralty business as well as to see them at the theatre. Hence everything and everybody on the stage appealed to him. His accounts of performances are, of course, for this reason peculiarly satisfactory; if there was a single novel or exceptional fact about the play, the players, the scenery, the music, the dancing, the audience, or the theatre itself, we feel certain that he has noted it. Whatever may be said of Pepys's critical acumen, remarks a recent writer, "no one has ever impeached his powers of observation."

The Diarist was not, to be sure, equally competent to judge in all these matters. It has been frequently charged that his criticisms of the plays are not so satisfactory as his criticisms of the acting, which seems often to have mattered to him more. In a certain instance, Pepys realized this himself. When Young, "but a bad actor at best," took Thomas Betterton's famous part in one of Pepys's favorite plays, *Macbeth,* the Diarist exclaims: "Lord! what a prejudice it wrought in me against the whole play!" But this does not mean that he was without literary taste or that he invariably judged a piece solely on its acting qualities. He could thoroughly appreciate a play like Jonson's *Catiline,* which he insisted had "much good sense and words to read," even though it appeared "the worst upon the stage, I mean, the least diverting, that ever I saw any." At any rate, he had his own theories of what was justifiable in tragedy, and of what was proper material for comedy, distinguishing between true "wit" and mere "fooling" or, as he calls it, "mirth fit for clowns." From his criticism of Etherege's *She Would if She Could,* it is evident that "witty" and "roguish" dialogue did not wholly blind him to deficiencies of plot; while in the case of Lord Orrery, whom he admired as a dramatist in many ways, he recognized the limitations which made one of his plays of "just the very same design, and words, and sense, and plot" as every other.

Pepys's literary judgment has been questioned mainly on the ground of his attitude towards Shakespeare, which is betrayed in certain "delicious bits of criticism," as Professor Lounsbury has called them, "whose impudent inappreciativeness later critics have occasionally equalled, but whose charm they have never been able even remotely to rival." In this connection, his wholesale condemnation of *A Midsummer-Night's Dream* as "the most insipid ridiculous play that ever I saw in my life," and his disparaging comparison of *Othello* with Tuke's *The Adventures of Five Hours* have usually been cited. Now, although, as Stevenson says, the Diarist's failure to appreciate these and other plays of Shakespeare on the stage is not "without either parallel or excuse," there is no need to minimize its import. Yet in passing judgment, two modifying circumstances must at the same time be borne in mind—on the one hand, the nature of the record Pepys kept, which attempted to do no more than jot down among a thousand other matters first impressions of plays, and, on the other hand, the nature of the Shakespearean productions he saw. Some of these were redeemed, we know, by the acting of the Bettertons, but others must have been hopelessly inadequate. Besides, it should not be forgotten in any final appraisal that Pepys never tired of seeing *Hamlet*—even trying at one time to get "To bee or not to bee" "without book"; that he held *Henry IV* "a good play"; and that he was "mightily pleased" with *Henry VIII*. In short, although it may be true that, as Sir Sidney Lee says, he "lived and died in complacent unconsciousness of Shakespeare's supreme excellence," there is little in his references to signify that Pepys wholly shared what has sometimes been assumed to be the conventional Restoration attitude towards Shakespeare, based upon such views as that expressed by Evelyn after seeing *Hamlet:* "Now the old plays began to disgust this refined age since his Majestie's being so long abroad."

As a dramatic historian, it should also be mentioned that Pepys was in two respects free from the prejudices of his time—or possibly, one should say, of the Court circle of his time. There is, first of all, his standpoint on the morality of the stage. This question, like the question of his feeling for Shakespeare, cannot fairly be considered apart from the general theory and practice of the *Diary* as a whole. It must be remembered that Pepys never aims at anything like such completeness or finality in his picture of a play on the stage as we are accustomed to expect from the modern dramatic reviewer. Neither is he writing for the edification of the public. He is only noting for his own private benefit the particular aspects of the production that for one reason or another stood out to him as of especial interest. Hence, quite naturally, we do not find the Diarist putting every play he sees, or indeed every play which might well be examined on this ground, to a rigid moral test. On the other hand, from the comments that Pepys makes from time to time on the moral issue, it would seem hardly justifiable to conclude, as does a recent writer, that "Pepys criticises the plays he so loved to frequent from almost every other point of view than the moral," or yet to assert that he is never "distressfully disturbed by the improprieties afterward discovered by Collier and his successors in the theatre."[1]   For one thing, he looked with disapproval upon the gross immorality of Thomas Killigrew's *The Parson's Wedding*.   Even though all the world commended Dryden's *Mock Astrologer,* he did "not like it, it being very smutty."   He came out positively in favor of Brome's *Jovial Crew* as "merry and the most innocent play that ever I saw"; while of Sir Samuel Tuke's *Adventures of Five Hours* he enthusiastically writes: "The play in one word, is the best . . . that ever I saw, or think ever shall, and all possible, not only to be done in the time, but in most other respects very admittable, and without one word of ribaldry." This testimony of Pepys, along with that of Evelyn, would seem to indicate that while the Court of the Merry Monarch countenanced gross immorality on the stage, and even fathered it—as Dryden later charged—the "City" was never wholly reconciled to it.

Again, Pepys's opinion differed from that which the Restoration Court is generally held to have imposed upon the contemporary stage, on the merits of the rhymed couplet for heroic plays.   In a reference to *The Indian Queen,* by Dryden and Sir Robert Howard, the Diarist appears emphatically

---

[1] Cf. John Palmer, *The Comedy of Manners,* 1913, pp. 5-6.

against its use. "The play good," he writes, "but spoiled with the ryme, which breaks the sense."

One habit of Pepys as a playgoer works to the especial good fortune of the modern student. This is his practice of going to see the same play several times over, at intervals varying from two or three days to two or three years. And since he is more concerned with fidelity to the immediate fact than with consistency to former statements, we are thus enabled to see one play from several different angles. Often he did not come to any definite conclusion about it until the second or third performance, meantime testing his preconceived prejudices, if he had any, noting the implication of new impressions, and, in general, keeping an open mind. This is well illustrated in his various accounts of a contemporary tragedy by Thomas Porter called *The Villain*. The first time Pepys saw it, he was "never less pleased with a play in my life"; the second time, he was "better pleased with the play than I was at first, understanding the design better than I did"; and the third time he records, "The more I see it, the more I am offended at my first undervaluing the play, it being very good and pleasant, and yet a true and allowable tragedy." With Dryden's popular comedy, *Sir Martin Mar-all,* his experience was just the reverse. He first saw it on August 16, 1667, the day after its *première,* and "never laughed so in all my life"; then on August 19 and 20, still finding it "a very ingenious play, and full of variety." Six weeks later he witnesses another performance "with great delight, though I have seen it so often"; then once more before the year is out, and three times in 1668. His enjoyment of it never lessens; the last time he mentions it, he writes: "Though I have seen it, I think, ten times, yet the pleasure I have is yet as great as ever." New details, if not fresh impressions, were generally gathered with each performance, and to his habit of seeing plays repeated, Pepys's record owes much of its value. Indeed, we are in so far indebted to the Diarist for this persistence in attending the theatre that we must even forgive him the absurd casuistry with which he manipulates his frequent vows to stay away.

In short, it cannot be said that Pepys was either a professed literary critic or a typical Restoration playgoer. Beyond the average man, he was open-minded and sincere in his appreciation of various types of plays, and many-sided and indefatigable in his interest in the theatre. Yet while he was too individual to subscribe in every matter to the stage conventions of the period, his power of observing closely others as well as himself, enabled him to body forth with peculiar realism the attitude of his age.

The intrinsic worth and unique interest of the evidence, as a whole, that Pepys has preserved for us can be grasped only by an examination of its full content. But perhaps the significance of a few of the comments on certain important groups of plays should be pointed out in advance.

At first glance, the entries in the *Diary* for the dramas of the pre-Restoration period point to the overwhelming popularity, during the decade succeeding the King's return, of the romances of Beau-

mont and Fletcher, over twenty-five of which Pepys
saw at one time or another. A reading of his criticisms in full will show, however, that he, at least, did
not admire them as he did the plays of Jonson. *The
Maid's Tragedy* he found on first hearing "too sad
and melancholy," though later he thought it "a good
play"; and *Philaster* was "far short of my expectations." But when it came to Jonson, his praise was
not thus tempered. *The Alchemist* he held to be "a
most incomparable play"; he declared that *The Silent
Woman* had "more wit in it than goes to ten new
plays"; *Volpone* was "the best I think I ever saw."
For Shirley, more of whose plays (nine in all) are
referred to as being produced than any other dramatist of his period excepting Beaumont and Fletcher
and Shakespeare, Pepys cared less, admiring only
The Traitor, as "a very good Tragedy." Along with
this should be mentioned Massinger's *The Bondman,*
which from the *Diary* would seem to have been among
the most successful plays of the time, perhaps because
it provided Betterton with one of his best parts. "To
the Opera," writes Pepys after a certain performance, "where we saw 'The Bondman,' which of old we
both did so doat on, and do still"; and again, "There is
nothing more taking in the world with me than that
play." Of the twelve plays of Shakespeare which
Pepys saw staged, at least eight seem to have been
acted substantially unaltered, four being given in
contemporary versions. From the *Diary* we learn
that the general popularity of *Hamlet, Henry VIII,*
and *Othello,* which were among the unaltered plays,
should be set over against the success of D'Avenant's

Macbeth and Dryden and D'Avenant's *The Tempest* in any consideration of the Restoration view of Shakespeare.

Pepys also supplies us with significant evidence as to the brief day of rhymed heroic drama. He applauds at length the success of the Earl of Orrery's plays—said to have been written at the instigation of Royalty—*The Black Prince, Henry the Fifth,* and *Mustapha,* this last, "a most admirable poem, and bravely acted." At the same time he dissents from the general opinion about other plays of this type. Besides feeling that *The Indian Queen* was "spoiled with the ryme," he calls the sequel, Dryden's *The Indian Emperor,* "a good play, but not so good as people cry it up." Moreover, on April 16, 1669, he notes a bit of gossip, which in its tone would seem to presage the coming of Buckingham's *Rehearsal* and the beginning of the end of heroic drama: "I did meet with Shadwell, the poet, who, to my great wonder, do tell me that my Lord of [Orrery] did write this play [*Guzman*], trying what he could do in comedy, since his heroique plays could do no more wonders." To certain of the dramatists, that is, it was already clear that the tide had turned.

With contemporary comedy, Pepys was perhaps more in sympathy. He describes among the earliest comic successes Cowley's satirical *Cutter of Coleman Street,* under December 16, 1661, and D'Avenant's *The Wits,* under August 15, 1661. Dryden's *Sir Martin Mar-all, or The Feign'd Innocence* (1667), he esteems "the most entire piece of mirth, a complete farce from one end to the other, that certainly ever

was writ"; he records that *Secret Love, or The
Maiden Queen* is "mightily commended for the regularity of it, and the strain and wit," though its success
was doubtless due in a measure to the "comical part"
of Florimel, done by Nell Gwyn. He has a long
notice of Etherege's first play, *The Comical Revenge,
or Love in a Tub,* January 4, 1665, which he calls
"very merry"; and of his second, *She Would if She
Could,* February 6, 1668, from the first performance
of which "there was 1,000 people put back that could
not have room in the pit," and about which the audience thought, so Pepys says, "there was something
very roguish and witty." It is especially interesting
to see from these entries in regard to Etherege the
attitude of his contemporaries towards this first
important writer of Restoration "society comedy."

If it is true that we do not understand a period
until we know its minor in addition to its major writers, we must acknowledge a still further debt to
Pepys's journal; for it has much to say of the lesser
contemporary dramatists. The fact is that the work
of mediocre men bulks as large in the *Diary* as it
usually does in the estimation of the contemporary
public. The plays mentioned by Pepys of the three
Howards—Edward, James, and Sir Robert—of the
Duke of Newcastle, Sir Charles Sedley, Thomas
Killigrew, John Lacy—the actor,—Thomas Porter,
Richard Rhodes, Sir Robert Stapylton, and Thomas
Shadwell—all are cases in point.

The most notable seem to have owed their success largely to contemporary allusions. Such was
Edward Howard's *The Change of Crowns* (1667),

in which John Lacy acted the part of the country gentleman who had the effrontery to attack "the Court with all the imaginable wit and plainness about selling places, and doing every thing for money." The King, who attended its first performance, was, we are told, so incensed at thus being abused to his face that he ordered the theatre closed and Lacy imprisoned. Finally, another actor got permission to reopen the theatre on condition that this play should not be repeated. Pepys pronounced *The Change of Crowns* "bitter indeed, but very true and witty." Curiously enough, Sir Robert Howard's *The Duke of Lerma* (1668), which, according to the Diarist, was "designed to reproach our King with his mistresses," did not arouse similar resentment in the royal spectator. Pepys fully expected that the first performance would be stopped, but although the whole Court was present, the play was allowed to take its course, and fortunately it "ended well, which salved all." Other plays, like Sedley's *The Mulberry Garden* (1668), drew crowded houses because of their author being "so reputed a wit"; and still others because, like James Howard's *All Mistaken* (1667), with its two "mad parts" immortalized by Hart and Nell Gwyn, they provided rôles that suited stage favorites. If these plays themselves have not stood the test of time, it is nevertheless instructive to learn from Pepys on what their popularity in their own day rested.

And here may be mentioned in passing the translations and adaptations referred to in the *Diary*, many from the Spanish, but most from the French, which flourished on the Restoration stage. Of the plays from Pierre Corneille, alone, Pepys saw five, each performed several times over,—*The Cid, Heraclius* ("an excellent play, to my extraordinary content"), *Horace, The Mistaken Beauty,* and *Pompey the Great. The Adventures of Five Hours,* based upon a Spanish play now ascribed to Antonio Coello, was, in Pepys's judgment, "the best, for the variety and the most excellent continuance of the plot to the very end, that ever I saw, or think ever shall." "And the house," he concludes, "by its frequent plaudits, did show their sufficient approbation."

Pepys and his companions also frequently attended puppet-shows. Of these *Polichinello* (the Italian *Punch*), mentioned nine times in all, seems to have been the most popular. One performance at least was graced by "Young Killigrew" and "a great many young sparks." After seeing *The Surprisal* at the King's theatre, Pepys went one day "to Polichinello, and there had three times more sport than at the play." Other puppet-plays referred to in the *Diary* are *The Modern History of Hero and Leander* (in *Bartholomew Fair,* Act V); "the story of Holofernes"; "Patient Grizill"; and the "show of Whittington." Of the last-named, Pepys remarks: "How that idle thing do work upon people that see it, and even myself too!"

Among the dramatists of the day, we read two or three times of Abraham Cowley, who was at his death "mightily lamented" as "the best poet of our nation, and as a good man"; of Sir William D'Avenant and his difficulties as manager of the Duke's company; and of "Dryden the poet," whom Pepys knew at Cambridge, and whom he saw "at the great Coffee-house," where "all the wits of the town" fore-gathered. The Diarist furnishes us with portraits of the unpopular Sir Robert Howard, ridiculed by Shadwell in *The Sullen Lovers;* of the popular and profligate Sir Charles Sedley, examples of whose witty repartees as a theatre-goer are carefully set down; of Tom Killigrew "the King's Foole or Jester," with his love of music and his managerial ambitions, his "raillery" and his "merry stories." Thus are the literary "lions" of the Restoration playhouse exhibited in Pepys's pages.

The next chapter will take up the conditions, as Pepys describes them, under which plays were pro-duced by D'Avenant and Killigrew, and the informa-tion which the *Diary* gives us on the general subject of the Restoration theatre.

III

PEPYS AND THE RESTORATION THEATRE

III

PEPYS AND THE RESTORATION
THEATRE

Historically, the decade covered by Pepys's *Diary*
is one of the most important in the development of
the English theatre. During the first few years after
the Restoration, improvements were introduced that
took from the stage its essentially Elizabethan aspect
and gave it those general features by which it is
known today. From this standpoint, Pepys may be
said to have witnessed the virtual modernization of
the English theatre. To be sure, the stage itself,
as in the pre-Restoration period, still projected in
the shape of a platform into the pit. But on account
of the regular employment of actresses for the
women's parts, the general use of movable scenery,
the elaboration of costumes and mechanical devices,
the illumination of the stage by chandeliers of candles, and the cutting off of the front of the stage at
the proscenium by flats or curtains, the Restoration
theatre resembles that of our own day more closely
than that of Shakespeare's. The placing in front of
the pit of a regular band of musicians, with the grow-
ing tendency towards more ambitious music both
during and between the acts, also contributed to
"this transformation," as Professor Thorndike has
called it, "from a half-medieval to a nearly modern

stage."[1]   As for the auditorium of the Restoration
playhouse, its plan was in general similar to that of
the typical London theatre of the present time.
There was the pit—somewhat curtailed, to be sure,
by the protrusion of the stage; above it the first tier
of boxes with the King's box occupying the centre;
then the so-called "middle gallery" with a few boxes
also, perhaps, in the centre; and finally above that the
shilling gallery with benches for the poorer class of
playgoers.

On nearly every one of the essential features of
the contemporary theatre, Pepys touches at some
point in his record.   Thus from the pages of the
Diary, it is possible to reconstruct in their main out-
lines the important playhouses of the period as well
as the productions that took place in them.

The first time that Pepys refers to the performance of a play is on June 6, 1660; he is still on board
The Charles—the ship which had just brought over
the King and was lying off Dover—when he hears in
a letter from London that "The two Dukes [York
and Gloucester] do haunt the Park much, and that
they were at a play, Madame Epicene, the other
day."   It is not clear where this performance of
Jonson's comedy was given—perhaps at the Red
Bull where the company of "old actors," to whose
repertory it belonged, was then playing.   On November 8 of this year, a company containing recruits from
the Red Bull removed to a theatre in Vere Street,
Clare Market, where in all probability Pepys saw the

[1] A. H. Thorndike, *Tragedy,* p. 244.

same play on December 4. The Diarist's statements throw much light upon the early history of the theatres opened immediately before the Restoration. Besides the Red Bull in St. John's Street, there is valuable information about the Cockpit in Drury Lane, and the rebuilt Salisbury Court theatre, White-friars—as well as about the companies of actors that gathered in them—though not enough to solve satis-factorily all the problems connected with these sub-jects. After the Royal grant of August 21, 1660, to Thomas Killigrew and Sir William D'Avenant of "full power and authority to Erect two Companies of Players" and the consequent formation of "the King's company" by Killigrew, and of "the Duke of York's" by D'Avenant—the comments upon them are more frequent. Thereafter the reader may follow somewhat closely their movements until they were established in the quarters they were to occupy throughout the period covered by the remainder of the *Diary*—the King's players in the Royal theatre, Drury Lane, the Duke's in the "Opera" in Portu-gal Street, Lincoln's Inn Fields.

Pepys also adds substantially to our knowledge of the Royal private theatre in Whitehall Palace. As this is a subject which has been generally passed over by stage historians, it is important to summarize the information he supplies. On November 20, 1660, he refers to the Cockpit, Whitehall, which stood, according to Edgar Sheppard, author of *The Old Royal Palace of Whitehall,* on the site "now occupied by the Privy Council Office." Pepys saw several plays acted here by both the Duke's and the King's companies, who, since the performances at the public theatres were in the afternoon, were free to appear at Court in the evening. He mentions this Cockpit for the last time by name on January 5, 1663. On February 23, 1663, and October 17, 1664, he speaks of plays given "at Court," without indicating definitely the place of performance. On April 20, 1665, he remarks: "I am told the first play is played in Whitehall noon-hall, which is now turned to a house of playing"; and in his next entry on the Court plays, which is in 1666, after the great plague, he says: "To Whitehall and into the new playhouse there, and the first time I was ever there." From these references, it is clear that the "theatre-room" in the palace was moved about. Sheppard has nothing to say on the subject except that the location of the "noon-hall" (which seems to be the "new play-house" Pepys mentions) is not known. H. B. Wheatley, in his *London, Past and Present,* asserts that "Charles built a new playhouse at Whitehall to which Pepys went." From this evidence, we may at least infer that the Court plays were given in the Cockpit adjoining the old palace (not to be confused with the Cockpit in Drury Lane) for the first three or four years of Charles the Second's reign, and also that from 1665 on they were probably given in what had previously been known as the "noon-hall."

Pepys first saw professional actresses at the King's theatre, Vere Street, on January 3, 1661, soon after the initial appearance of women on the English stage, if we except a few sporadic pre-Restoration performances. "To the Theatre," he records of the performance of this date, "where was acted 'Beggar's Bush,' it being very well done; and here the first time that ever I saw women come upon the stage." That their advent was not wholly pleasing to the actors of this company is suggested in the following reference in their petition of October 13, 1660, addressed to Sir Henry Herbert. Killigrew, they assert, "supprest us untill we had by covenant obleiged ourselves to Act with Woemen." Boys, however, still appeared in female rôles in the same company, as we learn from the Diarist's entry for January 7, which praises Edward Kynaston's acting of Epicoene in Jonson's *Silent Woman.* The second time Pepys mentions seeing women on the stage, which was on January 8— again at the King's theatre—the play was *The Widow,* and his pleasure in it was lessened because the women were "to seek in their parts." But after his third experience, February 12, he thought the acting of a woman, in *The Scornful Lady,* made "the play appear much better than ever it did to me." Some five years later in an account of *The English Monsieur,* his chief praise is reserved for the actresses who performed in it—"the women," he concludes, "doing better than ever I expected, and very fine women."

Unfortunately, Pepys does not furnish us with a clue to the name of the first English professional actress to take a speaking part; but through his descriptions, we become more or less intimately acquainted with the principal actresses of both the Duke's and the King's companies, who were soon afterward employed. Among these were Mrs. Corey,

Mrs. Betterton, the two Davenports, "Moll" Davis, Gosnell (who is not known outside the *Diary*), the famous Nell Gwyn, Mrs. Knepp (of whom little is otherwise known), the Marshall sisters, and Mrs. Norton.

It was Mrs. Corey, or "Doll Common"—as Pepys calls her from her part in Jonson's *Alchemist*—who deeply offended Lady Harvey by her "acting of Sempronia in 'Catiline' to imitate her." "For which," continues Pepys, "she got my Lord Chamberlain, her kinsman, to imprison Doll: when my Lady Castlemayne made the King to release her, and to order her to act it again, worse than ever, the other day, where the King himself was: and since it was acted again, and my Lady Harvy provided people to hiss her and fling oranges at her." As for the sequel, we are told that there were "real troubles at Court about it."

Mary Saunderson, who became in 1662 the wife of Betterton—prince of Restoration actors—is almost invariably mentioned in the same breath with her husband in terms of the highest praise. She first appears in the *Diary* in an account of a performance of Massinger's *The Bondman*, as "acting Cleora's part very well now Roxalana is gone." The original Roxalana was Elizabeth Davenport, whose imper- sonation of this rôle in the famous production of *The Siege of Rhodes*, lingered in Pepys's memory long after the impersonator had been "by force of love," as Downes says, "erept the stage." Of Moll Davis, "the pretty girle that sang and danced so well at the Duke's house," and "pretty witty Nell at the

King's house," there is abundant gossip. Pepys gives us glimpses of the latter off the stage as well as on it—"standing at her lodgings' door in Drury-Lane in her smock sleeves and bodice," and also in the "women's shift where Nell was dressing herself, and was all unready, and is very pretty, prettier than I thought." Her own opinion of her abilities as an actress seems largely to have been shared by the Diarist. He asserts, apropos of her spoiling the part of Samira in *The Surprisal* and then two days later playing to perfection Mirida in *The Mad Couple,* that it is a miracle to him "to think how ill she do any serious part, as, the other day, just like a fool or changeling; and, in a mad part, do beyond all imitation almost." But pretty, "mad-humoured" Mrs. Knepp, whom Killigrew, her manager, thought "like to make the best actor that ever come upon the stage," figures even more often in these gossipy pages in her double capacity of successful actress and intimate friend.

Pepys's accounts of the visits back and forth between the audience and the women players suggest that the but recently initiated actresses felt themselves from the first at home both on the stage and in the pit. The "gallants" and the women of the company were upon a most informal footing. On one occasion, Mrs. Knepp took the Diarist after a play up into "the tireing-rooms" at the King's theatre, where he proceeded to hear Knepp say "all her part of Flora's Figarys"; another time, she spied him "out of the tiring-room and come to the pit door." Again, Pepys records that Knepp "come, after her song in the clouds, to me in the pit." And at all times, "Orange Moll," the head orange-girl, acted as a go-between for the men in the auditorium and the actresses on the stage.

Pepys also testifies that the managers of the Restoration theatres soon learned to exploit the women of their companies in ways calculated to add a new zest to playgoing for the vulgar-minded. As early as October 28, 1661, we read of a woman who "acted Parthenia" in *Argalus and Parthenia,* and "came afterwards on the stage in men's clothes"—probably to recite a coarse epilogue. And on October 4, 1664, Pepys hears of Killigrew's *The Parson's Wedding,* which he calls a "bawdy loose play," about to be "acted all by women."

To turn from the women to the men of the companies—by the end of February, 1661, hardly two years after the reopening of the theatres, we find Pepys already observing that "the gallants do begin to be tyred with the vanity and pride of the theatre actors who are indeed grown very proud and rich." How difficult they were to deal with appears from the following story. Under July 22, 1663, we read of the versatile comedian, Henry Harris, a member of D'Avenant's company: "He demanded £20 for himself extraordinary, more than Betterton or anybody else, upon every new play, and £10 upon every revive; which with other things Sir W. Davenant would not give him, and so he swore he would never act there more in expectation of being received in the other House; but the King will not suffer it." Finally, as Pepys tells us on December 10, Harris was

G. Kneller pinx.   M. V^r Guche Sculp.

Mr. Thomas Betterton
Totus Mundus Agit Histrionem.

forced to go back to his old place. But it was doubt-less as much the fault of the public as his own that he was thus spoiled, to judge by an entry for April 29, 1668: "After the play done, I stepped up to Harris's dressing-room, where I never was, and there I observe much company come to him, and the Witts, to talk, after the play is done, and to assign meet-ings."

Another crisis arose when the popular comedian Lacy insulted Edward Howard—for acting in whose play he had been thrown into prison—telling him "he was more a fool than a poet," and giving him "a blow over the pate." An artist like Better-ton, who was always dignified, and was universally respected and admired, lived apparently in peace and quiet. But there were other more turbulent spirits who not infrequently became involved in quarrels that necessitated the temporary closing of their play-houses. That the actors did not always triumph over their opponents, we may infer from the fact that after Kynaston had taken a part in a play called *The Heiress* "in abuse to Sir Charles Sedley," he was "exceedingly beaten with sticks by two or three that assaulted him." The Diarist also records a sinister-sounding threat made by Sir William Cov-entry, when it was rumored that he was to be mim-icked on the stage. He immediately "told Killigrew that he should tell his actors whoever they were, that offer any thing like representing him . . . that he would cause his nose to be cut."

Of all the actors mentioned in the *Diary,* Thomas Betterton of the Duke's company seems most to have impressed Pepys, and in no rôle so much as in Hamlet. "Betterton did the prince's part beyond imagination" is a typical comment. Next to him stands Henry Harris in the estimation of the Diarist, who knew him personally perhaps better than any of the others. Besides inviting him frequently to his house, Pepys had his portrait painted as Henry V in Orrery's play of that name. Not only did he admire Harris's acting, but again and again he praises his intelligence, his wit, and his personal charm. "I do not know another better qualified for converse," we read, "whether in things of his own trade, or of other kinds, a man of great understanding and observation and very agreeable in the manner of his discourse, and civil as far as is possible." Of the actors in the King's company (which, on the whole, is not rated as high as its rival) we hear most about the versatile John Lacy. Lacy seems to have excelled in "character parts" such as a rustic "clown" in *Love in a Maze* and the "country-gentleman come up to Court" in *The Change of Crowns*. He appears also to have had a special gift for portraying national characteristics, for we read of his taking such diverse parts as "the French Dancing Master," an "Irish footman," and "Sawney the Scot." How much French and Irish he managed to speak is not told, but we know that he at least attempted Scotch, since as Sawney he succeeded in making himself quite unintelligible to Pepys. Edward Kynaston, of the King's company, also frequently receives honorable mention. He was one of the last of the "boy-actresses," and immediately after the Restoration Pepys twice praises him in women's parts. As Olympia in *The Loyal Subject,* he made—so the Diarist assures us— "the loveliest lady that ever I saw in my life, only her voice not very good." As Epicoene in *The Silent Woman,* he was "clearly the prettiest woman in the whole house."

Several times Pepys speaks of children on the stage, but does not give their names. In *The Slighted Maid,* he saw a little girl dance in boy's apparel; and in *The Sullen Lovers* "a little boy, for a farce, do dance Polichinelli the best that ever anything was done in this world." During the performance of *All Mistaken, or The Mad Couple* occurred an incident which must have been as embarrassing to Nell Gwyn and the rest of the company as it was entertaining to the Diarist. "It pleased us mightily," he writes, "to see the natural affection of a poor woman, the mother of one of the children brought on the stage: the child crying, she by force got upon the stage, and took up her child and carried it away."

Pepys usually notices the staging of plays, if there is anything novel or interesting about it. During the first two or three years after the Restoration, when movable scenery was practically an innovation in the London theatres for regular productions, the Diarist often puts down the mere presence of scenes as a noteworthy fact. The historically important setting for D'Avenant's *Siege of Rhodes,* Part II, which he saw on July 2, 1661, at the new "Opera" in Lincoln's Inn Fields, he describes as "very fine and magnificent." On August 15 he attended a performance, also at this theatre, of *The Wits,* "never acted yet

with scenes"; and there, on the twenty-fourth of this
month, a performance of *Hamlet,* "done with scenes
very well." Only in commenting upon *Henry VIII*
among the other plays of Shakespeare which were
revived at this time with elaborate settings, does
Pepys mention the scenery, in two of them his attention being taken up by the music. But he was
"mightily pleased" with the "shows" of *Henry VIII.*
He admired in Jonson's *Catiline* the scene "of the
Senate," and in Fletcher's *Island Princess,* the "good
scene of a town on fire." He listened with great
interest in August, 1664, to the ambitious plan which
Thomas Killigrew divulged to him for a new theatre
which was to "have the best scenes and machines, the
best musique, and every thing as magnificent as is in
Christendome; and to that end hath sent for voices
and painters and other persons from Italy." But
the contemporary interest in this side of theatrical
production may perhaps best be gauged from the
Diarist's entry for June 13, 1663, after he had seen
The Faithful Shepherdess, which he says was "much
thronged after, and often shown, but it is only for
the scene's sake, which is very fine indeed and worth
seeing." In spite of these ambitious efforts of
D'Avenant and Killigrew, Restoration scenery was,
of course, artistically crude, and it is therefore not
surprising that distance should have lent it enchant-
ment. When forced to sit in an "upper box," Pepys
observes with some interest, that "from this place the
scenes do appear very fine indeed, and much better
than in the pit."

One day in 1666, when the theatres were closed on

account of the great fire, which followed on the heels of the great plague, Pepys consoled himself by going behind the scenes at the King's playhouse and viewing at close range the stage properties. There he saw the "machines," the "paintings," and various other appurtenances—"here a wooden leg, there a ruff, here a hobby-horse, there a crown, would make a man split himself to see with laughing." But the actors at this time did not always have to ride hobby-horses; in Shirley's *Hyde Park,* at the King's theatre, Pepys saw real horses brought on the stage.

As for costumes, the Diarist particularly commends the richness of those in *The Tempest,* and in *Catiline;* for the latter play, he notes that the King was to give five hundred pounds, and that there were to be "sixteen scarlett robes." But when he visits the tiring-rooms at the Royal theatre, and sees there "Lacy's wardrobe and Shotrell's," he is amazed "to think how fine they show on the stage by candlelight and how poor things they are to look now." It has been said that "such costumes as Pepys saw made no pretension whatever to historical accuracy." Of course, the point of view towards historical accuracy is shifting ground, and "the garments" Pepys thought "like Romans very well" would probably not satisfy a modern theatre-goer's sense of archæological fitness. But *pretension* to historical accuracy there certainly was when the *Diary* was written. To substantiate this it is only necessary to quote further from the account of the performance of March 8, 1664, in which the "Romans" appeared (the play was a translation of Corneille's *Heraclius*) : "At the drawing up of the curtaine, there was the finest scene of the Emperor and his people about him, standing in their fixed and different postures in their Roman habitts, above all that ever I yet saw at any of the theatres." And we read in the description of a piece called *Queen Elizabeth's Troubles* that it "shews the true garbe of the Queen in those days just as we see Queen Mary and Queen Elizabeth painted."

But Pepys was probably more genuinely interested in the music than in the costuming of plays. "That which did please me beyond anything in the whole world," he writes after seeing *The Virgin Martyr* at the King's theatre, "was the wind musique when the angel comes down, which is so sweet that it ravished me." He often comments on the rendering of the songs, which were as frequent a feature of Restoration performances as the dances, and he was enough of a musician to write his own score for one of them, "Beauty Retire," from *The Siege of Rhodes*. When the theatre in Drury Lane was opened, in 1663, Pepys remarks on the new arrangement of having the music down in front of the pit instead of up in a gallery. But at first at least, this did not seem to work well. "The musique being below," he says, "and most of it sounding under the very stage, there is no hearing of the bases at all, nor very well, of the trebles, which sure must be mended." Apparently D'Avenant did not adopt this arrangement, for as late as 1669 Pepys refers to "the side balcony" at the Duke's theatre "over against the musick."

About the musicians, we learn from various entries that the most popular of them were foreigners.

Thomas Killigrew, who was so fond of music that he had been several times to Rome to hear it, led the way in importing them. He once told Pepys that before his time " 'Hermitt poore' and 'Chevy Chese' was all the musique we had; and yet no ordinary fiddlers get so much money as ours do here, which speaks our rudenesse still." In his effort to improve this state of things, he had "gathered our Italians from several Courts in Christendome, to come to make a concert for the King." According to his own account, the orchestra in his theatre contained "nine or ten of the best" fiddlers; while from Pepys's remarks on Killigrew's production of *The Virgin Martyr,* we infer that it also contained wind instruments. It appears from the *Diary*—as well as from other sources—that Sir William D'Avenant did his full share in his operatic productions towards bettering the music in the Restoration theatre.

As Pepys pictures the stage to us, so too he pictures the auditorium of the contemporary playhouse, peopling pit and gallery with the quaintly interesting figures of the day. Especially does he rejoice in the presence of "all the great ladies of the Court." "The sight of the ladies, indeed," he remarks of a particular audience, "was exceedingly noble." When it is "full of citizens," the theatre does not please him as much as it does when it is "full of gallants." He takes solid satisfaction when there are "many fine faces" in the pit, and is somewhat disturbed when he notices, as on January 1, 1668, at the Duke's playhouse, "that when I begun first to be able to bestow a play on myself, I do not remember that I saw so many by half of the ordinary 'prentices and mean people in the pit at 2*s*. 6*d*. a-piece as now; I going for several years no higher than 12*d*. . . . places, though I strained hard to go in them when I did: so much the vanity and prodigality of the age is to be observed in this particular." In view of the relations of Charles the Second's Court with the Continent, it is not surprising to read that Pepys's box at the theatre was once invaded by a company of Frenchmen who could understand no English and were forced to depend on "a pretty lady that they got among them" for a translation of the play.

The subject of dress at the theatre is also introduced. On May 8, 1663, Pepys goes home "a little ashamed that my wife and woman were in such a pickle, all the ladies being finer and better dressed in the pitt than they used" to be. About a month afterward, he and his wife notice at a play that Lady Mary Cromwell put on her vizard "when the House began to fill," and "so kept it on all the play; which of late is become a great fashion among the ladies, which hides their whole face"; whereupon nothing would do but immediately afterward they should go, as Pepys adds, "to the Exchange to buy things . . . with my wife; among others a vizard for herself." To what unfortunate consequences the revival of this custom of mask-wearing led, the Diarist suggests in an account of an experience at the King's theatre during a performance of *The Maid's Tragedy;* here he sat behind "two talking ladies and Sir Charles Sedley, . . . he being a stranger. And one of the ladies would and did sit with her mask on, all the play."

More than once Pepys records the fact that people in the audience talked throughout the play so loud that others were prevented from understanding it. On July 22, 1667, he hears of a fray at the Duke's playhouse, in which the Duke of Buckingham "did soundly beat [Henry Killigrew] and take away his sword." And in general, the behavior of Restoration playgoers appears to have been most informal. Once, he says, when I was sitting "in a dark place, a lady spit backward upon me by a mistake, not seeing me, but after seeing her to be a very pretty lady, I was not troubled at it at all." Yet another time at the private theatre in Whitehall Palace, Pepys thought the Duke of York and his Duchess overstepped the mark in informality—they "did show," he says, "some impertinent, and, methought, unnatural dalliances there, before the whole world, such as kissing, and leaning upon one another."

Apparently the Diarist never missed seeing the distinguished people in the theatre, and he somehow managed to watch them and the play at the same time. He was always interested in the effect produced by the play upon prominent spectators. "The King I did not see laugh," he notes with evident surprise at the first performance of the much-heralded *Mulberry Garden* by Sir Charles Sedley, "nor pleased the whole play from beginning to end, nor the company." And again—this time at *The Valiant Cid*—"Nor did the King or Queen once smile all the whole play, nor any of the company seem to take any pleasure but what was in the greatness and the gallantry of the company."

Here is a glimpse he gives of a brilliant audience gathered at the Duke's house for a performance of *Macbeth* on December 21, 1668: "The King and Court there; and we sat just under them and my Lady Castlemayne, and close to the woman that comes into the pit, a kind of loose gossip, that pretends to be like her, and is so, something. . . . The King and Duke of York minded me, and smiled upon me, at the handsome woman near me: but it vexed me to see Moll Davis, in the box over the King's and my Lady Castlemayne's head, look down upon the King, and he up to her; and so did my Lady Castlemayne once, to see who it was, but when she saw her, she looked fire." Pepys recognized the Queen of Bohemia at one performance, "the German Baron with his lady who is envoyé from the Emperour" at another, and at still another, the picturesque Duchess of Newcastle, who at the end of her husband's play, *The Humourous Lovers,* "made her respects to the players from her box."

When a new piece was on, the audience was sure to be a distinguished one, and the theatre was usually crowded. But there was this drawback about first days at the playhouse, that the would-be spectator must needs go hours beforehand to get a seat. Although at that time the plays at the public theatres did not begin before three or half past three in the afternoon, Pepys found on February 25, 1669, the Duke of York's playhouse "infinite full" at one o'clock on the occasion of the first presentation of Shadwell's *Royal Shepherdess.* For the *première* of another play, Shadwell's *The Sullen Lovers,* Pepys had the foresight to go "at a little past twelve, to get a good place in the pit, against the new play, and there setting a poor man to keep my place, I out, and spent an hour at Martin's, my bookseller's, and so back again, where I find the house quite full. But I had my place." For another play, however, even his arrival at the theatre before the doors were opened did not guarantee him first choice of seats. "To the King's playhouse," he notes, "where the doors were not then open, but presently they did open; and we in, and find many people already come in, by private ways, into the pit, it being the first day of Sir Charles Sidly's new play, so long expected, 'The Mullberry Guarden.'"

For these first performances, we learn from an entry about Cowley's *Cutter of Coleman Street,* under December 16, 1661, the prices of seats were increased—"It being the first time, the pay was doubled, and so to save money, . . . went up into the gallery, and there sat and saw very well." The "gallery" here referred to was the middle gallery where the seats were ordinarily eighteen pence. From the reference to a "box over the King's and my lady Castlemayne's head," in which the actress Moll Davis sat on December 21, 1668, we infer that this gallery also contained boxes, which would seem from this reference to have been in the centre rather than on the sides. Probably "the half-crown box" of Pepys's comment of January 19, 1661, was among them. Above this middle gallery in which Pepys sometimes sat, as he says, to hide himself, was the "upper gallery," chiefly frequented by servants and "the vulgar herd," while just under it was the main tier of boxes, including the King's. Here, too, at least in the Duke's theatre, was the box set aside for the manager of the rival company "sufficient"—so runs D'Avenant's stipulation—"to conteine six persons," who had "Liberty to enter without any Sallery or pay for their entrance." On October 19, 1667, Pepys tells us that he paid four shillings for a box seat; the seats were sold singly and this was the regular price. But for the most part, Pepys sat in the pit—just below the tier of boxes; and he finds no fault with it except when the only seat to be had is "almost out of sight at one end of the lower forms." This part of the auditorium, in which the seats were mere benches or "forms," was largely frequented by "gallants" and "ladies of quality," though by 1668, according to the Diarist, a good many "ordinary 'prentices and mean people" could afford the "2s. 6d." it cost to sit there.

Restoration playgoers are reported to have found various ways of getting around the regular charges. One was to go in late and take advantage of the rule that a gentleman could enter free towards the end of a play if he had friends whom he wished to meet afterward. Thus Pepys records on February 11, 1668, "Sent my wife and Deb. to see *Mustapha* acted, . . . so to the Duke of York's playhouse, and there saw the last act for nothing." Upon another custom which led to even greater abuse, Pepys looked with disapproval, as appears from the following story told under the date of December 30, 1667: "Sir Philip Carteret would fain have given me my going in to a play; but yet, when he come to the door, he had no money to pay for himself, I having refused to accept of it for myself, but was fain; and I perceive he is known there, and do run upon the score there for plays, which is a shame."

But the expense of an afternoon at the playhouse in Charles the Second's time did not end with the payment for seats. There were the refreshments. Once when Pepys took a party of people to the theatre, he states that it cost him "8s. upon them in oranges at 6d. a-piece." A sixpence was the regular price for an orange, which was evidently considered a part of the afternoon's pleasure. The fruit was peddled by so-called "orange-women," who stood in front of the pit with their backs to the stage and "broke jests" with the men during the progress of the play, and carried messages for them between the acts. That, however, they were not above blackmailing their patrons at times is to be seen from one of Pepys's own experiences. At the Duke's theatre, he writes on May 11, 1668, "there happened one thing which vexed me, which is, that the orange woman did come in the pit, and challenge me for twelve oranges, which she delivered by my order at a late play, at night, to give to some ladies in a box, which was wholly untrue, but yet she swore it to be true. But, however, I did deny it, and did not pay her; but for quiet did buy 4s. worth of oranges of her, at 6d. a-piece." "Orange Moll," as the head orange-woman was called, was indeed an important person in the Restoration theatre. Of the various offices which we hear of her performing, perhaps the most extraordinary is the following, described on November 2, 1667: "A gentleman of good habit, sitting just before us, eating of some fruit in the midst of the play, did drop down as dead, being choked; but with much ado Orange Moll did thrust her finger down his throat, and brought him to life again."

After the play was over, one of the players came out and announced what the bill would be for the following day. Thus we read under March 7, 1667: "Little Mis. Davis did dance a jig after the end of the play, and there telling the next day's play." In this way and by the posting of playbills upon the theatres and the street-posts—a custom to which Pepys several times refers—plays were advertised at this time. But even when the announcement of the next performance had been made, the audiences, of which the Diarist made one, did not always leave the theatre at once. After *She Would if She Could* on February 6, 1668, Pepys remarks that "it being dark and raining" he and the rest of the spectators stayed at the Duke's theatre an hour and a half "till the rain was over, and to talk."

The *Diary* leaves no room for doubt that Pepys made good use of his ample opportunities to familiarize himself with the details of the playhouses he frequented. We have seen that he knew from experience the advantages and disadvantages of every part of the auditorium, and that he had inspected "the inside of the stage and all the tiring-rooms and machines." At the King's theatre he was once ushered into the "women's shift." From here he walked "all up and down the house above, and then below into the scene-room." The intimate knowledge thus gained gives a certain weight to his criticisms of the various houses. In one theatre—that in Whitehall Palace—he was annoyed by the poor acoustics. "The House," he says, "though very fine, yet bad for the voice, for hearing." Hence it is not surprising to find that he does not like "a play so well here as at the common playhouse." In another, he is tried by the light of the candles, set in loops or branches which hung from the ceiling over the stage—especially so when he sits in a side balcony, a bad place indeed for the eyes, since the lights must have been about on a level with it and directly in front. The most detailed criticism which the Diarist has left us concerns the King's theatre in Drury Lane, built in 1663 at what was then considered the enormous expense of £1500. "The house," he informs us, "is made with extraordinary good contrivance, and yet hath some faults, as the narrowness of the passages in and out of the pitt, and the distance from the stage to the boxes, which I am confident cannot hear, but for all other things it is well." Evidently the stage of this theatre proved too small, for only three years later Pepys found the interior "all in dirt, they being altering of the stage to make it wider."

From the *Diary* we learn that improvements in the conduct and construction of the theatre were made between 1660 and 1670. What some of these were may be gathered from an interview which Pepys had in 1667 with Thomas Killigrew, who contrasted the King's house under his management with the stage before his day. "The stage," he tells Pepys, "is by his pains a thousand times better and more glorious" than before. "Now, wax-candles, and many of them; then, not above 3 lbs. of tallow: now, all things civil, no rudeness anywhere; then, as in a bear-garden: then two or three fiddlers; now nine or ten of the best: then, nothing but rushes upon the ground, and everything else mean; and now, all otherwise: then, the Queen seldom and the King never would come; now not the King only for state, but all civil people." Whether Killigrew was justified in taking to himself the credit for all these changes, the Diarist does not say. However that may be, his account may well stand as our final glimpse of the playhouse of his time.

Thus does Pepys bring vividly before us the interior of the Restoration theatre—the play, the players, and the playgoers. Many similar passages might be cited that help to make the decade the *Diary* covers stand out in a high light in English stage history. But it is not the author's intention to rob the reader of the pleasure of picking out for himself all the most diverting and illuminating of the details from the mass that is presented. Pepys's journal has always been a favorite with those who delight in seeing the people and events of a past age live again before their eyes. And it is hoped that in thus taking out of it a considerable portion dealing with one of its primary topics, little of its charm will have escaped for such readers, while much will have been gained for those more especially interested in the stage. Enough has perhaps been said to suggest the value of this material to the student, and to indicate how

even its hastiest comment, its sheerest gossip, serves
today to enhance our knowledge of English drama
and of conditions under which it has evolved. Indeed, there can be no doubt that the following assem-
blage of excerpts from Pepys's *Diary* constitutes a
body of information on the Restoration stage as
significant as it is racy.

REFERENCES IN PEPYS'S *DIARY* TO
THE RESTORATION STAGE

PART ONE

CHAPTER I

SHAKESPEARE'S PLAYS

[NOTE: For convenience of reference, certain works which must be frequently cited in the notes in this book will be mentioned as follows: John Downes's *Roscius Anglicanus, or An Historical Review of the Stage from 1660 to 1706*, Facsimile Reprint of the Rare Original of 1708, with an Historical Preface by Joseph Knight, London, 1886,—briefly, as *"Roscius Anglicanus"*; John Genest's *Some Account of the English Stage from the Restoration in 1660 to 1830*, 10 volumes, Bath, 1832,—as "Genest"; Gerard Langbaine's *An Account of the English Dramatic Poets*, Oxford, 1691,—as "Langbaine," and Edmond Malone's edition of the *Plays and Poems of William Shakspeare*, London, 1790,—as "Malone's *Shakspeare*." In every case, the page numbers given for these works apply to these editions.

Fuller entries and notes upon the actors, actresses, playwrights, and theatres mentioned in Part I, will be found under special chapters in Parts II and III.]

CHAPTER I

SHAKESPEARE'S PLAYS

HAMLET, PRINCE OF DENMARK

August 24, 1661. To the Opera,[1] and there saw "Hamlet, Prince of Denmark,"[2] done with scenes very well, but above all, Betterton did the prince's part beyond imagination.

November 27, 1661. To the Theatre,[3] and there saw "Hamlett" very well done.

[1] The "Opera" was the Duke of York's theatre in Lincoln's Inn Fields, built in 1660 and managed by Sir William D'Avenant until his death in 1668.

[2] *Hamlet* appears to have been performed unaltered. Downes (*Roscius Anglicanus,* p. 21) says: "No succeeding Tragedy for several Years got more Reputation, or Money to the Company than this,"—"*Hamlet,* being Perform'd by Mr. *Betterton,* Sir *William* [D'Avenant] (having seen Mr. *Taylor* of the Black-Fryars Company Act it, who being Instructed by the Author, Mr. *Shaksepeur*) taught Mr. *Betterton* in every Particle of it; which by his exact Performance of it, gain'd him Esteem and Reputation Superlative to all other Plays." Harris acted Horatio; Mrs. Davenport ("Roxalana"), the Queen, and Mrs. Saunderson (later Mrs. Betterton), Ophelia.

[3] Pepys generally uses the term "the Theatre" to refer to the House occupied by the King's company managed by Thomas Killigrew. At this time, this company was playing in a theatre in Vere Street, Clare Market. Evelyn had seen *Hamlet* on the preceding day, and comments thus upon the performance: "I

December 5, 1661.   To the Opera, and saw "Hamlett" well performed.

May 28, 1663.   To the Royall Theatre;[4] but that was so full they told us we could have no room.   And so to the Duke's House; and there saw "Hamlett" done, giving us fresh reason never to think enough of Betterton.   Who should we see come upon the stage but Gosnell, my wife's maid? but neither spoke danced, nor sung; which I was sorry for.   But she becomes the stage very well.

November 13, 1664.   Spent all the afternoon with my wife, within doors, and getting a speech out of Hamlett, "To bee or not to bee," without book.

August 31, 1668.   To the Duke of York's playhouse, . . . and saw "Hamlet," which we have not seen this year before, or more; and mightily pleased with it; but, above all, with Betterton, the best part, I believe, that ever man acted.

HENRY IV, PART I

December 31, 1660.   In Paul's Churchyard I bought the play of "Henry the Fourth,"[1] and so went to the new Theatre . . . and saw it acted; but my

saw Hamlet Prince of Denmark played, but now the old plays began to disgust this refined age, since his Majestie's being so long abroad" (*Diary of John Evelyn,* Wheatley ed., II, 139).

[4] The new theatre in Drury Lane occupied by Killigrew's company from April or May of this year throughout the period covered by Pepys.

[1] The cast for *Henry IV,* Part I,—presumably the part seen

expectation being too great, it did not please me, as otherwise I believe it would; and my having a book, I believe did spoil it a little.

June 4, 1661. From thence to the Theatre and saw "Harry the 4th" a good play.

November 2, 1667. To the King's playhouse, and there saw "Henry the Fourth"; and contrary to expectation, was pleased in nothing more than in Cartwright's speaking of Falstaffe's speech about "What is Honour?"[2] The house full of Parliament-men, it being holyday with them.

January 7, 1667-68. Into the pit, to gaze up and down to look for them, and there did by this means, for nothing, see an act in . . . "Henry the Fourth" at the King's house.

September 18, 1668. To the King's house, and saw a piece of "Henry the Fourth."

HENRY VIII

December 10, 1663. He [Wotton] tells me . . . of a rare play to be acted this week of Sir William

by Pepys on this date, as it certainly was on November 2, 1667—is given by John Downes (*Roscius Anglicanus,* p. 7) as follows: "King, Mr. Wintersel; Prince, Mr. Burt; Hotspur, Mr. Hart; Falstaff, Mr. Cartwright; Poyns, Mr. Shotterel." It was doubtless acted "as Shakespeare wrote it," as the only alteration known is Betterton's, which was used later at the Duke's playhouse and was printed in 1700. The "new theatre" was the King's in Vere Street.

[2] The last speech in Sc. 1, Act V, of *Henry IV*, Part I,

Davenant's: the story of Henry the Eighth[1] with all his wives.

December 22, 1663. I perceive the King and Duke and all the Court was going to the Duke's playhouse to see "Henry VIII" acted, which is said to be an admirable play.

December 24, 1663. By and by comes in Captain Ferrers to see us, and, among other talke, tells us of the goodness of the new play of "Henry VIII," which makes me think [it] long till my time is out.[2]

January 1, 1663-64. To the Duke's house, the first play I have been at these six months, according to my last vowe, and here saw the so much cried-up play of "Henry the Eighth"; which, though I went with resolution to like it, is so simple a thing made up of a great many patches, that, besides the shows and processions in it, there is nothing in the world good or well done. Thence mightily dissatisfied.

in which Sir John asks himself this question on the battlefield of Shrewsbury.

[1] Kilbourne (*Alterations and Adaptations of Shakespeare,* p. 112) says: "No alteration of this play appears ever to have been made." Perhaps Pepys simply mistook producer for author. Downes (*Roscius Anglicanus,* p. 24) gives a full account of this production. The play was "all new Cloath'd in proper Habits" and had "new scenes." "It continu'd Acting 15 Days together with general Applause." Betterton acted the King, having been coached in the part by D'Avenant, "who had it from old Mr. *Lowen,* that had his Instructions from Mr. *Shakespear* himself"; Harris was Wolsey; Mrs. Betterton, Queen Catherine.

[2] According to the terms of a vow to stay away from the theatre referred to again under January 1, 1664.

January 27, 1663-64. In the way observing the streete full of coaches at the new play, "The Indian Queene";[3] which for show, they say, exceeds "Henry the Eighth."

December 30, 1668. To the Duke's playhouse, and there did see "King Harry the Eighth"; and was mightily pleased, better than I ever expected, with the history and shows of it.

The Law Against Lovers

(D'Avenant's Alteration of *Measure for Measure*)

February 18, 1661-62. There[1] saw "The Law against Lovers,"[2] a good play and well performed, especially the little girl's (whom I never saw act before) dancing[3] and singing; and were it not for her, the loss of Roxalana would spoil the house.

[3] A tragedy by Dryden and Sir Robert Howard.

[1] At the Duke of York's playhouse.

[2] An alteration (1662) of *Measure for Measure,* with Benedick and Beatrice taken over from *Much Ado about Nothing,* printed in 1673. Evelyn saw it "acted before ye King" on December 17, 1662 (*Diary,* Wheatley ed., II, 156).

[3] Downes (*Roscius Anglicanus,* p. 26) mentions *The Law against Lovers* among the plays acted at the Duke's theatre between 1662 and 1665, but does not give the cast. It has been suggested that the actress here referred to was Mrs. Norton. "Roxalana" was Mrs. Davenport.

MACBETH

(D'Avenant's Alteration?)

November 5, 1664. To the Duke's house to a play, "Macbeth,"[1] a pretty good play, but admirably acted.

December 28, 1666. From hence to the Duke's house, and there saw "Macbeth" most excellently acted, and a most excellent play for variety.

January 7, 1666-67. To the Duke's house, and saw "Macbeth," which, though I saw it lately, yet appears a most excellent play in all respects, but especially in divertisement, though it be a deep tragedy; which is a strange perfection in a tragedy, it being most proper here, and suitable.

[1] It is not certain what version of Shakespeare's tragedy Pepys saw, though it was probably that of D'Avenant printed in 1673. Downes, after describing "the Tragedy of *Macbeth,* alter'd by Sir *William Davenant*" as it was given later, at the Dorset Garden theatre (*Roscius Anglicanus,* p. 33)—"drest in all it's Finery, as new Cloath's, new Scenes, Machines, as flyings for the Witches; with all the Singing and Dancing in it . . . it being all Excellently perform'd being in the nature of an Opera"—notes that "this Tragedy," and two others, "were *Acted* in *Lincolns-Inn-Fields.*" In a remark once passed by Charles the Second as it is repeated by Cibber, there is a suggestion as to the make-up of the Murderers in *Macbeth* at this time: "Turning to his People, in the Box about him, *Pray what is the Meaning,* said he, *that we never see a Rogue in a Play, but Godsfish! they always clap him on a black Perriwig?*" (*Apology for the Life of Mr. Colley Cibber,* Lowe ed., I, 133). Betterton played Macbeth; Harris, Macduff; Smith, Banquo; Mrs. Betterton, Lady Macbeth; Sandford, Banquo's Ghost, in the later performances (Genest, I, pp. 139-140).

April 19, 1667. So to the playhouse, not much company come, which I impute to the heat of the weather, it being very hot. Here we saw "Macbeth" which, though I have seen it often, yet it is one of the best plays for a stage, and variety of dancing and musique, that ever I saw. So, being very much pleased, thence home.

October 16, 1667. To the Duke of York's house. . . . I was vexed to see Young (who is but a bad actor at best) act Macbeth in the room of Betterton, who, poor man! is sick: but, Lord! what a prejudice it wrought in me against the whole play, and everybody else agreed in disliking this fellow.

November 6, 1667. To a play, . . . "Macbeth," which we still like mightily, though mighty short of the content we used to have when Betterton acted, who is still sick.

August 12, 1668. To the Duke of York's house, and saw "Mackbeth," to our great content.

December 21, 1668. Thence to the Duke's play-house, and saw "Macbeth." The King and Court there.

January 15, 1668-69. My wife to the Duke of York's house, to "Macbeth." . . . And having done my own business . . . I to the Duke of York's house, and saw the last two acts.

The Merry Wives of Windsor

December 5, 1660. After dinner I went to the new Theatre and there I saw "The Merry Wives of

Windsor"[1] acted, the humours of the country gentleman and the French doctor[2] very well done, but the
rest but very poorly, and Sir J. Falstaffe as bad as
any.

September 25, 1661.   Hence much against my
nature and will, yet such is the power of the Devil
over me I could not refuse it, to the Theatre, and saw
"The Merry Wives of Windsor," ill done.

August 15, 1667.   To the King's, and there saw
"The Merry Wives of Windsor": which did not
please me at all, in no part of it.

A Midsummer-Night's Dream

September 29, 1668.   Then to the King's Theatre,
where we saw "Midsummer Night's Dream,"[1] which
I had never seen before, nor shall ever again, for it
is the most insipid ridiculous play that ever I saw in
my life.   I saw, I confess, some good dancing and
some handsome women, which was all my pleasure.

[1] Shakespeare's comedy unaltered.

[2] William Cartwright presumably acted the part of Falstaff,
as he did in *Henry IV*, Part I, but neither Downes nor Genest
gives the names of the actors who took the parts of Justice
Shallow or Dr. Caius.

[1] "This seems to be the only mention of the acting of Shakespeare's play at the time" (*Pepys's Diary*, Wheatley ed., II,
326 n).   It was probably acted unaltered.

OTHELLO, THE MOOR OF VENICE

October 11, 1660. To the Cockpit to see "The Moore of Venice,"[1] which was well done. Burt acted the Moore; by the same token, a very pretty lady that sat by me, called out, to see Desdemona smothered.

August 20, 1666. To Deptford by water, reading "Othello, Moore of Venice," which I ever heretofore esteemed a mighty good play, but having so lately read "The Adventures of Five Houres," it seems a mean thing.

February 6, 1668-69. To the King's playhouse, and there . . . did see "The Moor of Venice": but ill acted in most parts; Mohun, which did a little surprise me, not acting Iago's part by much so well as Clun used to do; nor another Hart's which was Cassio's; nor, indeed, Burt doing the Moor's so well as I once thought he did.

ROMEO AND JULIET

March 1, 1661-62. Thence to the Opera, and there saw "Romeo and Juliet," the first time it was

---

[1] *Othello* does not appear to have been altered. Downes (*Roscius Anglicanus,* pp. 6-7) gives the cast as follows: "Brabantio, Mr. Cartwright; Moor, Mr. Burt; Cassio, Mr. Hart; Jago, Major Mohun; Roderigo, Mr. Beeston; Desdemona, Mrs. Hughs; Emilia, Mrs. Rutter." The Cockpit theatre here referred to was probably the old playhouse in Drury Lane.

ever acted;[1] but it is a play of itself the worst that
ever I heard in my life, and the worst acted that ever
I saw these people do,[2] and I am resolved to go no
more to see the first time of acting, for they were all
of them out more or less.

Sawney the Scot, or The Taming of the Shrew

(Lacy's Alteration of *The Taming of the Shrew*)

April 9, 1667. To the King's house, . . . and there
we saw "The Tameing of a Shrew,"[1] which hath some
very good pieces in it, but generally is but a mean
play: and the best part, "Sawny," done by Lacy,
hath not half its life, by reason of the words, I suppose, not being understood, at least by me.

November 1, 1667. To the King's playhouse and
there saw a silly play and an old one, "The Taming
of a Shrew."

[1] Pepys means, of course, since the Restoration.   This was
Shakespeare's play probably unaltered, as James Howard's
version was "made some time later" and was used "when the
Tragedy was Revived again."   (Cf. *Roscius Anglicanus*, p. 22.)

[2] According to Downes (*Ibid.*), Harris acted Romeo; Betterton, Mercutio; Mrs. Saunderson, Juliet.   R. W. Lowe (in his
Thomas Betterton, 1891 ed., p. 89) suggests "that this distribu-
tion of the two parts [Romeo and Mercutio] is somewhat curious
in view of Pepys's opinion"—inferring that Harris should have
made the better Mercutio and Betterton the better Romeo.

[1] "This was Lacy's alteration of Shakespeare's play.   Lacy
acted Sauny" (Genest, I, 69).   It was printed in 1698.   Sawney is Grumio turned into a coarse, officious Scotch servant to
Petruchio.

The Tempest, or The Enchanted Island
(Alteration of *The Tempest* by D'Avenant and Dryden)

November 7, 1667. Resolved with Sir W. Pen to go to see "The Tempest," an old play of Shakespeare's,[1] acted, I hear, the first day; . . . and forced to sit in the side balcone over against the musique-room at the Duke's house, close by my Lady Dorset,[2] and a great many great ones. The house mighty full; and the King and Court there: and the most innocent play that I ever saw; and a curious piece of musique[3] in an echo of half sentences, the echo repeating the former half, while the man goes on to the latter; which is mighty pretty. The play [has] no great wit, but yet good, above ordinary plays.

November 13, 1667. To the Duke of York's house, and there saw the Tempest again, which is very pleasant, and full of so good variety that I cannot be more pleased almost in a comedy, only the seamen's part[4] a little too tedious.

[1] In D'Avenant and Dryden's version (1667), with elaborate scenery, dancing, and music, as Downes (*Roscius Anglicanus,* p. 33) confirms: "This Tragedy, *King Lear,* and *The Tempest,* were Acted in *Lincolns-Inn-Fields;* . . . the *Tempest* alter'd by Sir *William Davenant* and Mr. *Dryden* before t'was made into an Opera."

[2] The wife of the fifth Earl of Dorset and mother of Lord Buckhurst.

[3] In Sc. 4, Act III, of this version, where Ferdinand sings to himself and Ariel echoes him. The music was by John Bannister.

[4] What Dryden called "the comical parts of the sailors," written by D'Avenant.

December 12, 1667. To the Duke of York's house, and saw "The Tempest," which, as often as I have seen it, I do like very well, and the house very full.

January 6, 1667-68. To the Duke's house; and, the house being full, was forced to carry them to a box, which did cost me 20*s.*, besides oranges, which troubled me, though their company did please me. Thence, after the play, stayed till Harris was undressed, there being acted "The Tempest."

February 3, 1667-68. To the Duke of York's house, to the play, "The Tempest," which we have often seen, but yet I was pleased again, and shall be again to see it, it is so full of variety, and particularly this day I took pleasure to learn the time of the seaman's dance,[5] which I have much desired to be perfect in, and have made myself so.

March 25, 1668. To see "The Storme"[6] . . . but a mean play compared with "The Tempest," at the Duke of York's house.

April 30, 1668. To the Duke of York's playhouse, and there saw "The Tempest," which still pleases me mightily.

May 11, 1668. To the Duke of York's playhouse, and there saw "The Tempest," and between two acts, I went out to Mr. Harris, and got him to repeat to me the words of the Echo, while I writ them down, having tried in the play to have wrote them; but, when I had done it, having done it without looking upon my paper, I find I could not read the blacklead. But

[5] In Act V.

[6] A comedy by Fletcher and Massinger.

now I have got the words clear, and, in going thither, had the pleasure to see the actors in their several dresses especially the seamen and monster,[7] which were very droll: so into the play again.

January 21, 1668-69. There[8] saw "The Tempest"; but it is but ill done by Gosnell in lieu of Moll Davis.

TWELFTH NIGHT, OR WHAT YOU WILL

September 11, 1661. He and I walking through Lincoln's Inn Fields observed at the Opera a new play, "Twelfth Night,"[1] was acted there, and the King there; so I, against my own mind and resolution, could not forbear to go in, which did make the play seem a burthen to me, and I took no pleasure at all in it; and so after it was done went home with my mind troubled for my going thither, after my swearing to my wife that I would never go to a play without her.

January 6, 1662-63. To the Duke's house, and there saw "Twelfth Night" acted well, though it be but a silly play, and not related at all to the name or day.

---

[7] Probably Caliban.

[8] At the Duke's playhouse.

[1] Without alterations. It "had mighty Success by its well Performance," says Downes, who, however, seems to be describing the occasion noted in Pepys's entry of *January 6, 1663,* as he adds, *"It was got up on purpose to be Acted on Twelfth Night"* (*Roscius Anglicanus,* p. 23). Betterton played Sir Toby Belch; and Harris, Sir Andrew Aguecheek.

January 20, 1668-69. To the Duke of York's house, and saw "Twelfth Night," as it is now revived; but, I think, one of the weakest plays that ever I saw on the stage.

CHAPTER II

OTHER PRE-RESTORATION PLAYS

CHAPTER II

OTHER PRE-RESTORATION PLAYS

Berkeley, Sir William   THE LOST LADY

January 19, 1660-61. Myself went to the Theatre, where I saw "The Lost Lady,"[1] which do not please me much. Here I was troubled to be seen by four of our office clerks, which sat in the half-crown box and I in the 1*s.* 6*d.*

January 28, 1660-61. To the Theatre, where I saw again "The Lost Lady," which do now please me better than before; and here I sitting behind in a dark place, a lady spit backward upon me by a mistake, not seeing me, but after seeing her to be a very pretty lady, I was not troubled at it at all.

[Beaumont and] Fletcher and Massinger (?)
         THE BEGGARS' BUSH

November 20, 1660. To the new Play-house near Lincoln's-Inn-Fields (which was formerly Gibbon's

---

[1] A tragi-comedy (1637?) by Sir William Berkeley, subsequently governor of Virginia. It is also mentioned in Sir Henry Herbert's list of plays produced by Killigrew's company, given in Malone's *Shakspeare*, Vol. I, Part II, p. 266, as having been acted on this date.

tennis-court), where the play of "Beggar's Bush"[1] was newly begun; and so we went in and saw it, it was well acted: and here I saw the first time one Moone,[2] who is said to be the best actor in the world, lately come over with the King, and indeed it is the finest play-house, I believe, that ever was in England.

January 3, 1660-61. To the Theatre, where was acted "Beggar's Bush," it being very well done; and here the first time that ever I saw women come upon the stage.[3]

October 8, 1661. Carried her[4] to the Theatre in a frolique, to my great expense, and there shewed her part of the "Beggar's Bush," without much pleasure, but only for a frolique.

April 24, 1668. Thence to the King's playhouse, and there saw a piece of "Beggar's Bush," which I have not seen some years.

[Beaumont and] Fletcher   THE CHANCES

April 27, 1661. To the Theatre to see "The Chances."[1]

[1] A comedy (1622) by [Beaumont and] Fletcher and Massinger (?) acted at the King's theatre, Vere Street. It is mentioned in the list of plays produced by Killigrew's company, given in Malone's *Shakspeare,* Vol. I, Part II, p. 266, as having been acted on this date.

[2] Michael Mohun probably played the part of Goswin, according to Genest (I, 377).

[3] Neither Downes nor Genest gives the cast of this performance.

[4] Martha, daughter of Sir W. Batten.

[1] A comedy (1615?) adapted by John Fletcher from Cer-

October 9, 1661. Took them to the Theatre, and shewed them "The Chances."

February 5, 1666-67. To the King's house, to show them a play, "The Chances." A good play I find it, and the actors most good in it,[2] and pretty to hear Knipp sing in the play very properly, "All night I weepe";[3] and sung it admirably. The whole play pleases me well: and most of all, the sight of many fine ladies.

Beaumont (?) and Fletcher   THE COXCOMB

March 17, 1668-69. To the King's playhouse, and saw "The Coxcomb,"[1] the first time acted, but an old play, and a silly one, being acted only by the young people.[2]

vantes's *La Señora Cornelia,* acted probably "with the alterations made in it by Villiers, Duke of Buckingham." Genest notes further (I, 67): "This is perhaps the happiest *material* alteration of any old play ever made."

[2] Downes mentions the play in the list of the "Principal Old Stock Plays" of the King's company (*Roscius Anglicanus,* p. 8), but does not give the cast, though he states that Don John was among the best parts of the actor Hart.

[3] Mrs. Knepp's song does not occur in this or in other known versions of the play.

[1] A comedy by Beaumont (?) and Fletcher (*circa* 1610). Langbaine (p. 208) says it "was reviv'd at the Theatre-Royal, the Prologue being spoken by Jo. Hains."

[2] That is, the company without the "stars."

[Beaumont and] Fletcher
Cupid's Revenge, or Love Despised

August 17, 1668. Thence to the Duke of York's house, and there saw "Cupid's Revenge," under the new name of "Love Despised,"[1] that hath something very good in it, though I like not the whole body of it. This day the first time acted here.

[Beaumont and] Fletcher and Massinger (?)
The Custom of the Country

September 25, 1664. Then I to read another play, "The Custome of the Country,"[1] which is a very poor one, methinks.

January 2, 1666-67. To the King's House, and there saw "The Custome of the Country," the second time of its being acted, wherein Knipp does the Widow[2] well; but of all the plays that ever I did see, the worst—having neither plot, language, nor anything in the earth that is acceptable; only Knipp sings a little song admirably. But fully the worst play that ever I saw or I believe shall see.

August 1, 1667. Upon a motion of the women, I was got to go to a play with them, the first I have

[1] A tragedy (1612) by John Fletcher. Downes (*Roscius Anglicanus*, p. 29) merely states that it was acted subsequent to Etherege's *She Would if She Could*.

[1] A coarse comedy (1619-1622) by Fletcher and Massinger (?). Langbaine (p. 208) mentions its revival.

[2] The "widow" was Guiomar, mother of Duarte.

seen since before the Dutch coming upon our coast, and so to the King's house, to see "The Custome of the Country." The house mighty empty—more than ever I saw it—and an ill play.

[Beaumont and] Fletcher   THE ELDER BROTHER

September 6, 1661. I went to the Theatre, and saw "Elder Brother,"[1] ill-acted.

[Beaumont and] Fletcher
                          THE FAITHFUL SHEPHERDESS

June 13, 1663. To the Royall Theatre. . . . Here we saw "The Faithful Sheepheardesse,"[1] a most simple thing, and yet much thronged after, and often shown, but it is only for the scene's sake, which is very fine indeed and worth seeing; but I am quite out of opinion with any of their actings, but Lacy's, compared with the other house.

October 12, 1668. To the King's playhouse, . . . and there we did hear the Eunuch (who, it seems, is a Frenchman, but long bred in Italy) sing, which

[1] A comedy by John Fletcher, revised by Massinger (1626?). The cast as given by Downes (*Roscius Anglicanus*, p. 6) included Burt as Charles, Kynaston as Eustace, and Mrs. Rutter and Mrs. Boutel in the women's parts.

[1] A pastoral drama by John Fletcher, acted in 1608, and revived with a setting by Inigo Jones in 1634. The cast is not given by Downes.

I seemed to take as new to me, though I saw him on Saturday last, but said nothing of it; but such action and singing I could never have imagined to have heard.

October 14, 1668. To the King's playhouse, and there saw "The Faythful Shepherdess" again, that we might hear the French Eunuch sing, which we did, to our great content; though I do admire his action as much as his singing, being both beyond all I ever saw or heard.

February 26, 1668-69. To the King's playhouse, to shew them that, and there saw "The Faithfull Shepherdesse." But, Lord! what an empty house, there not being, as I could tell the people, so many as to make up above £10 in the whole house! The being of a new play[2] at the other house, I suppose, being the cause, though it be a silly play, that I wonder how there should be enough people to go thither two days together, and not leave more to fill this house. The emptiness of the house took away our pleasure a great deal, though I liked it the better; for that I plainly discern the musick is the better by how much the house the emptier.

[Beaumont and] Fletcher   Father's Own Son

September 28, 1661. I and my wife to the Theatre, and there saw "Father's Own Son,"[1] a very good play and the first time I ever saw it.

[2] Shadwell's *The Royal Shepherdess* at the Duke's house.
[1] This play has been identified as Fletcher's *Monsieur Thomas,*

November 13, 1661. From thence to the Theatre, and there saw "Father's Own Son" again.

[Beaumont and] Fletcher

THE HUMOUROUS LIEUTENANT

April 20, 1661. So back to the Cockpitt, and there by the favour of one Mr. Bowman, he[1] and I got in, and there saw the King and the Duke of York and his Duchess (which is a plain woman, and like her mother, my Lady Chancellor). And so saw "The Humersome Lieutenant[2] acted before the King, but not very well done. But my pleasure was great to see the manner of it, and so many great beauties, but above all Mrs. Palmer,[3] with whom the King do discover a great deal of familiarity.

May 7, 1663. This day the new Theatre Royal

originally acted at the Cockpit and Blackfriars, and printed in 1639. W. C. Hazlitt (*A Manual for the Collector and Amateur of Old English Plays,* p. 160) states that "about 1660, it was reissued under the title of *Father's Own Son,* by which it is mentioned in the Lord Chamberlain's Accounts, as early as 1639." *Father's Own Son,* from the list of plays in Malone's *Shakspeare* (Vol. I, Part II, p. 267), appears to have been acted by the King's company on April 19, 1662.

[1] John Creed (?—1701?), a friend of Pepys, of humble origin, frequently mentioned in the *Diary;* he was made Secretary to the Commissioners for Tangier in 1662.

[2] A tragi-comedy (1619) by John Fletcher, performed in Whitehall Palace.

[3] Referred to later as Lady Castlemaine. Cf. p. 278 n.

begins to act[4] with scenes the Humourous Lieutenant, but I have not time to see it.

May 8, 1663. To the Theatre Royall, being the second day of its being opened. . . . The play was "The Humerous Lieutenant," a play that hath little good in it, nor much in the very part[5] which, by the King's command, Lacy now acts instead of Clun. In the dance, the tall devil's actions was very pretty.

January 23, 1666-67. Thence to the King's house, and there saw "The Humerous Lieutenant"; a silly play, I think; only the Spirit in it that grows very tall, and then sinks again to nothing, having two heads breeding upon one, and then Knipp's singing, did please us. . . . Knipp took us all in, and brought to us Nelly, a most pretty woman, who acted the part of Cœlia[6] to-day very fine, and did it pretty well: I kissed her, and so did my wife; and a mighty pretty soul she is. We also saw Mrs. Hall, which is my little Roman-nose black girl, that is mighty pretty: she is usually called Betty. Knipp made us stay in a box and see the dancing preparatory to to-morrow for "The Goblins,"[7] a play of Suckling's not acted these twenty-five years.

[4] On the authority of Downes (*Roscius Anglicanus,* p. 3) and a playbill which R. W. Lowe characterizes as "a not very astute forgery," it has also been asserted that the opening took place on April 8.

[5] The title part.

[6] According to Downes, in the original cast Mrs. Marshall was Celia. Mohun took the part of Leontius; Hart, Demetrius; Burt, Seleucus; and Wintersell, Antigonus. The play was "Acted Twelve Days successively" (*Ibid.,* p. 3).

[7] A comedy (1638?) by Sir John Suckling.

The Island Princess

[Beaumont and] Fletcher
The Island Princess, or The Generous Portugal

January 7, 1668-69. To the King's playhouse, and there saw "The Island Princesse,"[1] the first time I ever saw it; and it is a pretty good play, many good things being in it, and a good scene of a town on fire.[2]

February 9, 1668-69. To the King's playhouse, and there saw "The Island Princesse," which I like mighty well, as an excellent play: and here we find Kinaston[3] to be well enough to act again, which he do very well, after his beating by Sir Charles Sedley's appointment.

April 23, 1669. Thence to the King's playhouse, and saw "The Generous Portugalls," a play that pleases me better and better every time we see it.

Beaumont and Fletcher   A King and no King

March 14, 1660-61. To the Theatre, and there saw "King and no King,"[1] well acted.

September 26, 1661. With my wife by coach to

[1] A tragi-comedy (1621?) by John Fletcher, revived with alterations and additions, and published in 1669. According to Genest (I, 93), Kynaston (as King of Tidore), Cartwright (Governor of Ternata), Mrs. Marshall (Quisara), Hart (Armisia), and Mohun (Ruy Dias) were in the cast.

[2] Act II, Sc. 3, where the chief town in Ternata burns.

[3] Edward Kynaston in the rôle of the King.

[1] A tragi-comedy by Beaumont and Fletcher, licensed in 1611. In the cast of a later performance, were Hart as Arbaces;

the Theatre to shew her "King and no King," it being
very well done.

Beaumont and Fletcher (?)
The Knight of the Burning Pestle

May 7, 1662. To the Theatre, where I saw the last
act of the "Knight of the Burning Pestle,"[1] which
pleased me not at all.

[Beaumont and] Fletcher and Shirley
The Night Walker, or The Little Thief

April 2, 1661. So to White-fryars and saw "The
Little Thiefe,"[1] which is a very merry and pretty
play, and the little boy do very well.

March 31, 1662. Thence to the play, where coming late, and meeting with Sir W. Pen,[2] who had got
room for my wife and his daughter in the pit, he and

Mohun, Mardonius; Burt, Tygranes; Nell Gwyn, Panthea; and
Mrs. Corey, Arane. (Cf. *Roscius Anglicanus,* p. 5.)

[1] A comedy (before 1613) by Francis Beaumont and John
Fletcher (?). It is mentioned in the list of plays produced by
Killigrew's company, given in Malone's *Shakspeare,* Vol. II,
Part II, p. 267, as having been acted two days before, on May 5.

[1] A comedy by John Fletcher corrected by Shirley (1634).
Langbaine (p. 213) mentions having seen it "acted by the
King's Servants, with great applause."

[2] Sir William Penn (1621-1670), the distinguished naval
officer and later Commissioner of the Navy. He was the father
of William Penn, founder of Pennsylvania.

I into one of the boxes, and there we sat and heard "The Little Thiefe," a pretty play and well done.

May 19, 1662. To the Theatre, and there in a box saw "The little Thief" well done.

[Beaumont and] Fletcher   THE LOYAL SUBJECT

August 18, 1660. After dinner . . . to the Cockpitt play, the first that I have had time to see since my coming from sea,[1] "The Loyall Subject,"[2] where one Kinaston, a boy, acted the Duke's sister,[3] but made the loveliest lady that ever I saw in my life, only her voice not very good. After the play done, we three went to drink, and by Captain Ferrers' means, Kinaston and another[4] that acted Archas, the General, came and drank with us.

[Beaumont and] Fletcher   THE MAD LOVER

February 9, 1660-61. Creed and I to Whitefriars[1] to the Play-house, and saw "The Mad Lover,"[2]

[1] After his voyage to Holland on the ship that brought over the King.

[2] A tragi-comedy (1618) by John Fletcher, performed at the Cockpit in Drury Lane.

[3] Olympia.

[4] Lowe suggests that this was probably Betterton. (Cf. *Thomas Betterton,* 1891 ed., p. 61.)

[1] That is, to the Salisbury Court theatre, Whitefriars.

[2] A tragi-comedy (before 1619) by John Fletcher, mentioned

the first time I ever saw it acted, which I like pretty
well.

December 2, 1661. To the Opera to see "The Mad
Lover," but not much pleased with the play.

September 25, 1664. I spent all the morning reading of "The Madd Lovers," a very good play.

February 18, 1668-69. To the Duke of York's
house, to a play, and there saw "The Mad Lover,"
which do not please me so well as it used to do, only,
Betterton's part[3] still pleases me.

Beaumont and Fletcher   THE MAID'S TRAGEDY

May 16, 1661. So went away to the Theatre, and
there saw the latter end of "The Mayd's Tragedy,"[1]
which I never saw before, and methinks it is too sad
and melancholy.

December 7, 1666. To the King's playhouse,
where two acts were almost done when I come in; and
there I sat with my cloak about my face, and saw the
remainder of "The Mayd's Tragedy"; a good play,

in the list of plays produced by Killigrew's company, given in
Malone's *Shakspeare,* Vol. I, Part II, p. 266, as acted in February of this year.

[3] Memnon, the lunatic lover.

[1] A tragedy (1610?) by Beaumont and Fletcher. The usual
cast was, according to Downes (*Roscius Anglicanus,* p. 5):
Amintor, Hart; Melantius, Mohun; the King, Wintersell;
Calianax, Shotterel; Evadne, Mrs. Marshall [Rebecca]; Aspatia,
Mrs. Boutel.

and well acted, especially by the younger Marshall,[2] who is become a pretty good actor, and is the first play I have seen in either of the houses, since before the great plague,[3] they having acted now about fourteen days publickly. But I was in mighty pain, lest I should be seen by anybody to be at a play.

February 18, 1666-67. To the Duke of York's play-house, expecting a new play, and so stayed not more than other people, but to the King's house, to "The Mayd's Tragedy"; but vexed all the while with two talking ladies and Sir Charles Sedley.

April 15, 1668. To the King's playhouse, into a corner of the 18*d.* box, and there saw "The Maid's Tragedy," a good play, . . . play and oranges 2*s.* 6*d.*

May 9, 1668. Into the King's house, and there "The Mayd's Tragedy," a good play, but Knepp not there.

[2] Rebecca Marshall.

[3] The last play that Pepys mentioned seeing at a public theatre before the plague was *Love's Mistress,* at the King's house, May 15, 1665. R. W. Lowe (*Thomas Betterton,* 1891 ed., p. 103) states that the edict requiring the closing during the plague "remained in force for about a year and a half." Apparently the reason why Pepys did not wish to be seen at the theatre was that he felt that his presence there was owing to his weakness for plays, which he had reason to think might still be dangerous to the public. On November 20, he refers to "the thanksgiving-day for the cessation of the plague; but Lord! how the towne do say that it is hastened before the plague is quite over, there dying some people still, but only to get ground for plays to be publickly acted, which the Bishop would not suffer till the plague was over."

[Beaumont and] Fletcher and Rowley

THE MAID IN THE MILL

January 29, 1660-61.   Went to Blackfryers[1] (the
first time I ever was there since plays begun), and
there after great patience and little expectation, from
so poor beginning, I saw three acts of "The Mayd in
ye Mill,"[2] acted to my great content.

April 1, 1662.   To the playhouse, the Opera, and
saw "The Mayde in the Mill," a pretty good play.

September 10, 1668.   At the Duke's play-house,
and there saw "The Maid in the Mill," revived—a
pretty, harmless old play.

Beaumont and Fletcher

PHILASTER, OR, LOVE LIES A-BLEEDING

November 18, 1661.   To the Theatre to see
"Philaster,"[1] which I never saw before, but I found
it far short of my expectations.

May 30, 1668.   To the King's playhouse, and there

---

[1] To the theatre on the site of Apothecaries' Hall, Blackfriars.

[2] A comedy (1623) by Fletcher and William Rowley. "This
Play," says Langbaine (p. 211), "amongst others has likewise
been reviv'd by the Duke's House."

[1] A tragi-comedy (1609?) by Beaumont and Fletcher. Langbaine notes (p. 213): "This Play was One of those that were
represented at the old Theatre in *Lincolns-Inn-Fields,* when the
women acted alone."

saw "Philaster";[2] where it is pretty to see how I could remember almost all along, ever since I was a boy, Arethusa,[3] the part which I was to have acted at Sir Robert Cooke's; and it was very pleasant to me, but more to think what a ridiculous thing it would have been for me to have acted a beautiful woman.

[Beaumont and] Fletcher

THE BLOODY BROTHER, OR ROLLO, DUKE OF NORMANDY

March 28, 1661. Then . . . to the Theatre and saw "Rollo"[1] ill acted.

April 17, 1667. To the King's playhouse . . . and saw a piece of "Rollo," a play I like not much, but much good acting in it;[2] the house very empty.

September 17, 1668. To the King's playhouse, and saw "Rollo, Duke of Normandy," which for old

[2] In this year Hart played Philaster, and Nell Gwyn, Bellario—according to Genest (I, 82).

[3] The Princess Arethusa, with whom Philaster is in love.

[1] *The Bloody Brother, or Rollo, Duke of Normandy,* a tragedy by Fletcher and, perhaps, William Rowley, Jonson, and others, was printed in 1639.

[2] In the cast (*Roscius Anglicanus,* pp. 5-6) were Hart (in the title part), Kynaston (as Otto), Mohun (Aubrey), Burt (La Torch), Mrs. Marshall (Edith), and Mrs. Corey (the Duchess). From James Wright's *Historia Histrionica,* 1699 (in Dodsley's *Old English Plays,* Hazlitt ed., XV, 409), we learn that Hart and Burt were in the cast of the surreptitious performance of this play at the Cockpit in 1648, when the theatre was attacked by a "party of foot-soldiers who arrested the actors."

acquaintance, pleased me pretty well, and so home and to my business.

[Beaumont and] Fletcher
RULE A WIFE AND HAVE A WIFE

April 1, 1661. Then to Whitefryars, and there saw part of "Rule a wife and have a wife,"[1] which I never saw before, but do not like it.

February 5, 1661-62. I and my wife to the Theatre . . . and there saw "Rule a Wife and have a Wife" very well done.

Beaumont and Fletcher   THE SCORNFUL LADY

November 27, 1660. To a play,—"The Scornfull Lady,"[1] and that being done, I went homewards.

January 4, 1660-61. Mr. Moore and I to the Theatre, where was "The Scornful Lady," acted very well.

[1] A comedy (1624) by John Fletcher. Genest (I, 45) states that the cast as given by Downes (Don Leon, Mohun; Perez, Hart; Cacafago, Clun; Don John, Burt; Estifania, Mrs. Boutel; Margareta, Mrs. Marshall) "must be that of 1663 or 1664," but does not note earlier performances.

[1] A comedy (1609) by Beaumont and Fletcher, acted probably by the King's company as in the later references. Evelyn saw it soon afterwards. Under January 25, 1660-61 he writes as follows: "After divers yeares since I had seen any play, I went to see acted 'The Scornful Lady' at a new theater in Lincoln's Inn Fields" (*Diary*, Wheatley ed., II, 122).

February 12, 1660-61. By water to Salsbury Court playhouse, where not liking to sit we went out again, and by coach to the Theatre, and there saw "The Scornfull Lady," now done by a woman,[2] which makes the play appear much better than ever it did to me.

November 17, 1662. To the Cockpitt [Whitehall], and we had excellent places and saw the King, Queen, Duke of Monmouth, his son, and my Lady Castlemaine, and all the fine ladies; and "The Scornfull Lady," well performed. They had done by eleven o'clock.

December 27, 1666. To the King's playhouse, and meeting Creed took him up, and there saw "The Scornfull Lady" well acted; Doll Common doing Abigail most excellently, and Knipp the widow very well, and will be an excellent actor, I think. In other parts the play not so well done as used to be by the old actors.

September 16, 1667. To the King's play-house, to see "The Scornfull Lady"; but it being now three o'clock[3] there was not one soul in the pit, whereupon, for shame, we would not go in, but, against our wills, went all to see "Tu Quoque"[4] again . . . Thence to the King's house, upon a wager with my wife, that there would be no acting there to-day, there being no

[2] Downes (*Roscius Anglicanus,* p. 6) gives the cast of the women's parts, probably for the 1666 performance: "The Lady, Mrs. *Marshal;* Martha, Mrs. *Rutter;* Abigail, Mrs. *Corey.*"

[3] Plays at the public theatres began at three-thirty, according to the Prologue to Dryden's *The Wild Gallant* (1663).

[4] See p. 104 for a description of this performance.

company; so I went in and found a pretty good company there, and saw their dance at the end of the play.

June 3, 1668. To the King's house and there saw good part of "The Scornfull Lady."

[Beaumont and] Fletcher and Massinger (?)

THE SPANISH CURATE

March 16, 1660-61. So to Whitefriars and saw "The Spanish Curate,"[1] in which I had no great content.

January 1, 1661-62. Seeing that the "Spanish Curate" was acted, . . . sent to young Mr. Pen to go with my wife and I to the Theatre, . . . and by and by came the two young Pens, and after we had eat a barrel of oysters we went by coach to the play, and there saw it well acted, and a good play it is, only Diego the Sexton did overdo his part too much. From thence home, and they sat with us till late at night at cards very merry, but the jest was Mr. W. Pen[2] had left his sword in the coach.

May 17, 1669. To the King's playhouse,[3] and saw "The Spanish Curate" revived, which is a pretty good play, but my eyes troubled with seeing it mightily.

---

[1] A comedy (1622) by Fletcher and Massinger (?). The cast is not given by Downes or Genest.

[2] This was William Penn, the Quaker, founder of Pennsylvania.

[3] For the last performance mentioned in the *Diary*, which

[Beaumont and] Fletcher and Massinger (?)

THE STORM (THE SEA VOYAGE)

September 25, 1667. To the King's playhouse.
. . . The play was a new play; and infinitely full;
the King and all the Court almost there. It is "The
Storme,"[1] a play of Fletcher's; which is but so-so,
methinks; only there is a most admirable dance at the
end, of the ladies, in a military manner, which indeed
did please me mightily.

September 26, 1667. With my wife abroad to the
King's playhouse, to shew her yesterday's new play,
which I like as I did yesterday, the principal thing
extraordinary being the dance, which is very good.

March 25, 1668. To the King's playhouse, to see
"The Storme," which we did, but without much pleas-
ure, it being but a mean play compared with "The
Tempest," at the Duke of York's house, though
Knepp did act her part[2] of grief very well.

May 16, 1668. To the King's playhouse and there
saw the best part of "The Sea Voyage," where Knepp
I see do her part of sorrow very well.

Pepys brought to a close on May 31, from the fear that he was
losing his eyesight. Happily, his fears for his eyes proved to
be groundless.

[1] A comedy (1622) by Fletcher and Massinger (?) with
superficial resemblances to *The Tempest*—called by Pepys on
May 16, 1668, *The Sea Voyage*. For *The Widow*, in which
Fletcher is said to have collaborated with Jonson and Middleton,
see p. 119.

[2] "Mrs. Knipp acted Aminta" (Genest, I, 81).

[Beaumont and] Fletcher   THE WILD GOOSE CHASE

January 11, 1667-68.   To the King's house, there
to see "The Wild-goose Chase,"[1] which I never saw,
but have longed to see it, being a famous play, but as
it was yesterday I do find that where I expect most I
find least satisfaction, for in this play I met with
nothing extraordinary at all, but very dull inventions
and designs.

[Beaumont and] Fletcher   WIT WITHOUT MONEY

October 16, 1660.   And so . . . to the Cockpit,
where, understanding that "Wit without money"[1]
was acted, I would not stay.

April 22, 1663.   To the King's Playhouse, where
we saw but part of "Witt without mony," which I
do not like much, but coming late put me out of tune,
and it costing me four half-crowns for myself and
company.

---

[1] A comedy (1621) by John Fletcher. It is mentioned in the
list of plays performed by Killigrew's company, given in
Malone's *Shakspeare,* Vol. I, Part II, p. 266, as having been
acted in February, 1661.

[1] A comedy (1614) by John Fletcher. Langbaine (p. 216)
mentions having seen it "acted at the Old House in little *Lincolns-Inn-Fields* with very great applause; the part of *Valentine*
being play'd by that compleat Actor Major *Mohun* deceas'd."
This performance was probably at the Drury Lane Cockpit.

[Beaumont and] Fletcher
THE WOMAN'S PRIZE, OR THE TAMER TAMED

October 30, 1660. In the afternoon, to ease my mind, I went to the Cockpit all alone, and there saw a very fine play called "The Tamer tamed";[1] very well acted.

July 31, 1661. In the afternoon I went to the Theatre, and there I saw "The Tamer Tamed" well done.

[Beaumont and] Fletcher   WOMEN PLEASED

December 26, 1668. To a play, at the Duke of York's house, the house full of ordinary citizens. The play was "Women Pleased,"[1] which we had never seen before; and, though but indifferent, yet there is a good design for a good play.

Brome, Richard   THE ANTIPODES

August 26, 1661. To the Theatre, and saw the "Antipodes,"[1] wherein there is much mirth, but no great matter else.

[1] A comedy (1606?) in continuation of *The Taming of the Shrew*, by John Fletcher, acted probably at the Cockpit, Drury Lane, as plays at the Whitehall Cockpit were performed in the evening. It is also in the list of plays acted at the Drury Lane Cockpit given in *Roscius Anglicanus*, p. 18.

[1] A loosely constructed tragi-comedy (1620?) by John Fletcher.

[1] A comedy (1630) by Richard Brome.

Brome, Richard

The Jovial Crew, or The Merry Beggars

July 25, 1661. To the Theatre, and saw "The Jovial Crew,"[1] the first time I saw it, and indeed it is as merry and the most innocent play that ever I saw, and well performed.

August 27, 1661. Hence my wife and I to the Theatre, and there saw "The Joviall Crew," where the King, Duke and Duchess, and Madame Palmer, were, and my wife, to her great content, had a full sight of them all the while. The play full of mirth.

November 1, 1661. To the Theatre, to "The Joviall Crew."

January 11, 1668-69. To the King's playhouse, and there saw "The Joviall Crew"; but ill acted to what it was heretofore, in Clun's time, and when Lacy could dance.

Brome, Richard   The Northern Castle [Lass?]

September 14, 1667. To the King's playhouse to see "The Northerne Castle,"[1] which I think I never

---

[1] A comedy (1641) by Richard Brome, listed by Downes (*Roscius Anglicanus,* p. 8) among the "Principal Old Stock Plays" of the King's theatre.

[1] No play so called is known. The play which is nearest to it in point of title is Richard's Brome's comedy, *The Northern Lass,* printed in 1632; it has a pathetic heroine, Constance (the Northern Lass). That this was in the repertory of the King's company, we know from the list of plays given in Malone's *Shakspeare,* Vol. I, Part II, p. 267, according to which it was

did see before. Knipp acted in it, and did her part very extraordinary well; but the play is but a mean, sorry play; but the house very full of gallants. It seems, it hath not been acted a good while.

Chapman, George   Bussy D'Ambois

December 30, 1661. My wife has been at a play to-day and saw "D'Ambois,"[1] which I never saw.

November 15, 1662. After reading part of Bussy d'Ambois, a good play I bought to-day, to bed.

Cooke, John   Tu Quoque, or The City Gallant

September 12, 1667. At the Duke's house, where "Tu Quoque"[1] was the first time acted, with some

acted on April 4, 1662; and also from Langbaine, who says (p. 36) that *The Northern Lass* was "acted with great Applause at the Theatre Royal, by his Majestie's Servants, printed in quarto, *Lond.* 1663." W. C. Hazlitt states (*A Manual for the Collector and Amateur of Old English Plays,* p. 168) that "the 4to of 1663 describes it as acted with great applause at the Theatre Royal; and it seems to be the piece intended by Pepys, where he speaks of the *Northern Castle,* under the date of September 14, 1667."

[1] A tragedy (1595-1600) by George Chapman—"since the Restauration of King *Charles* the Second," says Langbaine (pp. 60-61), "acted at the Theatre-Royal with good applause." In the list of plays performed by Killigrew's company, in Malone's *Shakspeare,* Vol. I, Part II, p. 267, this play is mentioned as having been given on this date. According to Genest (I, 351), Hart usually took the title part.

[1] A comedy by John Cooke, in which the rôle of Bubble was

alterations of Sir W. Davenant's; but the play is a
very silly play, methinks: for I, and others that sat
by me, Mr. Povy and Mr. Progers, were weary of it;
but it will please the citizens.

September 16, 1667.   Against our wills, went all to
see "Tu Quoque" again, where there is pretty store
of company, and going with a prejudice the play
appeared better to us.   Here we saw Madam Moreland,[2] who is grown mighty fat, but is very comely.
But one of the best parts of our sport was a mighty
pretty lady that sat behind us, that did laugh so
heartily and constantly that it did me good to hear
her.

Ford, John   THE LADY'S TRIAL

March 3, 1668-69.   To the Duke of York's playhouse, and there saw an old play, the first time acted
these forty years, called "The Lady's Tryall,"[1] acted
only by the young people of the house; but the house
very full.   But it is but a sorry play, and the worse
by how much my head is out of humour by being a
little sleepy.

immortalized by Thomas Greene, printed in 1614; it is mentioned by Downes (*Roscius Anglicanus,* p. 26) as having been
acted at the Duke's theatre between 1662 and 1665.   It was
revived in 1667 with "alterations" by D'Avenant.   (Cf. *A Manual for the Collector and Amateur of Old English Plays,* by
W. C. Hazlitt, p. 99.)

   [2] The wife of Sir Samuel Moreland, and daughter of the Baron
of Boissay.

   [1] A tragi-comedy (1638) by John Ford.

Ford, John   'Tis Pity She's a Whore

September 9, 1661. Thence to Salisbury Court
playhouse, where was acted the first time " 'Tis pity
Shee's a Whore,"[1] a simple play and ill acted, only
it was my fortune to sit by a most pretty and
most ingenious lady, which pleased me much.

Glapthorne, Henry   Argalus and Parthenia

January 31, 1660-61. To the Theatre and there
sat in the pit among the company of fine ladys, &c.;
and the house was exceeding full, to see Argalus and
Parthenia,[1] the first time it hath been acted; and
indeed it is good, though wronged by my over great
expectations, as all things else are.

February 5, 1660-61. I went by coach to the playhouse at the Theatre, our coach in King Street breaking, and so took another. Here we saw Argalus and
Parthenia, which I lately saw, but though pleasant
for dancing and singing, I do not find good for any
wit or design therein.

October 28, 1661. To the Theatre, and there saw
"Argalus and Parthenia," where a woman acted
Parthenia,[2] and came afterwards on the stage in

[1] A tragedy (1626?) by John Ford.

[1] A pastoral drama (1638?) by Henry Glapthorne, based upon
an episode in Sidney's *Arcadia* (Book III). This performance
is also mentioned in the list of plays acted by Killigrew's company, given in Malone's *Shakspeare,* Vol. I, Part II, p. 266.

[2] Downes does not record the cast for this play.

men's clothes, and had the best legs that ever I saw, and I was very well pleased with it.

Glapthorne, Henry   WIT IN A CONSTABLE

May 23, 1662. To the Opera, where we saw "Witt in a Constable,"[1] the first time that it is acted; but so silly a play I never saw I think in my life.

Habington, William

CLEODORA, THE QUEEN OF ARRAGON

October 19, 1668. To the Duke of York's play-house; and there saw, the first time acted, "The Queene of Arragon," an old Blackfriars' play,[1] but an admirable one, so good that I am astonished at it, and wonder where it hath lain asleep all this while, that I have never heard of it before.

October 20, 1668. So to my tailor's, and the New Exchange, and so by coach home, and there, having this day bought "The Queene of Arragon" play, I did get my wife and W. Batelier to read it over this night by 11 o'clock.

[1] A comedy (1639) by Henry Glapthorne, mentioned by Downes (*Roscius Anglicanus*, p. 26) among the plays performed by the Duke's company between 1662 and 1665.

[1] A tragi-comedy by William Habington, staged with great expense at Blackfriars in 1640. Downes (*Roscius Anglicanus*, p. 29) merely notes that it was acted at the Duke's house subsequent to Etherege's *She Would if She Could.*

Heywood, Thomas
LOVE'S MISTRESS, OR THE QUEEN'S MASQUE

March 2, 1660-61. After dinner I went to the Theatre, where I found so few people (which is strange, and the reason I did not know) that I went out again, and so to Salsbury Court, where the house as full as could be; and it seems it was a new play, "The Queen's Maske,"[1] wherein there are some good humours: among others, a good jeer to the old story of the Siege of Troy, making it a common country tale. But above all it was strange to see so little a boy as that was to act Cupid, which is one of the greatest parts in it.

March 11, 1660-61. To the Theatre, and there saw "Love's Mistress" done by them, which I do not like in some things as well as their acting in Salsbury Court.

March 25, 1661. To Salisbury Court by water, and saw part of the "Queene's Maske."

May 15, 1665. To the King's playhouse, all alone, and saw "Love's Maistresse." Some pretty things and good variety in it, but no or little fancy in it.

August 15, 1668. To the King's playhouse, and there saw "Love's Mistresse" revived, the thing pretty good, but full of variety of divertisement.

---

[1] An allegorical drama (1634) by Thomas Heywood, originally produced by Inigo Jones.

Heywood, Thomas

IF YOU KNOW NOT ME, YOU KNOW NOBODY, OR THE TROUBLES OF QUEEN ELIZABETH

August 17, 1667. To the King's playhouse, where the house extraordinary full; and there was the King and Duke of York to see the new play, "Queen Elizabeth's Troubles, and the History of Eighty Eight."[1] I confess I have sucked in so much of the sad story of Queen Elizabeth, from my cradle, that I was ready to weep for her sometimes; but the play is the most ridiculous that sure ever come upon the stage; and, indeed, is merely a shew, only shews the true garbe of the Queen in those days, just as we see Queen Mary and Queen Elizabeth painted; but the play is merely a puppet play, acted by living puppets. Neither the design nor language better; and one stands by and tells us the meaning of things: only I was pleased to see Knipp dance among the milkmaids, and to hear her sing a song to Queen Elizabeth; and to see her come out in her night-gowne with no lockes on.

[1] An historical play in two parts (1604-1605) by Thomas Heywood. W. C. Hazlitt comments with reference to this entry that the play "was probably altered by some later hand, and the recent Dutch invasion had doubtless suggested its revival" (*A Manual for the Collector and Amateur of Old English Plays,* p. 113).

Jonson, Ben   THE ALCHEMIST

June 22, 1661. Then to the Theatre, "The Alchymist,"[1] which is a most incomparable play.

August 14, 1661. To the Theatre, and there saw "The Alchymist."

August 4, 1664. We hear that Clun, one of their best actors, was, the last night, going out of towne (after he had acted the Alchymist, wherein was one of his best parts) . . . set upon and murdered.

April 17, 1669. Learning that "The Alchymist," was acted, we did go, and took him [Pierce] with us to the King's house; and it is still a good play, having not been acted for two or three years before; but I do miss Clun, for the Doctor.[2]

Jonson, Ben   BARTHOLOMEW FAIR

June 8, 1661. To the Theatre and there saw "Bartholomew Faire,"[1] the first time it was acted now-a-days. It is a most admirable play and well acted, but too much prophane and abusive.

[1] A comedy (1610) by Ben Jonson.

[2] Clearly, Subtle, the alchemist. The cast given by Downes (*Roscius Anglicanus,* pp. 4-5) was probably the cast of this revival, and not, as Genest hazards, that of the 1664 performance. In it Wintersell acted Clun's old part of Subtle, and Mohun, Lacy, Cartwright, Burt, and Mrs. Corey (in the part of Doll Common), were in the cast.

[1] A comedy (1614) by Ben Jonson, which was popular on its revival after the Restoration partly because of its abuse of the Puritans. To Pepys, "the Puritan tailor's son," it was natural that it should have seemed too "prophane."

June 27, 1661. We went and saw "Bartholomew Fayre" acted very well.

September 7, 1661. I having appointed the young ladies at the Wardrobe[2] to go with them to the play to-day, . . . my wife and I took them to the Theatre, where we seated ourselves close by the King, and Duke of York, and Madame Palmer, which was great content; and, indeed, I can never enough admire her beauty. And here was "Bartholomew Fayre," with the puppet-show,[3] acted to-day, which had not been these forty years, (it being so satyricall against Puritanism, they durst not till now, which is strange they should already dare to do it, and the King to countenance it), but I do never a whit like it the better for the puppets, but rather the worse. Thence home with the ladies, it being by reason of our staying for the King's coming, and the length of the play, near nine o'clock before it was done.

August 2, 1664. Thence to the King's play-house, and there saw "Bartholomew Fayre," which do still please me; and is, as it is acted, the best comedy in the world, I believe. I chanced to sit by Tom Killigrew.

September 4, 1668. To the Fair: . . . my wife having a mind to see the play "Bartholomew-Fayre," with puppets. Which we did, and it is an excellent play; the more I see it, the more I love the wit of it;

[2] The daughters of Pepys's patron, Lord Sandwich.

[3] *The Modern History of Hero and Leander,* in Act V. From Pepys's comment on this occasion, we infer that the puppet-show had been omitted from the presentations of the play on June 8 and June 27 of this year.

only the business of abusing the Puritans begins to grow stale, and of no use, they being the people that, at last, will be found the wisest.

February 22, 1668-69. To White Hall, . . . and there by and by come the King and Queen, and they begin "Bartholomew Fayre." But I like no play here so well as at the common playhouse.

Jonson, Ben   CATILINE, HIS CONSPIRACY

December 18, 1664. Then to my chamber to read Ben Jonson's Cataline,[1] a very excellent piece.

December 7, 1667. She tells us that Catelin is likely to be soon acted, which I am glad to hear, but it is at the King's house. But the King's house is at present and hath for some days been silenced upon some difference [between] Hart and Moone.

December 11, 1667. I met Rolt and Sir John Chichly, and Harris, the player, and there we talked of many things, and particularly of "Catiline," which is to be suddenly acted at the King's house; and there all agree that it cannot be well done at that house, there not being good actors enow: and Burt acts Cicero,[2] which they all conclude he will not be able to

---

[1] A tragedy (1611) by Ben Jonson. Evelyn saw it on December 19, 1668. He records: "I went to see ye old play of Cataline acted, having ben now forgotten almost 40 yeares" (*Diary*, Wheatley ed., II, 233).

[2] Cicero became, however, one of Burt's most popular parts. Hart was Catiline; Mohun, Cethegus; and Mrs. Corey, Sempronia. (Genest, I, 84.)

do well. The King gives them £500 for robes, there being, as they say, to be sixteen scarlett robes.

January 11, 1667-68. She [Knepp] told me also of . . . "Catelin," which she thinks, for want of the clothes which the King promised them, will not be acted for a good while.

December 19, 1668. To the King's playhouse, and there, the pit being full, sat in a box above, and saw "Catiline's Conspiracy," yesterday being the first day: a play of much good sense and words to read, but that do appear the worst upon the stage, I mean, the least diverting, that ever I saw any, though most in fine clothes; and a fine scene of the Senate, and of a fight, that ever I saw in my life. But the play is only to be read.

Jonson, Ben   THE DEVIL IS AN ASS

July 22, 1663. So down to Deptford, reading Ben Jonson's "Devil is an asse."[1]

Jonson, Ben   EPICOENE, OR THE SILENT WOMAN

June 6, 1660. My letters tell me . . . that the two Dukes [York and Gloucester] . . . were at a play, Madame Epicene,[1] the other day.

[1] A comedy (1616) by Ben Jonson, mentioned among the "Principal Old Stock Plays" of the King's company in *Roscius Anglicanus,* p. 8.

[1] *Epicoene, or The Silent Woman,* a comedy (1610) by Ben

December 4, 1660. After dinner Sir Tho. [Crew] and my Lady to the Playhouse to see "The Silent Woman."

January 7, 1660-61. Tom and I and my wife to the Theatre, and there saw "The Silent Woman," the first time that ever I did see it, and it is an excellent play. Among other things here, Kinaston, the boy, had the good turn to appear in three shapes: first as a poor woman in ordinary clothes, to please Morose; then in fine clothes, as a gallant, and in them was clearly the prettiest woman in the whole house,[2] and lastly, as a man; and then likewise did appear the handsomest man in the house.

May 25, 1661. To the Theatre, where I saw a piece of "The Silent Woman," which pleased me.

June 1, 1664. To the King's house, and saw "The Silent Woman"; but me-thought not so well done[3] or so good a play as I formerly thought it to be, or else I am now a-days out of humour. Before the play was done, it fell such a storm of hayle, that we in the middle of the pit were fain to rise; and all the house in a disorder.

April 16, 1667. In haste to carry my wife to the

Jonson, mentioned in the list of plays "acted by the Red Bull Actors" given in Malone's *Shakspeare,* Vol. I, Part II, p. 265.

[2] Epicoene was one of Kynaston's famous parts.

[3] "The cast which Downes gives was probably the cast of this day," says Genest (I, pp. 49-50). It included Cartwright as Morose; Mohun as Truewit; Wintersell, Sir Amorous; Shotterel, Daw; Lacy, Captain Otter; Burt, Clerimont; Kynaston, Sir Dauphine; Mrs. Knepp, Epicoene; and Mrs. Corey, Mrs. Otter.

new play I saw yesterday,[4] she not knowing it.   But
there, contrary to expectation, find "The Silent
Woman." However, in. . . . I was never more taken
with a play than I am with this "Silent Woman," as
old as it is, and as often as I have seen it.   There is
more wit in it than goes to ten new plays.

September 18, 1668.   At the end of the play,
thinking to have gone abroad with Knepp, but it was
too late, and she to get her part against to-morrow, in
"The Silent Woman."

September 19, 1668.   To the King's playhouse,
and there saw "The Silent Woman," the best comedy,
I think, that ever was wrote; and sitting by Shadwell the poet, he was big with admiration of it. . . .
Knepp did her part mighty well.

Jonson, Ben   Every Man in his Humour

February 9, 1666-67.   Read a piece of a play,
"Every Man in his Humour,"[1] wherein is the greatest propriety of speech that ever I read in my life.

---

[4] Edward Howard's *The Change of Crowns.*

[1] A comedy (1598) by Ben Jonson; according to Downes
(*Roscius Anglicanus,* p. 8) one of the "Principal Old Stock
Plays" at the King's theatre.

Jonson, Ben   Volpone, or The Fox

January 14, 1664-65. To the King's house, there
to see "Vulpone,"[1] a most excellent play; the best I
think I ever saw, and well acted.[2]

Kyd, Thomas
          The Spanish Tragedy, or Hieronimo Is
                                    Mad Again

February 24, 1667-68. To the Nursery, where
none of us ever were before; where the house is better
and the musique better than we looked for, and the
acting not much worse, because I expected as bad as
could be: and I was not much mistaken, for it was so.
However, I was pleased well to see it once, it being
worth a man's seeing to discover the different ability
and understanding of people, and the different
growth of people's abilities by practise. Their play
was a bad one, called "Jeronimo is Mad Again,"[1] a
tragedy. Here was some good company by us, who
did make mighty sport at the folly of their acting,
which I could not neither refrain from sometimes,
though I was sorry for it.

[1] A comedy (1605-1606) by Ben Jonson. On October 16,
1662, Evelyn "saw 'Volpone' acted at Court before their Maties"
(*Diary,* Wheatley ed., II, 153).

[2] Downes (*Roscius Anglicanus,* p. 4) gives the following cast:
Volpone, Mohun; Mosca, Hart; Corbaccio, Cartwright; Corvino,
Burt; Sir Politique Would-be, Lacy; Peregrine, Kynaston; Lady
Would-be, Mrs. Corey; Celia, Mrs. Marshall.

[1] A tragedy (1586) by Thomas Kyd. It was performed perhaps at the "Nursery" for actors in Hatton Garden.

Marlowe, Christopher

THE TRAGICAL HISTORY OF DOCTOR FAUSTUS

May 26, 1662.   To the Redd Bull, where we saw "Doctor Faustus,"[1] but so wretchedly and poorly done, that we were sick of it, and the worse because by a former resolution it is to be the last play we are to see till Michaelmas.[2]

Massinger, Philip   THE BONDMAN

March 1, 1660-61.   To Whitefryars, and saw "The Bondman"[1] acted; an excellent play and well done. But above all that ever I saw, Betterton do the Bondman[2] best.

March 19, 1660-61.   To White-Fryars, where we saw "The Bondman" acted most excellently, and though I have seen it often, yet I am every time more and more pleased with Betterton's action.

March 26, 1661.   To Salisbury Court, where coming late . . . I and my wife sat in the pit, . . . and saw "The Bondman" done to admiration.

[1] Marlowe's tragedy (1588) probably as printed in the edition of 1663, which contained "several new scenes and the actors' names" (J. O. Halliwell [Phillipps], *Dictionary of Old English Plays,* p. 76).

[2] It may be of interest to note that on September 29 (Michaelmas), Pepys writes: "This day my oaths for drinking of wine and going to plays are out, and so I do resolve to take a liberty to-day, and then to fall to them again."

[1] A tragi-comedy (1623) by Philip Massinger.

[2] Marullo.

May 25, 1661. In my way bought "The Bond-man" in Paul's Churchyard.

November 4, 1661. To the Opera where we saw "The Bondman," which of old we both did so doat on, and do still; though to both our thinking not so well acted here (having too great expectations) as formerly at Salisbury-court. But for Betterton, he is called by us both the best actor in the world.

November 25, 1661. After dinner to the theatre, and there saw "The Country Captain"; and that being done . . . went to the Opera, and saw the last act of "The Bondman."

April 2, 1662. To the Opera and there saw "The Bondman" most excellently acted; and though we had seen it so often, yet I never liked it better than to-day, Ianthe[3] acting Cleora's part very well now Roxalana is gone.

July 28, 1664. Seeing "The Bondman" upon the posts,[4] I consulted my oath and find I may go safely this time without breaking it. . . . There I saw it acted. It is true, for want of practice, they had many of them forgot their parts a little; but Betterton and my poor Ianthe outdo all the world. There is nothing more taking in the world with me than that play.

November 2, 1666. And so home,[5] I reading all the way to make an end of the "Bondman" (which the oftener I read the more I like).

[3] Mrs. Betterton ("Ianthe") succeeded Elizabeth Davenport ("Roxalana") in this and other important parts.

[4] Where the playbills were placed.

[5] From Deptford where he frequently went on business for the Admiralty.

Massinger and Dekker   THE VIRGIN MARTYR

February 16, 1660-61.   To the Theatre, where I saw "The Virgin Martyr,"[1] a good but too sober a play for the company.

February 27, 1667-68.   To the King's House, to see "The Virgin Martyr," the first time it hath been acted a great while: and it is mighty pleasant; not that the play is worth much, but it is finely acted by Becke Marshal.[2]   But that which did please me beyond anything in the whole world was the wind musique when the angel comes down, which is so sweet that it ravished me.

March 2, 1667-68.   To the King's house to see the "Virgin Martyr" again, which do mightily please me, but above all the musique at the coming down of the angel,[3] which at this hearing the second time, do still commend me as nothing ever did, and the other musique is nothing to it.

May 6, 1668.   To the King's playhouse, and there saw "The Virgin Martyr," and heard the music that I like so well.

Mayne, Jasper   THE CITY MATCH

September 28, 1668.   Knepp's maid comes to me, to tell me that the women's day[1] at the playhouse is

---

[1] A tragedy by Massinger and Dekker, licensed in 1620.

[2] Rebecca Marshall played the part of St. Dorothea.   (Cf. Genest, I, 80.)

[3] The angel entertained by St. Dorothea as her page.

[1] The women's benefit.

to-day, and that therefore I must be there, to encrease
their profit. . . . Towards the King's playhouse, . . .
and there saw "The City Match";[2] not acted these
thirty years, and but a silly play; the King and
Court there; the house, for the women's sake, mighty
full.

Middleton, Thomas   THE MAYOR OF QUINBOROUGH

June 16, 1666. All the way down and up[1] reading of "The Mayor of Quinborough,"[2] a simple play.

Jonson (?), Fletcher (?), and Middleton
THE WIDOW

January 8, 1660-61. To the Theatre, and shewed
them "The Widdow,"[1] an indifferent good play, but
wronged by the women being to seek in their parts.

[2] A farcical comedy by Jasper Mayne, acted in 1639.

[1] To and from Deptford.

[2] An historical play (1596?) by Thomas Middleton, printed
in 1661. Langbaine (p. 372) says that it was "often acted with
much applause, by his Majesties Servants."

[1] A comedy by "Jonson, Fletcher, Middleton," acted between
1616 and 1625. Evelyn mentions a performance of it on January 16, 1661-62: "This night was acted before his Maty,
'The Widow,' a lewd play" (*Diary*, Wheatley ed., II, 143).
Langbaine (p. 298) says it "Was reviv'd not many Years ago,
at the King's House, with a new Prologue and Epilogue."

Middleton and W. Rowley   THE CHANGELING

February 23, 1660-61. Then by water to Whitefriars to the Play-house, and there saw "The Changeling,"[1] the first time it hath been acted these twenty
years, and it takes exceedingly. Besides, I see the
gallants do begin to be tyred with the vanity and
pride of the theatre actors who are indeed grown very
proud and rich.

Middleton and W. Rowley   THE SPANISH GYPSY

June 16, 1661. This afternoon . . . I spent in
reading "The Spanish Gypsey,"[1] a play not very
good, though commended much.

March 7, 1667-68. To the King's playhouse, and
there saw "The Spanish Gipsys," the second time of
acting, and the first that I saw it. A very silly play,
only great variety of dances, and those most excellently done, especially one part by one Hanes[2] only
lately come thither from the Nursery.

[1] A tragedy (1623) by Middleton and W. Rowley; its success
was undoubtedly due in part to the acting of Betterton in the
rôle of De Flores.

[1] A tragi-comedy (1623) by Middleton and W. Rowley.

[2] Joseph Haines's name occurs in Downes's list (*Roscius
Anglicanus,* p. 2) of actors who joined the King's company
"after they had begun in Drury-Lane."

Riley, Thomas (?)   CORNELIANUM DOLIUM

November 15, 1660. So to Paul's Churchyard and bought "Cornelianum dolium."[1]

December 3, 1660. I fell a reading Cornelianum dolium till 11 o'clock at night with great pleasure.

Rowley, William   ALL'S LOST BY LUST

March 23, 1660-61. At last into the pitt[1] where I think there was not above ten more than myself, and not one hundred in the whole house. And the play, which is called "All's lost by Lust,"[2] poorly done; and with so much disorder, among others, in the musique-room, the boy that was to sing a song, not singing it right, his master fell about his ears and beat him so, that it put the whole house into an uprore.

Shirley, James   THE CARDINAL

October 2, 1662. Hearing that there was a play at the Cockpit,[1] . . . I do go thither, and by very great fortune did follow four or five gentlemen who

[1] A Latin comedy (1638) "probably by Thomas Riley of Trinity College, Cambridge," asserts W. C. Hazlitt (*A Manual for the Collector and Amateur of Old English Plays*, p. 50).

[1] At the Red Bull Playhouse.

[2] A tragedy (1619?) by W. Rowley, mentioned in the list of plays performed by Killigrew's company, in Malone's *Shakspeare*, Vol. I, Part II, p. 266, as having been acted in March, April, and May of this year.

[1] In Whitehall Palace.

were carried to a little private door in a wall, and so crept through a narrow place and come into one of the boxes next the King's, but so as I could not see the King or Queene, but many of the fine ladies, who yet are really not so handsome generally as I used to take them to be, but that they are finely dressed. Here we saw "The Cardinall,"[2] a tragedy I had never seen before, nor is there any great matter in it. The company that came in with me into the box, were all Frenchmen that could speak no English, but, Lord! what sport they made to ask a pretty lady that they got among them that understood both French and English to make her tell them what the actors said.

August 24, 1667. Saw "The Cardinall" at the King's house, wherewith I am mightily pleased; but, above all, with Becke Marshall.[3]

April 27, 1668. To the King's playhouse, and there saw most of "The Cardinall," a good play.

Shirley, James THE CHANGES, OR LOVE IN A MAZE

May 22, 1662. To the Theatre and saw "Love in a Maze."[1] The play hath little in it but Lacy's part of a country fellow,[2] which he did to admiration.

June 10, 1663. To the Royal Theatre by water,

[2] A tragedy by James Shirley licensed in 1641, mentioned by Downes (*Roscius Anglicanus,* p. 8) among the "Principal Old Stock Plays" of the King's company.

[3] Rebecca Marshall doubtless acted the part of the Duchess Rosaura.

[1] A comedy (1632) by James Shirley.

[2] Langbaine records (p. 477): "As I remember, the deceas'd

and . . . we saw "Love in a Maze." The play is pretty good, but the life of the play is Lacy's part, the clown, which is most admirable; but for the rest, which are counted such old and excellent actors, in my life I never heard both men and women so ill pronounce their parts, even to my making myself sick therewith.

May 1, 1667. Thence away to the King's playhouse, . . . and saw "Love in a Maze": but a sorry play: only Lacy's clowne's part, which he did most admirably indeed; and I am glad to find the rogue at liberty again. Here was but little, and that ordinary company.

February 7, 1667-68. To the King's playhouse, and there saw a piece of "Love in a Maze," a dull, silly play, I think.

April 28, 1668. To the King's house, and there did see "Love in a Maze," wherein very good mirth of Lacy, the clown, and Wintersell, the country-knight, his master.[3]

Shirley, James   THE COURT SECRET

August 18, 1664. My wife going to-day to see a new play, "The Court Secret."[1] . . . My wife says the play she saw is the worst that ever she saw in her life.

Mr. *Lacy* acted *Jonny Thump,* Sir *Gervase Simple's* man, with general Applause."

    [3] Sir Gervase Simple was impersonated by William Wintersell.

    [1] A tragi-comedy by James Shirley, written before 1642 but not acted, according to Langbaine (p. 484), "till after it appeared in print, . . . 1653." Genest states (I, 351) that it "was brought out by the King's company."

Shirley, James   THE GRATEFUL SERVANT

February 20, 1668-69. To the Duke of York's
house, and there saw "The Gratefull Servant,"[1] a
pretty good play, and which I have forgot that ever
I did see.

Shirley, James   HYDE PARK

July 11, 1668. After dinner to the King's playhouse, to see an old play of Shirly's, called "Hide
Parke";[1] the first day acted; where horses are brought
upon the stage:[2] but it is a very moderate play, only
an excellent epilogue spoke by Beck Marshall.

[1] A tragi-comedy (licensed in 1629) by James Shirley.
Downes (*Roscius Anglicanus,* p. 27) mentions the production
of this play, which he says was "well Perform'd; especially
Dulcino the Grateful Servant, being Acted by Mrs. *Long;* and
the first time she appear'd in Man's Habit, prov'd as Beneficial
to the Company, as several succeeding new Plays."

[1] A comedy of contemporary London life by James Shirley,
licensed in 1632.

[2] Doubtless during the scene at the races laid in Hyde Park
in Act IV. Mr. Edmund Gosse, in commenting upon this entry
in Pepys's journal, remarks that "it would not appear that this
was attempted by Shirley, since the stage directions . . .
together with the fact that the personages enter to inform their
friends of their luck, seem to show that the horses were kept out
of sight of the audience." (Cf. *James Shirley,* in *The Mermaid
Series,* [1888] ed., Introduction, p. 22.)

Shirley, James   LOVE'S CRUELTY

December 30, 1667. To the King's playhouse,
there to see "Love's Cruelty,"[1] an old play, but which
I have not seen before, . . . and it proves to me a
very silly play, and to everybody else, as far as I could
judge.

April 14, 1668. Thence to a play, "Love's
Cruelty." . . . Play part 2*s.* Oranges 1*s.*

Shirley, James
    LOVE TRICKS, OR THE SCHOOL OF COMPLIMENT

August 5, 1667. To the Duke of York's house,
and there saw "Love Trickes, or the School of Compliments,"[1] a silly play, only Mis's [Davis's]dancing[2]
in the shepherds clothes did please us mightily.

January 7, 1667-68. To look for them, and there
by this means, for nothing, see an act in "The Schoole
of Compliments" at the Duke of York's house.

[1] A tragedy (1631) by James Shirley, evidently one of the
earliest plays to be revived after the Restoration, as it occurs
in the list of "plays acted by the Red Bull Actors," given in
Malone's *Shakspeare,* Vol. I, Part II, p. 265. Mohun played
the part of Bellamente.

[1] A comedy (1625) by James Shirley; its revival is noted by
Downes, *Roscius Anglicanus,* p. 27.

[2] In the part of Selina, who disguised as a shepherd dances
with Antonio, who is in women's clothes.

Shirley, James   THE TRAITOR

November 22, 1660. I to the new playhouse and saw part of the "Traitor,"[1] a very good Tragedy; Mr. Moon did act the Traitor[2] very well.

October 10, 1661. To the Theatre . . . where the King came to-day, and there was "The Traytor" most admirably acted; and a most excellent play it is.

January 13, 1664-65. To the King's house, to a play, "The Traytor," where, unfortunately, I met with Sir W. Pen, so that I must be forced to confess it[3] to my wife, which troubles me.

October 2, 1667. To the King's house to see "The Traytour," which still I like as a very good play.

Suckling, Sir John   AGLAURA

September 24, 1662. Bird[1] hath lately broke his leg, while he was fencing in "Aglaura."[2]

[1] A tragedy (1631) by James Shirley, mentioned in the list of plays performed by Killigrew's company, given in Malone's *Shakspeare,* Vol. I, Part II, p. 266, as having been acted on this date.

[2] Lorenzo, "Kinsman and Favourite" of the Duke of Florence; "Mr. Moon" is Michael Mohun.

[3] His playgoing in violation of a vow.

[1] R. W. Lowe mentions in this connection an actor named Theophilus Bird. (Cf. *Thomas Betterton,* 1891 ed., p. 78.)

[2] A pseudo-historical tragedy by Sir John Suckling, first acted as a tragedy in 1636, later acted as a tragi-comedy in 1637, with a new fifth act giving a happy ending to the intricate and sinister plot.

September 5, 1664. To Deptford, and so home, all the way reading Sir J. Suck[l]ing's "Aglaura," which, methinks, is but a mean play, nothing of design in it.

January 10, 1667-68. To the King's house, to see "Aglaura," which hath been always mightily cried up; and so I went with mighty expectation, but do find nothing extraordinary in it at all, and but hardly good in any degree.

Suckling, Sir John

BRENNORALT, OR THE DISCONTENTED COLONEL

July 23, 1661. I went to the Theatre, and saw "Brenoralt,"[1] I never saw before. It seemed a good play, but ill acted.

August 12, 1667. To the King's playhouse, and there . . . the play is "Brenoralt," which I do find but little in, for my part.

October 18, 1667. To the King's house, and saw "Brenoralt," which is a good tragedy that I like well.

March 5, 1667-68. To the King's house, and there saw part of "The Discontented Colonel," but could take no great pleasure in it, because of our coming in in the middle of it.

---

[1] A tragi-comedy (printed 1646) with a pseudo-historical background, by Sir John Suckling.

Suckling, Sir John   THE GOBLINS

January 23, 1666-67. Knipp made us stay in a box
and see the dancing preparatory to to-morrow for
"The Goblins,"[1] a play of Suckling's not acted these
twenty-five years; which was pretty.

January 24, 1666-67. But it was she [Knepp]
coming off the stage just as she acted this day in "The
Goblins."

May 22, 1667. To the King's house, where I did
give 18*d.*, and saw the last two acts of "The Goblins,"
a play I could not make any thing out of by these two
acts, but here Knipp spied me out of the tiring-room,
and come to the pit door.

Tomkis, Thomas   ALBUMAZAR

February 22, 1667-68. To the Duke's playhouse,
and there saw "Albumazar,"[1] an old play, this the
second time of acting. It is said to have been the
ground of B. Jonson's "Alchymist"; but, saving the
ridiculousnesse of Angell's part, which is called Trinkilo, I do not see anything extraordinary in it, but was

---

[1] A comedy (1638?) by Sir John Suckling. Neither Downes
nor Genest gives the cast.

[1] A comedy (1614) by a "Mr. Tomkis," erroneously referred
to, on its revival, by Dryden in the prologue he wrote for it as
being the "model" of *The Alchemist:*

> "Subtle was got by our Albumazar,
>   That Alchymist by this Astrologer. . . . "

(Cf. *The Works of John Dryden,* Scott-Saintsbury ed., X, 418.)

indeed weary of it before it was done. The King here, and, indeed, all of us, pretty merry at the mimique tricks of Trinkilo.

Webster, John   THE DUCHESS OF MALFI

September 30, 1662. To the Duke's playhouse, where we saw "The Duchess of Malfy"[1] well performed, but Betterton and Ianthe to admiration.[2]

November 2, 1666. Begun "The Duchess of Malfy," which seems a good play.

November 6, 1666. To Deptford, reading "Duchesse of Malfy," the play which is pretty good.

November 25, 1668. To the Duke of York's house, to see "The Duchesse of Malfy," a sorry play.

Webster, John

THE WHITE DEVIL, OR VITTORIA COROMBONA

October 2, 1661. We went to the Theatre, but coming late, and sitting in an ill place, I never had so little pleasure in a play in my life, yet it was the first

---

[1] A tragedy (printed 1623) by John Webster.

[2] Betterton played the part of Bosola, and "Ianthe" (Mrs. Betterton), the Duchess of Malfi; Harris, Duke Ferdinand; Smith, Antonio; and Young, the Cardinal,—according to Downes (*Roscius Anglicanus,* p. 25), who adds: "This Play was so exceedingly Excellently *Acted* in all Parts; chiefly, Duke *Ferdinand* and *Bosola:* It fill'd the House 8 Days Successively, it proving one of the Best of Stock Tragedies."

time that ever I saw it, "Victoria Corombona."[1]   Methinks a very poor play.

October 4, 1661.   To the Theatre, and there came too late, so we staid and saw a bit of "Victoria," which pleased me worse than it did the other day.

Unknown Author

THE MERRY DEVIL OF EDMONTON

August 10, 1661.   To the Theatre, and shewed them "The merry Devill of Edmunton,"[1] which is a very merry play, the first time I ever saw it, which pleased me well.

[1] A tragedy (1607-1608) by John Webster, mentioned in Downes's list (*Roscius Anglicanus,* p. 9) of "Principal Old Stock Plays" of the King's company.

[1] A comedy ascribed by Coxeter to Michael Drayton; nothing definite is known of its authorship. C. F. Tucker Brooke makes the following statement about it (*The Tudor Drama,* p. 276): "Registered for publication in 1607, it is known to have enjoyed marked popularity on the stage three years earlier and was presumably composed shortly before the end of Elizabeth's reign." It was one of the "Principal Old Stock Plays" of the King's company.

CHAPTER III

PLAYS OF UNCERTAIN DATE

CHAPTER III

PLAYS OF UNCERTAIN DATE

Unknown Author   Love's Quarrel

April 6, 1661. To Salisbury Court and there saw "Love's Quarrell"[1] acted the first time, but do not like the design or words.

Unknown Author   Merry Andrew

August 29, 1668. To Bartholomew Fair, and there did see a ridiculous, obscene little stage-play, called "Marry Andrey";[1] a foolish thing, but seen by everybody.

Unnamed Plays

November 20, 1660. I found my Lord Sandwich in bed late, he having been with the King, Queen, and Princesse, at the Cockpit[1] all night, where after supper a play.

---

[1] "The play is not known otherwise than by this notice" (Pepys's *Diary*, Wheatley ed., II, 3n).

[1] Probably the old folk play of *The Vagaries of Merry Andrew*, often acted by puppets.

[1] In Whitehall Palace.

February 20, 1662-63.   I met Madam Turner, she and her daughter having been at the play to-day at the Temple, it being a revelling time with them.

December 6, 1666.   After dinner my wife and brother . . . go out to see a play. . . . My wife not pleased with the play, but thinks that is it [*sic*] because she is grown more critical than she used to be, but my brother she says is mightily taken with it.

December 26, 1666.   I put the women into a coach, and they to the Duke's house, to a play which was acted, "The ——." It was indifferently done, but was not pleased with the song, Gosnell not singing, but a new wench, that sings naughtily.

February 13, 1666-67.   Dr. Clerke[2] fell to reading a new play, newly writ, of a friend's of his; but, by his disclosure and confession afterwards, it was his own.

July 22, 1667.   Creed tells me of the fray between the Duke of Buckingham at the Duke's playhouse the last Saturday (and it is the first day I have heard that they have acted at either the Duke's or the King's houses this month or six weeks) and Henry Killigrew.

April 13, 1668.   So with Creed to a play. Little laugh, 4*s.*

July 17, 1668.   To the King's House, to see a play revived called The ——; a sorry mean play, that vexed us to sit in so much heat of the weather to hear it.

---

[2] Timothy Clarke, appointed physician-in-ordinary to Charles the Second in 1667.

CHAPTER IV

CONTEMPORARY RESTORATION
PLAYS

CHAPTER IV

CONTEMPORARY RESTORATION PLAYS

[NOTE: In a few instances pre-Restoration works by authors, certain of whose plays were produced *after* 1660, are included in this section.]

Betterton, Thomas
THE ROMAN VIRGIN, OR THE UNJUST JUDGE

May 12, 1669. To the Duke of York's playhouse, and there, in the side balcony, over against the musick, did hear, but not see, a new play, the first day acted, "The Roman Virgin,"[1] an old play, but ordinary, I thought: but the trouble of my eyes with the candles did almost kill me.

Bristol, Earl of   WORSE AND WORSE

July 20, 1664. Went to a play, only a piece of it, which was at the Duke's house, "Worse and Worse";[1]

---

[1] A tragedy adapted from Webster's *Appius and Virginia* (printed 1654) by Thomas Betterton, the actor, and published as altered in 1679. Betterton acted the part of Virginius; Harris, Appius; and Mrs. Betterton, Virginia; "and all the other Parts *Exactly* perform'd, it lasted Successively 8 Days," records Downes (*Roscius Anglicanus*, p. 30).

[1] A lost adaptation from a comedy of Calderon, probably *Peor*

just the same manner of play, and writ, I believe, by
the same man, as "The Adventures of Five Hours";[2]
very pleasant it was, and I begin to admire Harris
more than ever.

Caryl, John

THE ENGLISH PRINCESS, OR RICHARD THE THIRD

March 7, 1666-67. Thence to the Duke's playhouse, and saw "The English Princesse, or Richard
the Third,"[1] a most sad, melancholy play, and pretty
good, but nothing eminent in it, as some tragedys are;
only little Mis. Davis did dance a jig after the end
of the play, and there telling the next day's play; so
that it come in by force only to please the company
to see her dance in boy's clothes; and, the truth is,
there is no comparison between Nell's[2] dancing the
other day at the King's house in boy's clothes and
this, this being infinitely beyond the other.

Está que Estaba, by George Digby, Earl of Bristol, acted between 1662 and 1665. (Cf. A. W. Ward, *A History of English
Dramatic Literature,* 2d ed., III, 305.)

[2] An adaptation (1663) by Sir Samuel Tuke from a play
ascribed to Antonio Coello.

[1] A tragedy (published 1667) by John Caryl. Downes states
(*Roscius Anglicanus,* p. 27) that it was "Excellently well Acted
in every Part; chiefly King *Richard* by Mr. *Betterton;* Duke of
Richmond, by Mr. *Harris;* Sir *William* Stanly, by Mr. *Smith,*"—
and that it "Gained them an Additional Estimation, and the
Applause from the Town, as well as profit to the whole Company."

[2] Nell Gwyn's dancing in *The Maiden Queen.*

Cowley, Abraham   CUTTER OF COLEMAN STREET

December 16, 1661. To the Opera, where there
was a new play ("Cutter of Coleman Street"[1]) made
in the year 1658, with reflections much upon the late
times; and it being the first time, the pay was
doubled, and so to save money, my wife and I went
up into the gallery, and there sat and saw very well;
and a very good play it is. It seems of Cowly's
making.

August 5, 1668. To the Duke of York's playhouse, and there saw "The Guardian"; formerly the
same, I find, that was called "Cutter of Coleman
Street"; a silly play.

Cowley, Abraham   NAUFRAGIUM JOCULARE

February 19, 1660-61. Spent the evening in reading of a Latin play, the "Naufragium Joculare."[1]

---

[1] A comedy (1661), by Abraham Cowley, based on his play
first acted at Cambridge in 1641 under the title of *The Guardian,*
"and several times after privately during the Troubles. . . .
The scene lies in London in the year 1658." (Cf. *Preface* to
1663 ed.) Betterton was Colonel Jolly; Harris, Truman Junior;
"Mrs. Betterton," Aurelia—in a later performance, perhaps, as
she was not then married. It "was Acted so perfectly Well and
Exact," that according to Downes (*Roscius Anglicanus,* p. 25),
"it was perform'd a whole Week with a full Audience."

[1] A comedy in Latin by Abraham Cowley, acted at Trinity
College, Cambridge, in 1638.

D'Avenant, Sir William
THE FIRST DAY'S ENTERTAINMENT AT RUTLAND HOUSE

February 7, 1663-64. With great mirth read Sir W. Davenant's two speeches in dispraise of London and Paris, by way of reproach to one another.[1]

D'Avenant, Sir William   LOVE AND HONOUR

October 21, 1661. And so against my judgment and conscience (which God forgive, for my very heart knows that I offend God in breaking my vows herein) to the Opera,[1] which is now newly begun to act again, after some alteracion of their scene, which do make it very much worse; but the play, "Love and Honour,"[2]

[1] These two speeches form the second part of *The First Days Entertainment at Rutland-House, by Declamations and Musick, after the Manner of the Ancients* (1656), immediately following "a concert of instrumental musick, after the French composition." The *Entertainment* is important historically as being the first notable step towards the revival of regular theatrical productions taken during the latter part of the dramatic interregnum. For D'Avenant's alteration of *Measure for Measure* (*The Law Against Lovers*), see p. 69; of *Macbeth*, see p. 70; of *The Tempest* (with Dryden), see pp. 75-77.

[1] The Duke of York's playhouse in Lincoln's Inn Fields, had been opened, according to Pepys, in June, 1661.

[2] A pre-Restoration heroic play (1634) by Sir William D'Avenant. Evelyn saw it on November 11, 1661. "I was so idle," he records, "as to go to see a play call'd 'Love and Honour'"(*Diary*, Wheatley ed., II, 153). Downes describes it as follows: "This Play was Richly C[l]oath'd; The King giving

being the first time of their acting it, is a very good plot, and well done.

October 23, 1661. So back to the Opera, and there I saw again "Love and Honour," and a very good play it is.

October 25, 1661. After dinner my wife and I to the Opera, and there saw again "Love and Honour," a play so good that it has been acted but three times and I have seen them all, and all in this week; which is too much, and more than I will do again a good while.

D'Avenant, Sir William   THE MAN'S THE MASTER

March 26, 1667-68. To the Duke of York's house, to see the new play, called "The Man is Master,"[1] where the house was, it not being above one o'clock, very full. But my wife and Deb. being there before, . . . they made me room; and there I sat, it costing me 8*s.* upon them in oranges, at 6*d.* a-piece. By and

Mr. *Betterton* his Coronation Suit, in which, he Acted the Part of Prince *Alvaro;* the Duke of *York* giving Mr. *Harris* his, who did Prince *Prospero;* And my Lord of *Oxford,* gave Mr. *Joseph Price* his, who did *Lionel,* the Duke of *Parma's* Son; The Duke was acted by Mr. *Lilliston; Evandra* by Mrs. Davenport, and all the other Parts being well done; The Play having a great run, Produc'd to the Company great Gain and Estimation from the Town" (*Roscius Anglicanus,* pp. 21-22).

[1] *The Man's the Master* (1668) was D'Avenant's last play. It is based upon two plays by Scarron—*Jodelet, ou le Maître Valet,* and *L'Héritière Ridicule.*

by the King come; and we sat just under him, so that I durst not turn my back all the play. The play is a translation out of French, and the plot Spanish, but not anything extraordinary at all in it, though translated by Sir W. Davenant, and so I found the King and his company did think meanly of it though there was here and there something pretty: but the most of the mirth was sorry, poor stuffe, of eating of sack posset and slabbering themselves, and mirth fit for clownes; the prologue but poor, and the epilogue little in it but the extraordinariness of it, it being sung by Harris[2] and another in the form of a ballet.

April 3, 1668. To the Duke's playhouse, and there saw the latter part of "The Master and the Man."

May 7, 1668. To the Duke of York's house, and there saw "The Man's the Master," which proves, upon my seeing it again, a very good play.

D'Avenant, Sir William   THE RIVALS

September 10, 1664. To the Duke's house, and there saw "The Rivalls,"[1] which is no excellent play,

---

[2] Harris's part was Don John; "another" was Sandford. Genest (I, 85) states that *The Man's the Master* was revived in 1726 and 1775, and "is the only one of Davenant's 16 plays which has been acted for many years."

[1] An alteration (1664) by Sir William D'Avenant of *The Two Noble Kinsmen*. Harris played the part of Theocles; Betterton that of Philander. Gosnell is not mentioned by Downes in his cast of the play (*Roscius Anglicanus*, p. 23); he notes, however, of the women's parts that they were "admirably Acted; chiefly

but good acting in it; especially Gosnell comes and sings and dances finely, but, for all that, fell out of the key, so that the musique could not play to her afterwards, and so did Harris also go out of the tune to agree with her.

December 2, 1664. To the Duke's house, and there saw, "The Rivalls," which I had seen before; but the play not good nor anything but the good actings of Betterton and his wife and Harris.

D'Avenant, Sir William   THE SIEGE OF RHODES

July 2, 1661. Went to Sir William Davenant's Opera; this being the fourth day that it hath begun, and the first that I have seen it. To-day was acted the second part of "The Siege of Rhodes."[1] We staid a very great while for the King and the Queen of

Celia, a Sheperdess being Mad for Love; especially in Singing several Wild and Mad Songs." "Moll" Davis was the Celia (should be Celania) here referred to.

[1] The first English opera—Part I, 1656. Evelyn mentions seeing "the Third [should be *second*] Part of the Siege of Rhodes," on January 9, 1661-62; "it was in recitaviva musiq" (*Diary,* Wheatley ed., II, 141). Downes (*Roscius Anglicanus,* pp. 20-21) describes it as "having new Scenes and Decorations, being the first that were e're Introduced in England." Betterton acted Solyman; Harris, Alphonso; Mrs. Saunderson, Ianthe; and Mrs. Davenport, Roxalana. In referring later (*ibid.,* p. 33) to the initial performance "*on the very first Day of opening the House,*" Downes states that in the audience were "*the King, Duke of York, and all the Nobility, . . . and the first time the King was in a Publick Theatre.*"

Bohemia;[2] and by the breaking of a board over our heads, we had a great deal of dust fell into the ladies' necks and the men's hair, which made good sport. The King being come, the scene opened; which indeed is very fine and magnificent, and well acted, all but the Eunuch, who was so much out that he was hissed off the stage.

November 15, 1661. To the Opera . . . and there did see the second part of "The Siege of Rhodes" very well done.

May 20, 1662. My wife and I by coach to the Opera, and there saw the 2nd part of "The Siege of Rhodes," but it is not so well done as when Roxalana[3] was there, who, it is said, is now owned by my Lord of Oxford.

December 27, 1662. To the Duke's Theatre, and saw the second part of "Rhodes," done with the new Roxalana;[4] which do it rather better in all respects for person, voice, and judgment, than the first Roxalana.

September 23, 1664. So home, and late reading "The Siege of Rhodes"[5] to my wife.

[2] Elizabeth, daughter of James I, widow of Frederick, Elector Palatine.

[3] Elizabeth Davenport. The story of the mock marriage into which the Earl of Oxford entrapped her is given in the *Memoirs of the Count de Gramont,* Vizetelly ed., II, 101.

[4] Mrs. Norton.

[5] From this reference as well as from the references of October 1, 1665, and December 19, 1668, it is, of course, impossible to say whether both parts of the play are meant or, if not, which part.

October 1, 1665. We spent most of the morning talking and reading of "The Siege of Rhodes," which is certainly (the more I read it the more I think so) the best poem that ever was wrote.

December 6, 1665. I spent the afternoon upon a song of Solyman's words to Roxalana[6] that I have set.

August 5, 1666. A fine day, reading over the second part of the "Siege of Rhodes," with great delight.

February 13, 1666-67. I do think and he [Dr. Clarke] confesses, "The Siege of Rhodes" as good as ever was writ.

May 21, 1667. But, Lord! how it went against my heart to go away from the very door of the Duke's play-house, and my Lady Castlemayne's coach, and many great coaches there, to see "The Siege of Rhodes."[7]

December 19, 1668. My wife read to me out of "The Siege of Rhodes."

D'Avenant, Sir William

THE UNFORTUNATE LOVERS

March 7, 1663-64. To the Duke's house, where we saw "The Unfortunate Lovers";[1] but I know not

---

[6] The song beginning "Beauty retire; thou doest my pity move," from *The Siege of Rhodes*, Part II, Act IV, Sc. 2.

[7] This was probably a revival of the second part of the play, first produced in 1661.

[1] A tragedy by Sir William D'Avenant, licensed in 1638.

whether I am grown more curious than I was or no, but I was not much pleased with it, though I know not where to lay the fault, unless it was that the house was very empty, by reason of a new play at the other house.

September 11, 1667.   To the Duke of York's playhouse, and there saw part of "The Ungrateful Lovers."[2]

April 8, 1668.   To the Duke of York's playhouse,[3] where we saw "The Unfortunate Lovers," no extraordinary play, methinks.

December 3, 1668.   To the Duke of York's playhouse, and saw "The Unfortunate Lovers"; a mean play, I think, but some parts very good, and excellently acted.

D'Avenant, Sir William   THE WITS

August 15, 1661.   Thence to the Opera, which begins again to-day with "The Witts,"[1] never acted yet with scenes; and the King and Duke and Duchess were there; . . . and indeed it is a most excellent play, and admirable scenes.

---

[2] No play of this title has been discovered.   It was perhaps *The Unfortunate Lovers.*

[3] This was on the day after D'Avenant's death.

[1] A comedy (1634) by Sir William D'Avenant.   According to Downes (*Roscius Anglicanus,* p. 21) Betterton played "Elder Pallatine"; Harris, "Younger Pallatine"; Mrs. Davenport, Lady Ample; and it "continu'd 8 Days Acting Successively."

August 17, 1661.   To the Opera, and saw "The Witts" again, which I like exceedingly.   The Queen of Bohemia was here brought by my Lord Craven.

August 23, 1661.   I took her [Mrs. Pepys] to the Opera, and shewed her "The Witts," which I had seen already twice, and was most highly pleased with it.

April 18, 1667.   To the Duke of York's house, and there saw "The Wits," a play I formerly loved, and is now corrected and enlarged;[2] but though I like the acting, yet I like not much the play now.

April 20, 1667.   Went to the Duke of York's house, and there saw "The Witts" again, which likes me better than it did the other day, having much wit in it.

January 18, 1668-69.   To the Duke of York's playhouse, and there saw "The Witts," a medley of things, but some similes mighty good, though ill mixed.

Dryden, John

AN EVENING'S LOVE, OR THE MOCK ASTROLOGER

June 19, 1668.   By and by comes my wife and Deb. home, have been at the King's playhouse to-day, thinking to spy me there; and saw the new play,

[2] "These alterations are not material—but the dialogue is considerably improved, and two short scenes are added" (Genest, I, 40).

"Evening Love,"[1] of Dryden's, which, though the world commends, she likes not.

June 20, 1668. To the King's house, and there I saw this new play my wife saw yesterday, and do not like it, it being very smutty, and nothing so good as "The Maiden Queen," or "The Indian Emperour," of his making, that I was troubled at it, and my wife tells me wholly (which he confesses a little in the epilogue) taken out of "Illustre Bassa."[2]

June 21, 1668. After dinner she to read in the "Illustre Bassa" the plot of yesterday's play, which is most exactly the same.

June 22, 1668. Saw an act or two of the new play again, but like it not. Calling this day at Herringman's[3] he tells me Dryden do himself call it but a fifth-rate play.

March 8, 1668-69. To the King's playhouse, and there saw "The Mocke Astrologer," which I have often seen, and but an ordinary play.

---

[1] *An Evening's Love, or the Mock Astrologer* (1668) "coarsens materials drawn from the younger Corneille and from Molière's *Le Dépit Amoureux*" (G. H. Nettleton, *English Drama of the Restoration and Eighteenth Century,* p. 57). Evelyn saw this performance and writes feelingly: "To a new play with several of my relations, 'The Evening Lover,' a foolish plot, and very prophane; it afflicted me to see how the stage was degenerated and polluted by ye licentious times" (*Diary,* Wheatley ed., II, 130). Hart played Wildblood; Mohun, Bellamy; Wintersell, Don Alonzo; Burt, Don Lopez; Nell Gwyn, Jacinta; Mrs. Knepp, Beatrix.

[2] *Ibrahim ou l'illustre bassa* (1641), by Mme. de Scuderi.

[3] The well-known bookseller and publisher at the "Blue Anchor" in the New Exchange.

Dryden, John   THE INDIAN EMPEROR

January 15, 1666-67. Here my Lord Bruncker
would have made me promise to go with him to a
play this afternoon where Knipp acts Mrs. Weaver's
part[1] in "The Indian Emperour,"[2] and he says is
coming to be a great actor. But I . . . will not go.

August 22, 1667. To the King's playhouse, and
there saw "The Indian Emperor"; where I find Nell
come again, which I am glad of; but was most infinitely displeased with her being put to act the Emperour's daughter; which is a great and serious part,
which she do most basely. The rest of the play,
though pretty good, was not well acted by most of
them, methought, so that I took no great content in it.

October 28, 1667. At the New Exchange, and
there buying "The Indian Emperour," newly printed.

November 11, 1667. To the King's playhouse, and
there saw "The Indian Emperour," a good play, but
not so good as people cry it up, I think, though above
all things Nell's ill-speaking of a great part made me
mad.

January 14, 1667. They fell to discourse of the
last night's work at Court, where the ladies and the
Duke of Monmouth and others acted "The Indian

---

[1] Downes (*Roscius Anglicanus,* p. 9) states that Mrs. Marshall
played Almeria and Nell Gwyn, Cydaria. It is not clear to
which part Pepys is here referring. Mohun was Montezuma;
Hart, Cortez; Burt, Vasquez; Wintersell and Kynaston, Odmar
and Guyomar; and Cartwright, the High Priest.

[2] A sequel (1665), also in heroic couplets, to *The Indian
Queen.*

Emperour"; wherein they told me these things most remarkable: that not any woman but the Duchess of Monmouth and Mrs. Cornwallis did any thing but like fools and stocks, but that these two did do most extraordinary well: that not any man did anything well but Captain O'Bryan, who spoke and did well, but, above all things did dance most incomparably.

March 28, 1668. To the King's house, and there saw the "Indian Emperour," a very good play indeed.

April 21, 1668. To the King's house, and saw "The Indian Emperour."

Dryden, John

Secret Love, or The Maiden Queen

March 2, 1666-67. After dinner with my wife, to the King's house to see "The Mayden Queene,"[1] a new play of Dryden's, mightily commended for the regularity of it, and the strain and wit; and the truth is, there is a comical part done by Nell,[2] which is Florimell, that I never can hope to see the like done again, by man or woman.

March 25, 1667. To the King's playhouse. . . . Sir W. Pen and I in the pit, and here saw "The

---

[1] An heroic drama (1667) with comic under-plot. Evelyn saw this play—to which he refers as "The Virgin Queene, a play written by Mr. Dryden,"—on March 14 of this year (*Diary*, Wheatley ed., II, 215).

[2] Florimel, beloved of Celadon, was one of Nell Gwyn's most popular impersonations.

Mayden Queene" again; which indeed the more I see
the more I like, and is an excellent play, and so done
by Nell, her merry part, as cannot be better done in
nature, I think.

May 24, 1667. To the King's playhouse, and there
saw "The Mayden Queene," which, though I have
often seen, yet pleases me infinitely, it being impossible, I think, ever to have the Queen's part, which is
very good and passionate, and Florimel's part, which
is the most comicall that was ever made for woman,
ever done better than they two are done by young
Marshall[3] and Nelly.

August 23, 1667. To the King's house, and saw
"The Mayden Queene," which pleases us mightily.

January 18, 1667-68. I bought "The Mayden
Queene," a play newly printed, which I like at the
King's house so well, of Mr. Dryden's, which he himself, in his preface, seems to brag of,[4] and indeed is
a good play.

January 24, 1667-68. I to the King's playhouse,
to fetch my wife, and there saw the best part of "The
Mayden Queene," which, the more I see, the more I
love, and think one of the best plays I ever saw, and
is certainly the best acted of any thing ever the House
did, and particularly Becke Marshall, to admiration.

[3] Rebecca Marshall played the heroic Queen of Sicily. The
other principal parts were taken as follows, according to *Roscius
Anglicanus* (p. 7): Philocles by Mohun; Lysimantes, Burt;
Celadon, Hart; Asteria, Mrs. Knepp; Melissa, Mrs. Corey.

[4] In his dedication of the play to the King, Dryden remarks
that he has "ever valued" it "above the rest of my follies of this
kind," and proceeds to defend it against the critics.

January 1, 1668-69.   To the King's playhouse, and there in a box saw "The Mayden Queene."

January 13, 1668-69.   To the King's playhouse, and there saw, I think, "The Mayden Queene."

Dryden, John

SIR MARTIN MAR-ALL, OR THE FEIGN'D INNOCENCE

August 16, 1667.   To the Duke's playhouse, where we saw the new play acted yesterday, "The Feign Innocence, or Sir Martin Marr-all";[1] a play made by my Lord Duke of Newcastle, but as everybody says, corrected by Dryden.   It is the most entire piece of mirth, a complete farce from one end to the other, that certainly ever was writ.   I never laughed so in all my life.   I laughed till my head [ached] all the

[1] *Sir Martin Mar-all, or The Feign'd Innocence,* an adaptation of Molière's *L'Etourdi,* which was entered on the books of the Stationers' Company as the production of the Duke of Newcastle, was published in 1668.   Downes says (*Roscius Anglicanus,* p. 28): "The Duke of *Newcastle* giving Mr. *Dryden* a bare Translation of it, out of a Comedy of the Famous *French* Poet *Monsieur Moleiro;* he Adapted the Part purposely for the Mouth of Mr. *Nokes,* curiously Polishing the Whole. . . . This and Love in a Tub got the Company more Money than any preceding Comedy."   The part of Sir Martin was taken by Nokes; Harris was Warner; Smith, Sir John Swallow; Young, Lord Dartmouth; and Mrs. Davis, Mrs. Millicent.   Downes makes the further statement that the Dorset Gardens theatre was opened November 9, 1671, with *Sir Martin Mar-all* "notwithstanding it had been Acted 30 Days before in *Lincolns-Inn Fields,* and above 4 times at Court."   Langbaine and later dramatic historians ascribe this play to Dryden.

evening and night with the laughing; and at very good wit therein, not fooling. The house full.

August 19, 1667. To the Duke of York's house, all alone, and there saw "Sir Martin Marr-all" again, though I saw him but two days since, and do find it the most comical play that ever I saw in my life.

August 20, 1667. Thence, . . . to the Duke's Playhouse, . . . and there saw "Sir Martin Marr-all" again, which I have now seen three times, and it hath been acted but four times, and still find it a very ingenious play, and full of variety.

September 28, 1667. To the Duke of York's playhouse, and there saw a piece of "Sir Martin Marrall," with great delight, though I have seen it so often, and so home.

October 8, 1667. Some other pleasant simplicities of the fellow did give occasion to us to call him Sir Martin Marrall. . . . Away to Cambridge, it being foul, rainy weather, and there did take up at the Rose for the sake of Mrs. Dorothy Drawwater, the vintner's daughter, which is mentioned in the play of Sir Martin Marrall.[2]

October 14, 1667. To the Duke of York's House, and there went in for nothing into the pit, at the last act, to see Sir Martin Marr-all, still being pleased with the humour of the play, almost above all that ever I saw.

January 1, 1667-68. To the Duke of York's playhouse, and there saw "Sir Martin Mar-all"; which I have seen so often, and yet am mightily

[2] Cf. Act. V, Sc. 1: "Her name was Dorothy, daughter to one Draw-water, a vintner at the Rose."

pleased with it, and think it mighty witty, and the fullest of proper matter for mirth that ever was writ; and I do clearly see that they do improve in their acting of it.   Here a mighty company of citizens, 'prentices, and others.

April 25, 1668.   To the Duke of York's playhouse, and there saw "Sir Martin Marr-all," which, the more I see, the more I like.

May 22, 1668.   Thence to the Duke of York's house to a play, and saw Sir Martin Marr-all, where the house is full; and though I have seen it, I think, ten times, yet the pleasure I have is yet as great as ever, and is undoubtedly the best comedy ever was wrote.

Dryden, John   THE RIVAL LADIES

August 4, 1664.   He [Sir W. Pen] did carry me to a play, and pay for me at the King's house, which is "The Rivall Ladys,"[1] a very innocent and most pretty witty play.   I was much pleased with it, and it being given me, I look upon it as no breach to my oathe.

July 18, 1666.   To Woolwich, reading "the Rivall Ladys" all the way, and find it a most pleasant and fine writ play.

August 2, 1666.   To Woolwich, reading and making an end of the "Rival Ladys," and find it a very pretty play.

[1] A tragi-comedy (1664) by John Dryden, based on a Spanish plot.   Genest (I, 50) says of this play under this date, "Not first time."

Dryden, John   THE WILD GALLANT

February 23, 1662-63. We took coach and to Court, and there got good places, and saw "The Wilde Gallant,"[1] performed by the King's house, but it was ill acted, and the play so poor a thing as I never saw in my life almost, and so little answering the name, that from beginning to end, I could not, nor can at this time, tell certainly which was the Wild Gallant. The King did not seem pleased at all, all the whole play, nor any body else, though Mr. Clerke whom we met here did commend it to us.

Dryden and Sir Robert Howard
                            THE INDIAN QUEEN

January 27, 1663-64. In the way observing the streete full of coaches at the new play "The Indian Queene";[1] which for show, they say, exceeds "Henry the Eighth."

February 1, 1663-64. To the King's Theatre, it

[1] Dryden's first comedy (1663). Evelyn had seen its first performance on February 5 of this year. (Cf. *Diary,* Wheatley ed., II, 158.) Genest (I, 35) asserts that "it was unsuccessful at this time, and was brought out again in 1667." For Dryden's alteration of *The Tempest* (with D'Avenant), see pp. 75-77 of this book.

[1] A rhymed heroic tragedy (1664) by Sir Robert Howard and Dryden. Evelyn saw it acted on February 5 of this year. He calls it "a tragedie well written, so beautified with rich scenes as the like had never ben seen here, or haply (except rarely) elsewhere on a mercenary theater" (*Diary,* Wheatley ed., II, 163).

being a new month, and once a month I may go,[2] and
there saw "The Indian Queene" acted; which indeed
is a most pleasant show, and beyond my expectation;
the play good, but spoiled with the ryme, which
breaks the sense.[3]   But above my expectation most,
the eldest Marshall[4] did do her part most excellently
well as I ever heard woman in my life; but her voice
not so sweet as Ianthe's; but, however, we came home
mightily contented.

[2] According to the terms of one of his several "vows against
plays."

[3] It will be seen from this entry that Restoration spectators
did not without exception welcome the heroic couplet in tragedy.

[4] Anne Marshall, doubtless in the title part.   Mrs. Aphra
Behn gives the following interesting description of the Queen's
realistic costume in *The History of Oroonoko: Or, The Royal
Slave,* in an account of the trade with the natives of Surinam:
"We trade for Feathers, which they order into all Shapes, make
themselves little short Habits of 'em, and glorious Wreaths for
their Heads, Necks, Arms and Legs, whose Tinctures are incon-
ceivable.   I had a set of these presented to me, and I gave 'em
to the *King's Theatre;* it was the Dress of the *Indian Queen,*
infinitely admir'd by Persons of Quality; and was inimitable."
Like other statements made by Mrs. Behn which would seem
to show that she had actually visited Oroonoko, this has been
challenged by Mr. Ernest Bernbaum, who thus laughs it out of
court: "To think of Nell Gwynn in the true costume of a Carib
belle is indeed ludicrous" (*Mrs. Behn's Oroonoko,* in *The George
Lyman Kittredge Anniversary Papers,* p. 432).   The matter
cannot, however, be so briefly dismissed.   It is improbable that
Mrs. Behn would have gone out of her way to expose herself to
contradiction upon so easily verifiable a statement.   And we may
infer from the play itself that there was some attempt at realism
in the costumes, however slight or "ludicrous" it may have been.
The stage direction before Act V reads: "Four Priests in habits

June 27, 1668. To the King's playhouse, and saw "The Indian Queene," but do not doat upon Nan Marshall's acting therein, as the world talks of her excellence therein.

Etherege, Sir George
THE COMICAL REVENGE, OR LOVE IN A TUB

January 4, 1664-65. To "Love in a Tubb,"[1] which is very merry, but only so by gesture, not wit at all, which methinks is beneath the [Duke's] House.

October 29, 1666. To White Hall and into the new play-house there, the first time I ever was there, and the first play I have seen since before the great plague.[2] . . . By and by the King and Queene, Duke and Duchesse, and all the great ladies of the Court; which, indeed, was a fine sight. But the play being "Love in a Tub," a silly play, and though done by the Duke's people, yet having neither Betterton nor his wife,[3] and the whole thing done ill, and being ill

of white and red Feathers"; and in the Epilogue, spoken by Montezuma, there is this reference to the play:

"Our naked Indians then, when Wits appear,
  Would as soon chuse to have the Spaniards here."

[1] *The Comical Revenge, or Love in a Tub* (1664), Etherege's first play. Evelyn mentions it on April 27, 1664: "Saw a facetious comedy called 'Love in a Tub'" (*Diary*, Wheatley ed., II, 164).

[2] Since May 15, 1665,—to be exact,—when he had seen *Love's Mistress* at the King's theatre.

[3] Betterton usually acted Lord Beaufort. Mrs. Betterton (as

also, I had no manner of pleasure in the play. Besides, the House, though very fine, yet bad for the voice, for hearing. The sight of the ladies, indeed, was exceedingly noble; and above all my Lady Castlemayne. The play done by ten o'clock. I carried them all home, and then home myself, and well satisfied with the sight, but not the play, we with great content to bed.

April 29, 1668. To the Duke of York's playhouse, and there saw "Love in a Tubb"; and, after the play done, I stepped up to Harris's dressing-room, where I never was, and there I observe much company come to him, and the Witts, to talk, after the play is done, and to assign meetings.

Etherege, Sir George   SHE WOULD IF SHE COULD

February 6, 1667-68. To the Duke of York's playhouse; where a new play of Etherige's, called "She Would if she Could,"[1] and though I was there by two o'clock, there was 1000 people put back that could not have room in the pit: and I at last, because my wife was there, made shift to get into the 18*d.* box and there saw; but, Lord! how full was the house, and how silly the play, there being nothing in the world good in it, and few people pleased in it. The

Graciana), Harris (as Sir Frederick Frolic), Smith, Nokes, Sandford, and Mrs. Davis (as Aurelia) were in the cast. According to *Roscius Anglicanus* (pp. 24-25), the play brought the house £1,000 in a month.

[1] The second comedy (1668) by Sir George Etherege.

King was there; but I sat mightily behind, and could see but little, and hear not all. The play being done, I into the pit. . . . There I found . . . Sidly, and Etherige, the poet; the last of whom I did hear mightily find fault with the actors,[2] that they were out of humour, and had not their parts perfect, and that Harris did do nothing, nor could so much as sing a ketch in it; and so was mightily concerned; while all the rest did, through the whole pit, blame the play as a silly, dull thing, though there was something very roguish and witty; but the design of the play, and end, mighty insipid.

February 1, 1668-69. To the Duke of York's playhouse, and there saw "She Would if She Could."

Evelyn, John   THYRSANDER (?)

November 5, 1665. By water to Deptford, and there made a visit to Mr. Evelyn. . . . He read me part of a play[1] or two of his making, very good, but not as he conceits them, I think, to be.

[2] Harris was Sir Joslin Jolly; Nokes, Sir Oliver Cockwood; Smith, Courtall; Young, Freeman; Mrs. Shadwell, Lady Cockwood; Mrs. Davis, Gatty. "It took well," says Downes (*Roscius Anglicanus,* pp. 28-29), "but Inferior to Love in a Tub."

[1] In a letter of February 9, 1664-65, to Lord Cornebery, Evelyn writes: "You know, my Ld, that I (who have written a play & am a scurvy poet too some times) am far from Puritanisme" (*Diary,* Wheatley ed., III, 302). The play here referred to and one of those later read to Pepys was probably "Thyrsander" a "Tragy-Comedy," mentioned in one of the MSS. at Wotton in a list entitled "Things I would write out faire and reform if I had leasure" (*Ibid.,* III, 194).

Falkland, Lord   THE MARRIAGE NIGHT

March 21, 1666-67. I alone out and to the Duke of
York's playhouse, where unexpectedly I come to see
only the young men and women of the house act; they
having liberty to act for their own profit on Wednesdays and Fridays this Lent: and the play they did
yesterday, being Wednesday, was so well-taken, that
they thought fit to venture it publickly to-day; a
play of my Lord Falkland's called "The Wedding
Night"[1] a kind of tragedy, and some things very
good in it, but the whole together, I thought, not so.
I confess I was well enough pleased with my seeing it:
and the people did do better, without the great actors,
than I did expect, but yet far short of what they do
when they are there, which I was glad to find the
difference of.

Flecknoe, Richard (?)   THE LADIES A LA MODE

September 15, 1668. To the King's playhouse, to
see a new play, acted but yesterday, a translation out
of French by Dryden, called "The Ladys à la
Mode":[1] so mean a thing as, when they come to say

[1] Should be *The Marriage Night,* a tragi-comedy by Henry
Cary, Viscount Falkland, published in 1664. (Cf. Genest, I,
75.) It has been generally stated that this play was never acted.

[1] Pepys appears to have been wrongly informed. The play
which seems best to fit the requirements of date, title, and suggestion of French origin is Richard Flecknoe's *Damoselles à la
Mode,* printed in 1667, which according to the preface was

it would be acted again to-morrow, both he that said it, Beeson,[2] and the pit fell a-laughing, there being this day not a quarter of the pit full.

Green, Alexander   THE POLITICIAN CHEATED

July 29, 1663. To see Sir W. Pen at Deptford, reading by the way a most ridiculous play, a new one, called "The Politician Cheated."[1]

Holden, T.   THE GHOSTS

April 17, 1665. We all to a play, "The Ghosts,"[1] at the Duke's house, but a very simple play.

"taken out of several Excellent pieces of Molière." Langbaine, on the authority of this preface, states (p. 201) that it was designed "to have been acted by the King's Servants . . . but I know not for what reason they refus'd it." Langbaine's statement would, however, have no bearing upon the performance described by Pepys, which took place the year *after* Flecknoe's *Damoselles à la Mode* was printed.

[2] William Beeston.

[1] A comedy by Alexander Green, published in 1663, is mentioned by Genest (X, 138) in his chapter on plays "printed but never acted."

[1] Downes (*Roscius Anglicanus*, p. 26) attributes this comedy (1665?) to Holden. Hazlitt (*A Manual for the Collector and Amateur of Old English Plays,* p. 95) states that it was by T. Holden and was "not printed."

Howard, Edward   THE CHANGE OF CROWNS

April 15, 1667. To the King's house by chance, where a new play: so full as I never saw it; I forced to stand all the while close to the very door till I took cold, and many people went away for lack of room. The King, and Queene, and Duke of York and Duchesse there, and all the Court, and Sir W. Coventry.[1] The play called "The Change of Crownes";[2] a play of Ned Howard's, the best that ever I saw at that house, being a great play and serious; only Lacy did act the country-gentleman come up to Court, who do abuse the Court with all the imaginable wit and plainness about selling of places, and doing everything for money. The play took very much. . . . Then home, . . . mightily pleased with the new play.

April 16, 1667. Knipp tells me the King was so angry at the liberty taken by Lacy's part to abuse him to his face, that he commanded they should act no-more, till Moone[3] went and got leave for them to act again, but not this play.

Howard, Edward   THE USURPER

January 2, 1663-64. To the King's house, and there met Mr. Nicholson, my old colleague, and saw

[1] Sir William Coventry (1628-1686), Commissioner of the Navy, and Privy Councillor, often mentioned in the *Diary* in terms of praise.

[2] "This play," says Genest (I, 69), "is not printed—it seems to have been a T.C. by E. Howard."

[3] Michael Mohun.

"The Usurper,"[1] which is no good play, though better than what I saw yesterday.

December 2, 1668. To the King's playhouse, . . . and there saw "The Usurper"; a pretty good play, in all but what is designed to resemble Cromwell and Hugh Peters,[2] which is mighty silly.

Howard, James
All Mistaken, or The Mad Couple

September 20, 1667. To the King's playhouse, and there saw "The Mad Couple,"[1] which I do not remember that I have seen; it is a pretty pleasant play.

December 28, 1667. To the King's house, and there saw "The Mad Couple," which is but an ordinary play; but only Nell's and Hart's mad parts[2] are most excellently done, but especially her's: which makes it a miracle to me to think how ill she do any serious part, as, the other day, just like a fool or changeling; and in a mad part, do beyond all imitation almost. It pleased us mightily to see the natural

[1] A tragedy (1664) by Edward Howard, printed in 1668. Pepys had seen *Henry VIII* on January 1.

[2] The character supposed to resemble Cromwell was Damocles, while Hugo de Petra was intended for Hugh Peters, and "Cleomenes probably for General Monck" (Genest, I, 72).

[1] *All Mistaken, or The Mad Couple* (1667), was a comedy by James Howard.

[2] The "mad couple" were Philidor and Mirida, acted by Hart and Nell Gwyn respectively.

affection of a poor woman, the mother of one of the children[3] brought on the stage: the child crying, she by force got upon the stage, and took up her child and carried it away off of the stage from Hart. Many fine faces here to-day.

July 29, 1668. To the King's house, and saw "The Mad Couple," a mean play altogether.

Howard, James   THE ENGLISH MONSIEUR

December 8, 1666. To the King's playhouse, which troubles me since, and hath cost me a forfeit of 10*s.*, which I have paid, and there did see a good part of "The English Monsieur,"[1] which is a mighty pretty play, very witty and pleasant. And the women do very well; but, above all, little Nelly,[2] that I am mightily pleased with the play, and much with the House, more than ever I expected, the women doing better than ever I expected, and very fine women.

April 7, 1668. To the King's playhouse, and there saw "The English Monsieur"; sitting for privacy sake in an upper box: the play hath much mirth in it as to that particular humour.

[3] In an attempt to collect money from their father, Philidor, several babes in arms, his illegitimate offspring, are brought on the stage by their nurses at various times during the play.

[1] A comedy by James Howard, printed in 1674. The forfeit was paid in accordance with one of Pepys's vows.

[2] Nell Gywn played the part of Lady Wealthy. This is the year following her début in the rôle of Cydaria in *The Indian Emperor,* and is the first time Pepys mentions seeing her on the stage.

Howard, Sir Robert   THE COMMITTEE

June 12, 1663. To the Royall Theatre, and there saw "The Committee,"[1] a merry but indifferent play, only Lacey's part, an Irish footman,[2] is beyond imagination.

August 13, 1667. To the King's house, and there saw "The Committee," which I went to with some prejudice, not liking it before, but I do now find it a very good play, and a great deal of good invention in it; but Lacy's part is so well performed that it would set off anything.

October 28, 1667. To the King's house, and there saw "The Committee," a play I like well.

May 15, 1668. To the King's house, and there saw the last act of "The Committee," thinking to have seen Knepp there, but she did not act.

[1] *The Committee* (1662) was Sir Robert Howard's most popular comedy. Evelyn had seen this play on November 29, 1662, at the "Queene Mother's Court." He calls it "a ridiculous play of Sir R. Howard, where ye mimic Lacy acted the Irish footeman to admiration" (*Diary*, Wheatley ed., II, 155). *The Cambridge History of English Literature* (VIII, 121) gives the date of its production as 1665, which Pepys and Evelyn show is an ·error, as Professor Nettleton has recently pointed out (*English Drama of the Restoration and Eighteenth Century*, p. 111).

[2] "Teague, an early Irish comic character, if deficient in dialect, has Irish wit enough to 'take the Covenant' by stealing a copy of it from a bookseller" (*Ibid.*). For *The Indian Queen,* in which Sir Robert Howard collaborated with Dryden, see p. 155 of this book.

Howard, Sir Robert

THE GREAT FAVOURITE, OR THE DUKE OF LERMA

January 11, 1667-68. She [Knepp] told me also of . . . another play called, "The Duke of Lerma."[1]

February 20, 1667-68. By one o'clock to the King's house: a new play, "The Duke of Lerma" of Sir Robert Howard's: where the King and the Court was; and Knepp and Nell spoke the prologue most excellently, especially Knepp, who spoke beyond any creature I ever heard. The play designed to reproach our King with his mistresses, that I was troubled for it, and expected it should be interrupted; but it ended all well, which salved all. The play a well-writ and good play, only its design I did not like of reproaching the King, but altogether a very good, and most serious play.

April 18, 1668. To the King's playhouse, 1*s.*, and to the play of the "Duke of Lerma," 2*s.* 6*d.*, and oranges 1*s.*

Howard, Sir Robert   THE SURPRISAL

April 8, 1667. To the King's house, and saw the latter end of the "Surprisall,"[1] wherein was no great matter, I thought, by what I saw there.

August 26, 1667. To the King's playhouse, . . .

---

[1] *The Great Favourite, or the Duke of Lerma* (1668), is a tragedy with "some scenes in blank Verse, others in Rhime."

[1] A comedy by Sir Robert Howard, previously published in *Foure New Plays* (1665).

and saw "The Surprizall," a very mean play, I thought: or else it was because I was out of humour, and but very little company in the house.

December 26, 1667. To the King's playhouse, and there saw "The Surprizall"; which did not please me to-day, the actors not pleasing me; and especially Nell's acting of a serious part,[2] which she spoils.

April 17, 1668. To the King's house, and saw "The Surprizall," where base singing, only Knepp,[3] who come, after her song in the clouds, to me in the pit, and there oranges, 2*s.*

May 1, 1668. To the King's play-house, and there saw "The Surprizall": and a disorder in the pit by its raining in, from the cupola at top.

Killigrew, Thomas   CLARACILLA

July 4, 1661. In the afternoon I went to the Theatre, and there saw "Claracilla,"[1] (the first time I ever saw it), well acted. But strange to see this house, that used to be so thronged, now empty since the Opera begun;[2] and so will continue for a while, I believe.

January 5, 1662-63. To the Cockpitt,[3] where we

---

[2] This "serious part" was Samira.

[3] Mrs. Knepp played the part of Emelia.

[1] A tragi-comedy by Thomas Killigrew, which had been acted before the Restoration in 1636.

[2] The Opera had "begun" towards the end of June, 1661, according to Pepys.

[3] In Whitehall Palace.

saw "Claracilla," a poor play, done by the King's house (but neither the King nor Queen were there, but only the Duke and Duchess . . .); but to my very little content, they not acting in any degree like the Duke's people.

March 9, 1668-69.   Towards the King's playhouse, and . . . to see "Claricilla," which do not please me almost at all, though there are some good things in it.

Killigrew, Thomas

The Princess, or Love at First Sight

November 29, 1661.   To the Theatre, but it was so full that we could hardly get any room, so he .went up to one of the boxes, and I into the 18*d*. places, and there saw "Love at first sight,"[1] a play of Mr. Killigrew's, and the first time that it hath been acted since before the troubles, and great expectation there was, but I found the play to be a poor thing, and so I perceive everybody else do.

Killigrew, Thomas   The Parson's Wedding

October 4, 1664.   To-morrow they told us should be acted, or the day after, a new play, called "The Parson's Dreame," acted all by women.[1]

October 11, 1664.   He [Luellin] tells me what a

[1] *The Princess, or Love at First Sight,* a tragi-comedy by Thomas Killigrew, acted before the Restoration in 1637-1638.

[1] Evidently *The Parson's Wedding* (1640), referred to on October 11, 1664.

bawdy loose play this "Parsons Wedding,"[2] is, that is acted by nothing but women at the King's house, and I am glad of it.

Lacy, John   THE OLD TROOP, OR MONSIEUR RAGGOU

July 31, 1668.   To the King's house, to see the first day of Lacy's "Monsieur Ragou,"[1] now new acted.   The King and Court all there, and mighty merry—a farce.

August 1, 1668.   To the King's house again, coming too late yesterday to hear the prologue, and do like the play better now than before; and, indeed, there is a great deal of true wit in it, more than in the common sort of plays.

Newcastle, Duke of   THE COUNTRY CAPTAIN

October 26, 1661.   My wife and I to the Theatre, and there saw "The Country Captain,"[1] the first time

---

[2] A comedy by Thomas Killigrew acted before the Restoration and chiefly distinguished for ribaldry and obscenity of dialogue.   Lovewit, in James Wright's *Historia Histrionica,* 1699 (in Dodsley's *Old English Plays,* Hazlitt ed., XV, 412), remarks that at this time it was "presented by all women as formerly by all men"; and Langbaine (p. 313), commenting upon this revival of the play, adds—"a new Prologue and Epilogue being spoken by Mrs. Marshal in Man's Cloaths."

[1] *The Old Troop, or Monsieur Raggou* (1664?), the best play by this well-known actor.   Lacy probably acted the title part. For his alteration of *The Taming of the Shrew,* see p. 74.

[1] A comedy by William Cavendish, Duke of Newcastle, acted

it hath been acted these twenty-five years, a play of my Lord Newcastle's, but so silly a play as in all my life I never saw, and the first that ever I was weary of in my life.

November 25, 1661. To the Theatre, and there saw "The Country Captain," a dull play.

August 14, 1667. To the King's playhouse, and there saw "The Country Captain," which is a very ordinary play. Methinks I had no pleasure therein at all.

May 14, 1668. Then into the [King's] playhouse again, and there saw "The Country Captain," a very dull play, that did give us no content, and besides, little company there, which made it very unpleasing.

Newcastle, Duke of (?)   THE HEIRESS

February 1, 1668-69. To the King's playhouse, thinking to have seen "The Heyresse,"[1] first acted on Saturday last; but when we come thither, we find no play there; Kinaston, that did act a part therein, in

at Blackfriars about 1639; Pepys's damning of the play has been deemed unjust. Among modern critics, Professor F. E. Schelling says of it: *"The Country Captain is far from a contemptible performance, and its lively scenes of contemporary English country life must have proved readily actable by the King's Company at Blackfriars"* (*Elizabethan Drama,* II, 184).

[1] "'The Heiress' does not appear in the list of the Duke of Newcastle's works, nor has any play of that name and date been traced" (Pepys's *Diary,* Wheatley ed., VIII, 204). It would seem from the reference to the part in abuse to Sedley to have been a contemporary play.

abuse to Sir Charles Sedley, being last night exceedingly beaten.[2]

February 2, 1668-69. To the King's playhouse, where "The Heyresse," notwithstanding Kinaston's being beaten, is acted: and they say the King is very angry with Sir Charles Sedley for his being beaten, but he do deny it. But his part is done by Beeston, who is fain to read it out of a book all the while, and thereby spoils the part, and almost the play, it being one of the best parts in it; and though the design is, in the first conception of it, pretty good, yet it is but an indifferent play, wrote, they say, by my Lord Newcastle. But it was pleasant to see Beeston come in with the others, supposing it to be dark, and yet he is forced to read his part by the light of the candles: and this I observing to a gentleman that sat by me, he was mightily pleased therewith, and spread it up and down. But that, that pleased me most in the play is, the first song that Knepp sings, she singing three or four; and, indeed, it was very finely sung, so as to make the whole house clap her.

Newcastle, Duke of   THE HUMOUROUS LOVERS

March 30, 1667. Did by coach go to see the silly play of my Lady Newcastle's, called "The Humourous Lovers";[1] the most silly thing that ever come upon

---

[2] For this story, see Doran's *Annals of the English Stage,* Lowe ed., I, 71-72.

[1] W. C. Hazlitt describes *The Humourous Lovers* as "A comedy by the Duke of Newcastle, acted at the Duke's Theatre"

a stage. I was sick to see it, but yet would not but have seen it, that I might the better understand her.

April 11, 1667. To White Hall, thinking there to have seen the Duchess of Newcastle. . . . [She] was the other day at her own play, "The Humourous Lovers"; the most ridiculous thing that ever was wrote, but yet she and her Lord mightily pleased with it; and she, at the end, made her respects to the players from her box, and did give them thanks.

Orrery, Earl of   THE BLACK PRINCE

October 19, 1667. Full of my desire of seeing my Lord Orrery's new play this afternoon at the King's house, "The Black Prince,"[1] the first time it is acted; where, though we come by two o'clock, yet there was no room in the pit, but we were forced to go into one of the upper boxes, at 4*s.* a piece, which is the first time I ever sat in a box in my life, . . . and this pleasure I had, that from this place the scenes do appear very fine indeed, and much better than in the pit. The house infinite full, and the King and Duke of York was there. By and by the play begun, and in it nothing particular but a very fine dance for variety of figures, but a little too long. But, as to the con-

(*A Manual for the Collector and Amateur of Old English Plays,* p. 111). He gives the date of publication as 1677. Langbaine, who also attributes the play to the Duke, not the Duchess, comments (p. 387) that it "equals most of the Comedies of this Age."

[1] A tragedy (1667) with a happy ending, written in rhyme.

trivance, and all that was witty (which, indeed, was much, and very witty), was almost the same that had been in his two former plays of "Henry the 5th"[2] and "Mustapha,"[3] and the same points and turns of wit in both, and in this very same play often repeated, but in excellent language, and were so excellent that the whole house was mightily pleased with it all along till towards the end he comes to discover the chief of the plot of the play by the reading of a long letter,[4] which was so long and some things (the people being set already to think too long) so unnecessary that they frequently begun to laugh, and to hiss twenty times, that, had it not been for the King's being there, they had certainly hissed it off the stage. But I must confess that, as my Lord Barkeley says behind me, the having of that long letter was a thing so absurd that he could not imagine how a man of his parts could possibly fall into it; or, if he did, if he had but let any friend read it, the friend would have told him of it; and, I must confess, it is one of the most remarkable instances that ever I did or expect to meet with in my life of a wise man's not being wise at all times, and in all things, for nothing could be more ridiculous than this, though

[2] *The History of Henry the Fifth* (1664).

[3] *Mustapha, the Son of Solyman the Magnificent* (1665).

[4] Read by Hart in Act V, and afterwards omitted as will be seen from Pepys's entry for October 23. According to Downes (*Roscius Anglicanus*, p. 14), Hart acted the part of Lord Delaware; Mohun, Edward III; Kynaston, the Black Prince; Wintersell, King John of France; Burt, Count Guesclin; Mrs. Marshall, Plantagenet; Nell Gwyn, Alizia.

the letter of itself at another time would be thought an excellent letter, and indeed an excellent Romance, but at the end of the play, when every body was weary of sitting, and were already possessed with the effect of the whole letter, to trouble them with a letter a quarter of an hour long, was a most absurd thing. After the play done, and nothing pleasing them from the time of the letter to the end of the play, people being put into a bad humour of disliking (which is another thing worth the noting), I home by coach, and could not forbear laughing almost all the way home, and all the evening to my going to bed, at the ridiculousness of the letter.

October 23, 1667. To the King's playhouse, and there saw "The Black Prince," again: which is mightily bettered by that long letter being printed and so delivered to every body at their going in, and some short reference made to it in heart in the play, which do mighty well; but, when all is done, I think it the worst play of my Lord Orrery's. . . . The play done I . . . to my chamber, to read the true story, in Speed,[5] of the Black Prince.

April 1, 1668. To the King's house, and there sat in an upper box, to hide myself, and saw "The Black Prince," a very good play; but only the fancy, most of it, the same as in the rest of my Lord Orrery's plays; but the dance very stately; . . . I did fall asleep the former part of the play, but afterwards did mind it and did like it very well.

[5] John Speed's *Historie of Great Britaine,* book IX, chapter XII.

Orrery, Earl of   THE GENERAL

September 28, 1664. To a play, and so we saw,
coming late, part of "The Generall";[1] my Lord
Orrery's (Broghill) second play; but Lord! to see
how no more either in words, sense, or design, it is
to his "Henry the 5th" is not imaginable, and so
poorly acted, though in finer clothes, is strange.

October 4, 1664. After dinner to a play, to see
"The General"; which is so dull and so ill-acted, that
I think it is the worst I ever saw or heard in all my
days. I happened to sit near to Sir Charles Sidly;
who I find a very witty man, and he did at every line
take notice of the dullness of the poet and badness of
the action, and that most pertinently; which I was
mightily taken with; and among others where by
Altemire's command Clarimont, the General, is commanded to rescue his Rivall, whom she loved, Lucidor,
he, after a great deal of demurre, broke out, "Well,
I'll save my Rivall and make her confess, that I
deserve while he do but possesse." "Why, what,

---

[1] A play entitled *The General* appears in the list of pieces performed by Killigrew's company, given in Malone's *Shakspeare,*
Vol. I, Part II, p. 268, as having been acted about this time.
In Rufus Chetwood's *British Theatre* (Dublin, 1750) *"Altemira,
a Tragedy. 1685"* is mentioned among the anonymous plays (p.
137). This was doubtless the "Altemira, Trag. in rhyme, by
Roger Boyle, Earl of Orrery," described by the *Biographia*   .
Dramatica (1812 ed., II, 21-22) as having been "left unfinished"
and later drastically revised and curtailed by the grandson of
the poet, Charles Boyle, Earl of Orrery. In the revision of the
play (1702) Altemire is Altemira; Clarimont, the General, is
Clorimon; and Lucidor, his rival, Lycidor.

pox," says Sir Charles Sydly, "would he have him have more, or what is there more to be had of a woman than the possessing her?"[2]

April 24, 1669. After dinner to the King's house, and there saw "The General"[3] revived—a good play, that pleases me well.

Orrery, Earl of GUZMAN

April 16, 1669. My wife being gone . . . to see the new play to-day at the Duke of York's house, "Guzman,"[1] . . . I thence presently to the Duke of York's playhouse, and there, in the 18*d.* seat, did get room to see almost three acts of the play, but it seemed to me but very ordinary. After the play done, I into the pit, and . . . here I did meet with Shadwell,[2] the poet, who, to my great wonder, do tell me that my

[2] In the 1702 version, the first part of Act III comes very close to this description. The lines, as Pepys remembered them, on which Sedley comments, were published practically unaltered. Clorimon says:

"I'll save my Rival, and make her Confess
'Tis I Deserve what he does but Possess."

[3] Either a revival of Orrery's tragedy, or, as W. C. Hazlitt asserts, a tragi-comedy with the same title by James Shirley, printed from a MS. in 1853. (Cf. *A Manual for the Collector and Amateur of Old English Plays,* p. 93.)

[1] A comedy (1669). This entry is of particular interest as indicating how fleeting was the popularity of the heroic drama of the Restoration. According to Downes (*Roscius Anglicanus,* p. 28), Guzman "took very well."

[2] Thomas Shadwell.

Lord of [Orrery] did write this play, trying what he could do in comedy, since his heroique plays could do no more wonders. This do trouble me; for it is a mean thing, and so he says, as hath been upon the stage a great while; and Harris, who hath no part in it, did come to me, and told me in discourse that he was glad of it, it being a play that will not take.

Orrery, Earl of

The History of Henry the Fifth

August 13, 1664. Mr. Creed dining with me I got him to give my wife and me a play this afternoon, lending him money to do it, which is a fallacy that I have found now once, to avoyde my vowe with, but never to be more practised I swear, and so to the new play, at the Duke's house, of "Henry the Fifth";[1] a most noble play, writ by my Lord Orrery, wherein Betterton, Harris, and Ianthe's[2] parts are most incomparably wrote and done, and the whole play the most full of height and raptures of wit and sense, that ever I heard; having but one incongruity, or what did

[1] A rhymed heroic drama (1664), "Splendidly Cloath'd," according to Downes (*Roscius Anglicanus,* pp. 27-28),—"The King in the Duke of *York's* Coronation Suit: *Owen Tudor,* in King *Charle's:* Duke of *Burgundy,* in the Lord of *Oxford's,* and the rest all New. It was Excellently Perform'd, and Acted 10 Days Successively."

[2] Betterton played Owen Tudor; Harris, King Henry; "Ianthe" (Mrs. Betterton), Princess Katherine; and Mrs. Davis, Anne of Burgundy.

not please me in it, that King Harry promises to plead for Tudor to their Mistresse, Princesse Katherine of France, more than when it comes to it he seems to do; and Tudor refused by her with some kind of indignity, not with a difficulty and honour that it ought to have been done in to him.

August 17, 1664. Very merry discoursing of the late play of Henry the 5th, which they conclude the best that ever was made, but confess with me that Tudor's being dismissed in the manner he is is a great blemish to the play.

December 28, 1666. To White Hall, and got my Lord Bellasses to get me into the playhouse; and there, after all staying above an hour for the players, the King and all waiting, which was absurd, saw "Henry the Fifth"[3] well done by the Duke's people, and in most excellent habits, all new vests, being put on but this night. But I sat so high and far off, that I missed most of the words, and sat with a wind coming into my back and neck, which did much trouble me. The play continued till twelve at night.

February 13, 1666-67. But what I wondered at, Dr. Clerke did say that Sir W. Davenant is no good judge of a dramatick poem, finding fault with his choice of Henry the 5th and others for the stage.

July 6, 1668. My wife and company to the [Duke's] house, to see "Henry the Fifth." . . . Thence I to the playhouse, and saw a piece of the play, and glad to see Betterton.

---

[3] It seems probable that in this and the following entries Pepys is again referring to Orrery's and not Shakespeare's play.

Orrery, Earl of

MUSTAPHA, THE SON OF SOLYMAN THE MAGNIFICENT

April 3, 1665. To a play at the Duke's, of my Lord Orrery's, called "Mustapha,"[1] which being not good, made Betterton's part and Ianthe's[2] but ordinary too, so that we were not contented with it at all. . . . All the pleasure of the play was, the King and my Lady Castlemayne were there; and pretty witty Nell, at the King's house, and the younger Marshall[3] sat next us; which pleased me mightily.

[1] *Mustapha, the Son of Solyman the Magnificent* (1665). Evelyn saw this play three days later and again on October 18, 1666. Under the latter date he makes the following interesting comment: "This night was acted my Lord Broghill's tragedy called 'Mustapha' before their Majesties at Court, at which I was present, very seldom going to the publiq theaters for many reasons, now as they were abused to an atheistical liberty, fowle and undecent women now (and never till now) permitted to appear and act, who inflaming severall young noblemen and gallants, became their misses, and to some their wives; witness ye Earl of Oxford, Sir R. Howard, P. Rupert, the Earl of Dorset, and another greater person than any of them, who fell into their snares, to ye reproch of their noble families, and ruine of both body and soule. I was invited by my Lo. Chamberlaine to see this tragedy, exceedingly well written, tho' in my mind I did not approve of any such pastime in a time of such judgments and calamities" (*Diary*, Wheatley ed., II, pp. 210-211). The "judgments and calamities" were the fire, which was just over, and the plague not yet abated.

[2] For the complete cast, see *Roscius Anglicanus,* p. 26. Betterton played Solyman; Harris, Mustapha; W. Smith, Zanger; Sandford, Rustan; Mrs. Davenport—and later Mrs. Betterton—Roxalana; and Mrs. Davis, Queen of Hungaria.

[3] Nell Gwyn and Rebecca Marshall.

January 5, 1666-67.   To the Duke's house, and there saw "Mustapha" a most excellent play for words and design as any ever I did see.   I had seen it before but forgot it, so it was wholly new to me, which is the pleasure of my not committing these things to my memory.

September 4, 1667.   To the Duke of York's play house, and there saw "Mustapha," which, the more I see the more I like; and is a most admirable poem, and bravely acted; only both Betterton and Harris could not contain from laughing in the midst of a most serious part, from the ridiculous mistake of one of the men upon the stage; which I did not like.

February 11, 1667-68.   Sent my wife and Deb. to see "Mustapha" acted, . . . and so to the Duke of York's playhouse, and there saw the last act for nothing, where I never saw such good acting of any creature as Smith's part of Zanger; and I do also, though it [Solyman] was excellently acted by ——, do yet want Betterton mightily.

June 15, 1668.   My wife pleased with all, this evening reading of "Mustapha" to me till supper.

June 16, 1668.   To Reading, and then heard my wife read more of "Mustapha."

Orrery, Earl of   TRYPHON

December 8, 1668.   My wife tells me of my Lord Orrery's new play "Tryphon,"[1] at the Duke of

---

[1] A tragedy (1668).   Evidently the Earl of Orrery felt the

York's house, which, however, I would see . . . and therefore . . . went thither, where, with much ado, at half-past one, we got into a blind hole in the 18*d.* place, above stairs, where we could not hear well, but the house infinite full, but the prologue most silly, and the play, though admirable, yet no pleasure almost in it, because just the very same design, and words, and sense, and plot, as every one of his plays have, any one of which alone would be held admirable, whereas so many of the same design and fancy do but dull one another; and this, I perceive, is the sense of every body else, as well as myself, who therefore showed but little pleasure in it.

December 9, 1668.   To the Duke of York's house where mighty full again, but we come time enough to have a good place in the pit, and did hear this new play again, where, though I better understood it than before, yet my sense of it and pleasure was just the same as yesterday, and no more, nor any body else's about us.

Porter, Thomas (?)   THE GERMAN PRINCESS

April 15, 1664.   To the Duke's house, and there saw "The German Princess"[1] acted, by the woman

force of such criticism.   It is interesting to note that in his next dramatic venture, the comedy of *Guzman* (1669), he broke away from the rhymed heroic tragedy.

[1] Genest states (I, pp. 51-52) that the play referred to here was *A Witty Combat, or the Female Victor, a Trage-Comedy,* "as it was acted by persons of quality in Whitsun-week with great

herself; but never was anything so well done in earnest, worse performed in jest upon the stage; and indeed the whole play, abating the drollery of him that acts her husband, is very simple, unless here and there a witty sprinkle or two.

.   Porter, Thomas   THE VILLAIN

October 20, 1662.   Among other discourse young Killigrew did so commend "The Villaine,"[1] a new play made by Tom Porter, and acted only on Saturday at the Duke's house, as if there never had been any such play come upon the stage.   The same yesterday was told me by Captain Ferrers; and this morning afterwards by Dr. Clerke, who saw it. . . . To the Duke's house, and there was the house full of company: but whether it was in over-expecting or what, I know not, but I was never less pleased with

applause . . . written by T. P. [Thomas Porter ?] Gent."
(1663). It was obviously based upon the adventures of a notorious impostor, Mary Moders, who masqueraded about this time under the name of "the German princess." After D'Avenant had exploited her on the stage, she returned to her former occupations, and in 1673 was executed for theft. Pepys refers to her again on May 29 and June 7, 1663. On the latter occasion, he defends "her wit and spirit" against Lady Batten. For an account of the publications based upon her career, see Ernest Bernbaum, *The Mary Carleton Narratives, 1663-1673.*

[1] A tragedy by Thomas Porter, published in the following year.

a play in my life. Though there was good singing and dancing, yet no fancy in the play, but something that made it less contenting was my conscience that I ought not to have gone by my vow, and, besides, my business commanded me elsewhere.

October 27, 1662. Here [at Whitehall] we staid some time, thinking to stay out the play before the King to-night, but it being "The Villaine," . . . I had no mind.

December 26, 1662. To the Duke's house and saw "The Villaine," which I ought not to do without my wife, but that my time is now out that I did undertake it for. But, Lord! to consider how my natural desire is to pleasure, which God be praised that he has given me the power by my late oaths to curb so well as I have done, and will do again after two or three plays more. Here I was better pleased with the play than I was at first, understanding the design better than I did.

January 1, 1662-63. To the Duke's House, where we saw "The Villane" again; and the more I see it, the more I am offended at my first undervaluing the play, it being very good and pleasant, and yet a true and allowable tragedy. The house was full of citizens, and so the less pleasant, but that I was willing to make an end of my gaddings, and to set to my business for all the year again to-morrow.

September 7, 1665. Thence to Brainford, reading "The Villaine," a pretty good play, all the way.

October 24, 1667. To the Duke of York's playhouse; but there Betterton not being yet well, we would not stay, though since I hear that Smith do act his part[2] in "The Villaine," which was then acted, as well or better than he, which I do not believe.

Rhodes, Richard   FLORA'S VAGARIES

August 8, 1664.   So my wife and I abroad to the King's playhouse, she giving me her time of the last month, she having not seen any then; so my vowe is not broke at all. . . .   Here we saw "Flora's Figarys."[1]   I never saw it before, and by the most ingenuous performance of the young jade Flora, it seemed as pretty a pleasant play as ever I saw in my life.

October 5, 1667.   Here[2] I read the questions to Knepp, while she answered me, through all her part of Flora's Figary's[3] which was acted to-day. . . . By

[2] Betterton's part was Monsieur Brisac. In the original cast were also Sandford (Maligni, the Villain); Harris (Beaupres); Young (Bontefeu), Mrs. Betterton, "late Saunderson," (Belmont). "This Play," says Downes (*Roscius Anglicanus,* p. 23), "by its being well perform'd, had Success Extremely beyond the Company's Expectation. . . . It Succeeded 10 Days with a full House, to the last."

[1] A comedy (1663) by Richard Rhodes, previously acted, according to the list of plays performed by Killigrew's company, given in Malone's *Shakspeare,* Vol. I, Part II, p. 268, on November 23, 1663. The part of Flora was later played by Nell Gwyn.

[2] In the greenroom at the King's theatre, which like the "tiringroom" of the Restoration playhouse was accessible to the friends of the players.

[3] Mrs. Knepp played the part of Otrante. The other principal

and by into the pit, and there saw the play, which is pretty good, but my belly was full of what I had seen in the house.

February 18, 1667-68. To the King's house, and there, in one of the upper boxes saw "Flora's Vagarys," which is a very silly play; and the more, I being out of humour, being at a play without my wife.

Sedley, Sir Charles

THE MULBERRY GARDEN (THE WANDERING LADIES (?))

January 11, 1667-68. She [Knepp] told me also of a play shortly coming upon the stage, of Sir Charles Sidly's, which, she thinks, will be called "The Wandering Ladys,"[1] a comedy that, she thinks, will be most pleasant.

May 7, 1668. Thither comes Bannister with a song of her's [Knepp's], that he hath set in Sir Charles Sidley's play for her.[2]

May 18, 1668. To the King's playhouse, where the doors were not then open,[3] but presently they did open; and we in, and find many people already come

actors were Beeston as Ludovico; Mohun, Alberto; Burt, Francisco; Cartwright, Grimani. (Cf. Genest, I, 70.)

[1] Probably *The Mulberry Garden.* No play of this name is known.

[2] The song beginning, "Ah, Cloris, that I now could sit," Bannister's music to which has not been discovered.

[3] This was at twelve o'clock, when the doors of the theatre were usually opened.

in, by private ways, into the pit, it being the first day
of Sir Charles Sidly's new play, so long expected,
"The Mullberry Guarden,"[4] of whom, being so reputed a wit, all the world do expect great matters. I
having sat there a while . . . did slip out, getting a
boy to keep my place; and to the Rose Tavern. . . .
And so to the play again, where the King and Queen,
by and by, come, and all the Court; and the house
infinitely full. But the play, when it come, though
there was, here and there, a pretty saying, and that
not very many neither, yet the whole of the play had
nothing extraordinary in it, at all, neither of language
nor design, insomuch that the King I did not see
laugh, nor pleased the whole play from the beginning
to the end, nor the company; insomuch that I have not
been less pleased at a new play in my life, I think.
And which made it the worse was, that there never
was worse musick played—that is, worse things composed, which made me and Captain Rolt, who happened to sit near me, mad. So away thence, very
little satisfied with the play, but pleased with my
company.

May 20, 1668. Thence walked to the King's playhouse, and saw "The Mulberry-Garden" again, and
cannot be reconciled to it, but only to find here and
there an independent sentence of wit, and that is all.

June 29, 1668. With my wife to the King's playhouse—"The Mulberry Garden," which she had not
seen.

---

[4] A comedy (1668) which met with great success in spite of
Pepys's disapproval.

St. Serfe, Sir Thomas
TARUGO'S WILES, OR THE COFFEE HOUSE

October 5, 1667. To the Duke of York's play-house, but the house so full, it being a new play, "The Coffee House,"[1] that we could not get in, so to the King's house. . . . But to see how Nell cursed, for having so few people in the pit, was pretty; the other house carrying away all the people at the new play.

October 15, 1667. To the Duke of York's house, where, after long stay, the King and Duke of York come, and there saw "The Coffee-house," the most ridiculous, insipid play that ever I saw in my life, and glad we were that Betterton had no part in it.

Shadwell, Thomas   THE ROYAL SHEPHERDESS

February 25, 1668-69. To the Duke of York's house, and there before one, but the house infinite full, where, by and by, the King and Court come, it being a new play, or an old one new vamped by Shadwell, called "The Royall Shepherdesse,"[1] but the silliest

---

[1] *Tarugo's Wiles, or The Coffee House* (1667), a comedy based upon Moreto's *No puede ser,* which "Expir'd the third Day" (*Roscius Anglicanus,* p. 31). John Dennis (*Original Letters, Familiar, Moral, Critical,* I, 51) remarks of the Spanish play that it was "translated and acted and damned, under the title of Tarugo's Wiles, or the Coffee House."

[1] A pastoral tragi-comedy (1669) based upon John Fountain's *The Rewards of Virtue,* which "liv'd Six days" according to Downes (*Roscius Anglicanus,* p. 31).

for words and design, and everything, that ever I saw
in my whole life, there being nothing in the world
pleasing in it, but a good martial dance of pikemen,
where Harris and another do handle their pikes in a
dance to admiration; but never less satisfied with a
play in my life.

Shadwell, Thomas

The Sullen Lovers, or The Impertinents

May 2, 1668.   To the Duke of York's playhouse,
at a little past twelve, to get a good place in the pit,
against the new play, and there setting a poor man
to keep my place, I out, and spent an hour at Martin's, my bookseller's, and so back again, where I find
the house quite full.   But I had my place, and by and
by the King comes and the Duke of York; and then
the play begins, called "The Sullen Lovers; or, The
Impertinents,"[1] having many good humours in it, but
the play tedious, and no design at all in it.   But a
little boy, for a farce, do dance Polichinelli, the best
that ever anything was done in this world, by all
men's report: most pleased with that, beyond anything in the world, and much beyond all the play.

May 4, 1668.   To the Duke of York's house, and
there saw "The Impertinents" again, and with less

---

[1] Shadwell's first comedy (1668), based upon Molière's *Les
Fâcheux*.   Smith acted the part of Stanford; Harris, Sir Positive
At-all; Nokes, Ninny; and Mrs. Shadwell, Emilia.   "This Play,"
Downes records (*Roscius Anglicanus*, p. 29), "had wonderful
Success, being Acted 12 Days together."

pleasure than before, it being but a very contemptible play, though there are many little witty expressions in it; and the pit did generally say that of it.

May 5, 1668. To the Duke of York's playhouse; and there coming late, he and I up to the balcony-box, where we find my Lady Castlemayne and several great ladies; and there we sat with them, and I saw "The Impertinents" once more, now three times, and the three only days it hath been acted. And to see the folly how the house do this day cry up the play more than yesterday! and I for that reason like it, I find, the better, too; by Sir Positive At-all, I understand is meant Sir Robert Howard.

May 6, 1668. Among other things understand that my Lord St. John is meant by Mr. Woodcocke in "The Impertinents."

May 8, 1668. But Lord! to see how this play of Sir Positive At-All, in abuse of Sir Robert Howard, do take, all the Duke's and everybody's talk being of that, and telling more stories of him, of the like nature, that it is now the town and country talk, and, they say, is most exactly true. The Duke of York himself said that of his playing at trap-ball is true, and told several other stories of him.

June 24, 1668. To the Duke of York's playhouse, and there saw "The Impertinents," a pretty good play.

August 29, 1668. Thence carried Harris to his playhouse, where, though four o'clock, so few people there at "The Impertinents," as I went out, and do believe they did not act though there was Lord Arlington and his company there.

April 14, 1669. To the Duke of York's play-house, and there saw "The Impertinents," a play which pleases me still.

Southland, Thomas (?)   Love a la Mode

July 19, 1663. Then I fell to read over a silly play writ by a person of honour (which is, I find, as much as to say a coxcomb), called "Love a la Mode."[1]

Stapylton, Sir Robert   The Slighted Maid

February 23, 1662-63. Walked out to see what play was acted to-day, and we find it "The Slighted Mayde."[1] But, Lord! to see that though I did know myself to be out of danger, yet I durst not go through the street, but round by the garden into Tower Street. By and by took coach, and to the Duke's house, where we saw it well acted, though the play hath little good in it, being most pleased to see the little girl dance in boy's apparel, she having very fine legs, only bends in the hams, as I perceive all women do.

May 29, 1663. To the Royall Theatre, but they not acting to-day, then to the Duke's house, and there saw "The Slighted Mayde," wherein Gosnell acted

---

[1] *Love à la Mode,* a comedy by "T. S."—supposedly Thomas Southland—was printed in 1663.

[1] *The Slighted Maid* (1663), a comedy by Sir Robert Stapylton.

Pyramena,[2] a great part, and did it very well, and I believe will do it better and better, and prove a good actor. The play is not very excellent, but is well acted, and in general the actors, in all particulars, are better than at the other house.

July 28, 1668. To the Duke of York's playhouse, and there saw "The Slighted Maid," but a mean play; and thence home, there being little pleasure now in a play, the company being but little. Here we saw Gosnell, who is become very homely, and sings meanly I think, to what I thought she did.

Tatham, John
The Rump, or The Mirrour of the Late Times

November 10, 1660. After reading of . . . the comedy of the Rump,[1] which is also very silly, I went to bed.

Taylor, Captain Silas
The Serenade, or Disappointment

May 7, 1669. So home, and there met with a letter from Captain Silas Taylor, and, with it, his written

[2] According to Genest (I, 46), Mrs. Betterton had taken the part of Pyramena on May 28. Betterton was Iberio; Harris, Salerno; Smith, Lugo; Young, Corbulo; Sandford, Vindex.

[1] *The Rump, or the Mirrour of the Late Times,* a satire of the Cromwellian régime, was privately produced in 1660 at Dorset Court, and published later in the same year.

copy of a play that he hath wrote and intends to have acted. It is called "The Serenade or Disappointment,"[1] which I will read, not believing he can make any good of that kind. He did once offer to show Harris it, but Harris told him he would judge by one Act, whether it were good or no, which is indeed a foolish saying. . . . This made Taylor say he would not shew it him, but is angry, and hath carried it to the other house, and he thinks it will be acted there, though he tells me they are not agreed upon it.

Tuke, Sir Samuel

THE ADVENTURES OF FIVE HOURS

January 8, 1662-63. There being the famous new play acted the first time to-day, which is called "The Adventures of Five Hours,"[1] at the Duke's house, being, they say, made or translated by Colonel Tuke, I did long to see it, . . . and so we went; and though early, were forced to sit almost out of sight at one end of the lower forms, so full was the house. And

[1] This play does not seem to be otherwise known. The author (?—1688), who had been made keeper of the King's stores at Harwich in 1665, was a well-known antiquary and something of a musician.

[1] An adaptation from a Spanish comedy of intrigue, *Los Empeños de Seis Horas,* ascribed to Antonio Coello. Evelyn had already seen it. His entry for December 23, 1662, reads: "I went with Sr George Tuke to hear the comedians con and repeat his new comedy, 'The Adventures of 5 Hours,' a play whose plot was taken out of the famous Spanish poet Calderon"

the play, in one word, is the best, for the variety and the most excellent continuance of the plot to the very end, that ever I saw, or think ever shall, and all possible, not only to be done in the time, but in most other respects very admittable, and without one word of ribaldry; and the house, by its frequent plaudits, did show their sufficient approbation.

January 17, 1662-63. To the Duke's playhouse, where we did see "The Five Hours" entertainment again, which indeed is a very fine play, though through my being out of order, it did not seem so good as at first, but I could discern it was not any fault in the play.

June 1, 1663. Begun again to rise betimes by 4 o'clock, and make an end of "The Adventures of Five Houres," and it is a most excellent play.

August 15, 1666. So down the river, reading "The Adventures of Five Houres," which the more I read the more I admire.

August 17, 1666. I walking alone from Green-

(*Diary,* Wheatley ed., II, 156). Evelyn saw the play again on the day on which Pepys first saw it. It is interesting to compare his record of the performance with the above: "I went to see my kinsman Sir Geo. Tuke's comedy acted at ye Duke's Theatre, which took so universally, that it was acted for some weekes every day, and 'twas believ'd it would be worth to the comedians 4 or £500. The plot was incomparable but the language was stiffe and formal" (*Ibid.,* II, 157). Downes, who ascribes the play to the Earl of Bristol and Sir Samuel Tuke, adds: "It took Successively 13 Days together"; "Mr. *Betterton,* Acting *Don Henriq;* Mr. *Harris, Antonio;* Mr. *Young, Octavio; . . .* Mrs. *Davenport, Camilla;* Mrs. *Betterton, Portia*" (*Roscius Anglicanus,* p. 22).

wich thither, making an end of the "Adventures of Five Hours," which when all is done is the best play, that ever I read in my life.

August 20, 1666. Reading "Othello, Moore of Venice," which I ever heretofore esteemed a mighty good play, but having so lately read "The Adventures of Five Houres," it seems a mean thing.

January 27, 1668-69. To the Duke of York's playhouse, and there saw "The Five Hours' Adventure," which hath not been acted a good while before, but once, and is a most excellent play, I must confess.

February 15, 1668-69. To White Hall; and there, by means of Mr. Cooling, did get into the play, the only one we have seen this winter: it was "The Five Hours' Adventure": but I sat so far I could not hear well, nor was there any pretty woman that I did see, but my wife, who sat in Lady Fox's pew, with her. The house very full; and late before done, so that it was past eleven before we got home. But we were well pleased with seeing it.

CHAPTER V

FOREIGN PLAYS AND TRANSLATIONS

CHAPTER V

FOREIGN PLAYS AND TRANSLATIONS

Comenius, Johann Amos   SCHOLA LUDUS

June 25, 1666. All this day on the water entertained myself with the play[1] of Commenius.

Corneille, Pierre   THE CID

December 1, 1662. To the Cockpitt, with much
crowding and waiting, where I saw "The Valiant
Cidd,"[1] acted, a play I have read with great delight,
but is a most dull thing acted, which I never understood before, there being no pleasure in it, though
done by Betterton and by Ianthe, and another fine

[1] *Schola Ludus seu Encyclopædia Viva (hoc est) Januæ Lin-
guarum Praxis Scenica* (1655), a school drama in 5 acts and 21
scenes, by Johann Amos Comenius, or Komensky (1592-1671),
the noted Moravian educator and theologian. The *Schola Ludus*
was written for the instruction of the boys of the author's school
at Patak, chiefly in natural history; among its 52 characters are
a chemist, a geographer, and personifications of the elements.

[1] A translation of *Le Cid* (1637) presumably by Joseph
Rutter. D. F. Canfield (*Corneille and Racine in England*,
p. 13) cites Pepys's statement as evidence that "Rutter's translation held the stage as late as 1662."

wench that is come in the room of Roxalana;[2] nor did the King or Queen once smile all the whole play, nor any of the company seem to take any pleasure but what was in the greatness and the gallantry of the company.

Corneille, Pierre HERACLIUS, EMPEROR OF THE EAST

March 8, 1663-64. "Heraclius" being acted,[1] (which my wife and I have a mighty mind to see). . . . The play hath one very good passage well managed in it, about two persons pretending, and yet denying themselves, to be son to the tyrant Phocas,

[2] That is, by Betterton and his wife ("Ianthe") and an actress who succeeded Elizabeth Davenport ("Roxalana").

[1] A translation of Corneille's *Heraclius*, brought out at the Duke's theatre. It has been attributed to Lodovick Carlell, author of the only known printed version. This is, however, expressly denied by Carlell in "The Author's Advertisement" to *"Heraclius, Emperour of the East. A Tragedy. Written in French by Monsieur de Corneille. Englished by Lodovick Carlell, Esq. London. 1664"*—a copy of which is in the library of the Elizabethan Club, Yale University. The "Advertisement" begins: "Another Translation formerly design'd (after this seem'd to be accepted of) was perfected and acted, this, not returned to me until that very day." It is noteworthy that Carlell's translation bears the date of "March 9, 1664,"—the day following the performance Pepys describes. It also contains a "Prologue Intended for the Play."

The scene of the tragedy is laid in Constantinople, and the plot is based upon the struggle of Heraclius against the usurper Phocas for the throne of the Eastern Empire.

and yet heire of Mauricius to the crowne. The garments like Romans very well. The little girle is come to act very prettily, and spoke the epilogue most admirably. But at the beginning, at the drawing up of the curtaine, there was the finest scene of the Emperor and his people about him, standing in their fixed and different postures in their Roman habitts, above all that ever I yet saw at any of the theatres.

February 4, 1666-67. To the Duke's playhouse, and there saw "Heraclius," an excellent play, to my extraordinary content; and the more from the house being very full, and great company. . . . Mightily pleased with the play.

September 5, 1667. To the Duke of York's house, and there saw "Heraclius," which is a good play; but they did so spoil it with their laughing, and being all of them out, and with the noise they made within the theatre, that I was ashamed of it, and resolve not to come thither again a good while, believing that this negligence, which I never observed before, proceeds only from their want of company in the pit, that they have no care how they act.

Corneille, Pierre   HORACE

January 19, 1668-69. To the King's house, to see "Horace";[1] this is the third day of its acting—a silly

[1] A translation of Pierre Corneille's tragedy left "unfinished" by Mrs. Katharine Philips at her death, the last act being "afterward translated by Sir John Denham" before 1668. (Cf. Can-

tragedy; but Lacy hath made a farce of several dances—between each act, one: but his words are but silly, and invention not extraordinary, as to the dances; only some Dutchmen come out of the mouth and tail of a Hamburgh sow.

Corneille, Pierre

The Mistaken Beauty, or the Liar

November 28, 1667. To the King's playhouse, and there sat by my wife, and saw "The Mistaken Beauty,"[1] which I never, I think, saw before, though an old play; and there is much in it that I like, though the name is but improper to it—at least, that name, it being also called "The Lyer," which is proper enough.

field, *Corneille and Racine in England,* pp. 45-48.) Evelyn saw the play on February 4, 1667-68 and on February 15, 1668-69. The entry of February 4 reads: "I saw ye tragedy of 'Horace' (written by ye *virtuous* Mrs. Phillips) acted before their Maties. 'Twixt each act a masq and antiq daunce" (*Diary,* Wheatley ed., II, 229).

[1] A translation of *Le Menteur* by an unknown author, printed in 1685. The *Biographia Dramatica* (1812 ed., III, 48) states that "there is an earlier edition of it, under the latter title alone, in 1661." In comparing Corneille with native dramatists in his *Essay of Dramatic Poesy,* 1668, Dryden comments: "What has he produced except *The Liar,* and you know how it was cried up in France; but when it came upon the English Stage, though well translated, and that part of Dorant acted [by Mr. Hart] to so much advantage as I am confident it never received in its own country, the most favourable to it would not put it in competition with many of Fletcher's or Ben Jonson's" (*The Works of John Dryden,* Scott-Saintsbury ed., XV, 330).

Corneille, Pierre   POMPEY THE GREAT

June 23, 1666. Down to Deptford, all the way reading Pompey the Great (a play translated from the French by several noble persons; among others, my Lord Buckhurst),[1] that to me is but a mean play, and the words and sense not very extraordinary.

Corneille, Thomas (?)

THE LABYRINTH, OR THE FATAL EMBARRASSMENT

May 2, 1664. To the King's play-house to . . . "The Labyrinth,"[1] the poorest play, methinks, that ever I saw, there being nothing in it but the odd accidents that fell out, by a lady's being bred up in man's apparel, and a man in a woman's.

[1] A translation (1663) of Corneille's *La Morte de Pompée,* by "certain Persons of Honour"—Waller, Earl of Dorset; Sir Charles Sedley; Sidney Godolphin; and Sir Edward Filmore.

[1] Neither Downes, nor Genest, nor Langbaine, throws light on this piece. The only play of this name recorded is a translation of *Ariane,* by Thomas Corneille, by Rev. M. Stratford, published in 1795. The *Biographia Dramatica* (1812 ed., II, 660) gives it as *"The Labyrinth, or The Fatal Embarrassment. Trag. from Corneille. Dublin printed, 8vo. 1795."*

Unknown Author   "French Comedy"

August 30, 1661. Then my wife and I to Drury
Lane[1] to the French comedy;[2] which was so ill done,
and the scenes and company and everything also so
nasty and out of order and poor, that I was sick all
the while in my mind to be there . . . There being
nothing pleasant but the foolery of the farce, we went
home.

Guarini, Battista   The Faithful Shepherd

February 25, 1667-68. To the Nursery, where I
was yesterday, and there saw them act a comedy, a
pastorall, "The Faythful Shepherd,"[1] having curiosity to see whether they did a comedy better than a
tragedy;[2] but they do it both alike, in the meanest
manner, that I was sick of it, but only for to satisfy
myself once in seeing the manner of it, but I shall see
them no more, I believe.

[1] Evidently the Cockpit theatre in Drury Lane.

[2] In Act I of D'Avenant's *A Playhouse to be Let* (1663?),
there is a Frenchman who has brought over a troupe of his
countrymen to act a farce. Dr. Doran (*Annals of the English
Stage,* 1865 ed., pp. 15-16) refers thus to such a company: "In
1661, £300 was given to M. Channoyeux, as the King's bounty
to the French Comedians, and in 1663, a *pass* was granted to
them to bring over new scenes and decorations."

[1] A pastoral drama from Battista Guarini's *Il Pastor Fido,* the
first English translation of which appeared anonymously in
1602. (Cf. Tucker Brooke, *The Tudor Drama,* p. 289, for an
account of the several translations.)

[2] He had recently seen them act *The Spanish Tragedy,* by
Thomas Kyd.

CHAPTER VI
DROLLS AND PUPPET-PLAYS

CHAPTER VI

DROLLS AND PUPPET-PLAYS

Drolls   THE FRENCH DANCING MASTER

May 21, 1662. We went to the Theatre to "The French Dancing Master."[1] . . . The play pleased us very well; but Lacy's part, the Dancing Master, the best in the world.

Puppet-Shows   POLICHINELLO

August 22, 1666. By coach to Moorfields, and there saw "Polichinello,"[1] which pleases me mightily.

---

[1] A "droll" according to W. C. Hazlitt (*A Manual for the Collector and Amateur of Old English Plays,* p. 91) based on the Duke of Newcastle's comedy *The Variety.* Malone, *Shakspeare,* Vol. I, Part II, p. 267, mentions a piece of this title acted on March 11, 1662, in the list of plays performed by Killigrew's company.

[1] The most popular of the puppet-plays of Italian origin, widely known in France in the reign of Louis XIV, is first heard of in England soon after the Restoration. (Cf. Charles Magnin, *Histoire des Marionettes en Europe.*) It seems to have been much patronized by the Court at this time, but is more frequently alluded to after 1688. Probably this was the "Italian puppet play" Pepys saw on May 9, 1662; Evelyn saw it on August 21, 1667 (*Diary,* Wheatley ed., II, 223).

August 29, 1666. To Moorfields, and shewed Batelier, with my wife, "Polichinello," which I like the more I see it.

September 1, 1666. To "Polichinelly," but were there horribly frighted to see Young Killigrew come in with a great many young sparks; but we did hide ourselves, so as we think they did not see us.

March 20, 1666-67. To Polichinelli at Charing Crosse, which is prettier and prettier, and so full of variety that it is extraordinary good entertainment.

April 8, 1667. Thence away to Polichinello, and there had three times more sport than at the play.[2]

September 4, 1667. To Bartholomew fayre, and there Polichinelli.

October 24, 1667. To Charing Cross, there to see Polichinelli. But, it being begun, we in to see a Frenchman.

May 2, 1668. But a little boy, for a farce do dance Polichinelli,[3] the best ever anything was done in the world, by all men's report: most pleased with that, beyond anything in the world, and much beyond all the play.

August 31, 1668. Thence to the Fayre, and saw "Polichinelle."

[2] Sir R. Howard's *The Surprisal.*

[3] At the Duke's theatre in a performance of *The Impertinents, or The Sullen Lovers.*

Puppet-Shows   MISCELLANEOUS

September 7, 1661. Here [at the "Theatre"] was "Bartholomew Fayre," with the puppet-show,[1] acted to-day, . . . but I do never a whit like it the better for the puppets, but rather the worse.

November 12, 1661. To "Bartholomew Fayre," with puppets, which I had seen once before, and the play without puppets often, but though I love the play as much as ever I did, yet I do not like the puppets at all, but think it to be a lessening to it.

May 9, 1662. Thence to see an Italian puppet play,[2] that is within the rayles there [Covent Garden] which is very pretty, the best that ever I saw, and great resort of gallants.

---

[1] Shows by puppets had been popular from the time when like the contemporary drama for the "legitimate" stage they were based on stories from the Bible. *Jonah and the Whale* and *The Prodigal Son* were popular sixteenth-century puppet-plays. Jonson's *Bartholomew Fair,* containing in Act V the puppet-show of *The Modern History of Hero and Leander,* had been acted with puppets as early as 1641. Popular plays of this period were *The Sorrows of Griselda, Dick Whittington,* and *The Vagaries of Merry Andrew.* From *The Actor's Remonstrance,* 1643 (reprinted in *The English Drama and Stage under the Tudor and Stuart Princes, 1543-1664,* Roxburghe Library, p. 262), we learn that puppet-plays were "still up with uncontrolled allowance" during the dramatic interregnum. And they held their own with the regular theatre after the actors were permitted to play again: in Etherege's *She Would if She Could* (1668), Act III, Sc. 3, Courtall says to Sir Joslin Jolly: "How the people would throng about you if you were but mounted on a few deal boards in Covent Garden now!"

[2] Probably *Polichinello.*

May 23, 1662.   To the puppet play in Covent Garden, which I saw the other day, and indeed it is very pleasant.

October 8, 1662.   He [Lord Sandwich] is at White Hall with the King, before whom the puppet plays I saw this summer in Covent-garden are acted this night.

November 10, 1662.   To Charing Cross, and there showed her the Italian motion, much after the nature of what I showed her a while since in Covent Garden.   Their puppets here are somewhat better, but their motions not at all.

August 6, 1663.   Having in our way, though nine o'clock at night, carried them into a puppet play in Lincolnes Inn Fields, where there was the story of Holofernes, and other clockwork, well done.

August 30, 1667.   To Bartholomew fayre, to walk up and down; and there, among other things, find my Lady Castlemayne at a puppet-play, "Patient Grizill."

September 4, 1668.   To the Fair, . . . my wife having a mind to see the play "Bartholomew-Fayre" with puppets.   Which we did.

September 21, 1668.   To Southwarke-Fair, very dirty, and there saw the puppet-show of Whittington, which was pretty to see; and how that idle thing do work upon people that see it, and even myself too!

PART TWO

CHAPTER VII
THE ACTORS

CHAPTER VII

THE ACTORS

[NOTE: In order to avoid unnecessary repetitions in Parts II
and III of material already presented in Part I, all details in
the following Chapters not falling under their respective special
topics—e.g., *Actors, Actresses,* etc.— have been as far as possible suppressed. It will be noted that a full account of each play
mentioned has been given in Part I. Minor details in regard
to individuals, not bearing upon the history or the literature of
the stage, have, also, generally been omitted.]

Angel, ———

February 22, 1667-68. Saving the ridiculousnesse
Angell's[1] part, which is called Trinkilo,[2] I do not see
anything extraordinary in it.

[1] Angel's name appears in Downes's list (*Roscius Anglicanus,*
p. 18) of original actors of the Duke's company who "Commonly
Acted Women's Parts" immediately after the Restoration.
Genest (I, 158) states that he "originally played female parts,
and became in time an actor of consequence"; also that no mention of his name occurs after 1673 when he played De Boastado
in Ravenscroft's *The Careless Lovers.*

[2] In *Albumazar,* at the Duke's theatre.

Beeston, William

September 15, 1668.   When they come to say it would be acted again to-morrow, both he that said it, Beeson,[1] and the pit fell a-laughing.

February 2, 1668-69.   But his part[2] is done by Beeston, who is fain to read it out of a book all the while, and thereby spoils the part, and almost the play. . . .   But it was pleasant to see Beeston come in with others, supposing it to be dark, and yet he is forced to read his part by the light of the candles.

Betterton, Thomas

March 1, 1660-61.   But above all that ever I saw, Betterton do the Bondman best.[1]

March 19, 1660-61.   Saw "The Bondman" acted most excellently, and though I have seen it often, yet

[1] William Beeston (?-1682) was according to Downes (*Roscius Anglicanus,* p. 2) among those who "come not into the [King's] Company, till after they had begun in *Drury-Lane.*" The reference is to *The Ladies à la Mode* at the King's theatre.

[2] Kynaston's part in *The Heiress.*

[1] The title part in Massinger's play, performed on this date at the Salisbury Court theatre.   Thomas Betterton (1635?-1710) was easily the greatest actor of the Restoration period. He was distinguished in comic as well as tragic characters, "created" some one hundred and thirty parts, of which his Hamlet seems most to have impressed the public of this period as, according to Cibber, his Falstaff did that of a later time. Steele, Pope, and Cibber are among those who delighted to praise him.

I am every time more and more pleased with Betterton's action.

August 24, 1661.   Betterton did the prince's part[2] [in *Hamlet*] beyond imagination.

November 4, 1661.   But for Betterton [in *The Bondman*] he is called by us both the best actor in the world.

September 30, 1662.   Saw the "Duchess of Malfy" well performed, but Betterton[3] and Ianthe to admiration.

December 1, 1662.   There being no pleasure in it [*The Cid*] though done by Betterton and by Ianthe, and another fine wench that is come in the room of Roxalana.

May 28, 1663.   And so to the Duke's House; and there saw "Hamlett" done, giving us fresh reason never to think enough of Betterton.

July 22, 1663.   He[4] grew very proud and demanded £20 for himself extraordinary, more than Betterton or any body else, upon every new play.

July 28, 1664.   Betterton and my poor Ianthe [in *The Bondman*] outdo all the world.

August 13, 1664.   Wherein Betterton,[5] Harris,

---

[2] Downes (*Roscius Anglicanus,* p. 21) says: "Sir *William* [D'Avenant] (having seen Mr. *Taylor* of the Black-Fryars Company Act it, who being Instructed by the Author, Mr. Shakespeur) taught Mr. *Betterton* in every Particle of it; which by his exact Performance, gain'd him Esteem and Reputation Superlative to all other plays."

[3] As Bosola.

[4] Henry Harris.

[5] Betterton's part was Owen Tudor.

and Ianthe's parts [in Orrery's *Henry V*] are most incomparably wrote and done.

December 2, 1664.   Saw "The Rivalls," which I had seen before; but the play not good, nor anything but the good actings of Betterton[6] and his wife and Harris.

April 3, 1665.   To a play . . . called "Mustapha," which being not good, made Betterton's part[7] and Ianthe's but ordinary too.

September 4, 1667.   Saw "Mustapha" . . . bravely acted; only both Betterton and Harris could not contain from laughing in the midst of a most serious part . . . which I did not like.

October 15, 1667.   To the Duke of York's house, . . . and there saw "The Coffee-house,"[8] the most ridiculous, insipid play that ever I saw in my life, and glad we were that Betterton had no part in it.

October 16, 1667.   I was vexed to see Young . . . act Macbeth in the room of Betterton, who, poor man! is sick.

October 24, 1667.   Betterton not being well yet.

November 6, 1667.   Mighty short of the content [in *Macbeth*] we used to have when Betterton acted, who is still sick.

February 11, 1667-68.   Do yet want Betterton mightily [in *Mustapha*].

July 6, 1668.   Here comes Harris, and first told us

---

[6] As Philander.

[7] Solyman the Magnificent.

[8] *Tarugo's Wiles, or The Coffee House* (1667), by Sir Thomas St. Serfe.

how Betterton is come again upon the stage: whereupon my wife and company to the [Duke's] house
to see "Henry the Fifth." . . . I to the playhouse,
and saw a piece of the play, and glad to see Betterton.

August 31, 1668.   Mightily pleased with it [*Hamlet*]; but, above all, with Betterton, the best part, I
believe, that ever man acted.

February 18, 1668-69.   Only Betterton's part[9] still
pleases me.

Bird, Theophilus

September 24, 1662.   He told me how Bird[1] hath
lately broke his leg, while he was fencing in
"Aglaura," upon the stage.

Burt, Nicholas

October 11, 1660.   To see "The Moore of Venice,"
which was well done.   Burt[1] acted the Moore.

[9] Memnon, in *The Mad Lover.*

[1] Theophilus Bird, who "belonged to the former race of actors,
and did not long survive the Restoration." (Cf. P. Cunningham, *The Story of Nell Gwyn*, Wheatley ed., p. 14.)

[1] Nicholas Burt was one of the original actors of principal
rôles in the King's company.   Before the Restoration he had
played women's parts.   According to Thomas Davies, he afterward soon "resigned the part of Othello to Hart, who had previously acted Cassio when Burt took the Moor" (*Dramatic
Miscellanies*, 1785 ed., I, 221).

December 11, 1667. And Burt acts Cicero,[2] which they all conclude he will not be able to do well.

February 6, 1668-69. Nor, indeed, Burt doing the Moor's [part] so well as I once thought he did.

Cartwright, William.

November 2, 1667. To the King's playhouse, and there saw "Henry the Fourth": and contrary to expectation, was pleased in nothing more than in Cartwright's speaking of Falstaffe's speech about "What is Honour?"[1]

Clun, Walter

May 8, 1663. The play was "The Humerous Lieutenant" [at the King's Theatre], a play that hath little good in it, nor much in the very part which, by the King's command, Lacy now acts instead of Clun.[1]

[2] Burt was, however, well liked in this part in Jonson's *Catiline* when the play was produced.

[1] The last speech in Act V, Sc. 1, of *Henry IV*, Part I. William Cartwright (?-1687) had been a player before the Civil War. After the Restoration he became one of the original members of the King's company and was known as a "respectable" actor. Among his other rôles were Morose in *The Silent Woman*, Brabantio in *Othello*, Major Oldfox in *The Plain Dealer*, and Thunder in *The Rehearsal*. (Cf. Genest, I, 378-379.)

[1] Walter Clun (?-1664), one of the original members of the King's company, had acted female characters before the Civil War. His best parts after the Restoration were those which Pepys praises—Subtle in *The Alchemist* and Iago in *Othello*.

JOE HAINES SPEAKING A PROLOGUE

August 4, 1664. We hear that Clun, one of their best actors, was, the last night, going out of towne (after he had acted the Alchymist, wherein was one of his best parts that he acts) to his country-house, set upon and murdered; one of the rogues taken, an Irish fellow. It seems most cruelly butchered and bound. The house will have a great miss of him.

August 5, 1664. In the way, at Kentish-towne, he showing me the place and manner of Clun's being killed and laid in a ditch, and yet he was not killed by any wounds, having only one in his arm, but bled to death through his struggling. He told me, also, the manner of it, of his going home so late [from] drinking with his whore, and manner of having found it out.

February 6, 1668-69. Mohun, which did a little surprise me, not acting Iago's part by much as well as Clun used to do.

April 17, 1669. It [*The Alchemist*] is still a good play, having not been acted for two or three years before; but I do miss Clun for the Doctor.

Haines, Joseph

March 7, 1667-68. The dances . . . excellently done, especially one part by one Hanes,[1] only lately come thither from the Nursery, an understanding

---

[1] Joseph Haines (?-1701), the popular comedian, dancer, and coffee-house wit, had just joined the King's company. "Joe Haines," says Anthony Ashton in his *Brief Supplement* to Colley Cibber's *Apology* (Lowe ed., II, 314), "is more remark-

fellow, but yet, they say, hath spent £1000 a year before he come thither.

May 7, 1668. Here [at Knepp's lodgings] was also Haynes, the incomparable dancer of the King's house, and a seeming civil man, and sings pretty well.

Harris, Henry

July 22, 1663. At Wotton's, the shoe-maker's, who tells me the reason of Harris's[1] going from Sir Wm. Davenant's house, that he grew very proud and demanded £20 for himself extraordinary, more than Betterton or any body else, upon every new play, and £10 upon every revive; which with other things

able for the witty, tho' wicked, Pranks he play'd, and for his Prologues and Epilogues, than for Acting." His best parts, such as Sparkish in *The Country Wife* and Captain Bluff in Congreve's *Old Bachelor,* were created after Pepys had brought his *Diary* to a close. The reference here is to a performance of *The Spanish Gypsy* at the King's theatre.

[1] Henry Harris (?-1681), originally a "painter," appears to have been the "matinee idol" of his day and was somewhat spoiled, according to Pepys's entries concerning him for this date and for February 6, 1667-68. It is expressly stated in the Letters Patent issued to D'Avenant, January 15, 1662, that an actor who withdrew from either one of the two companies could not be received into the other. Harris proved, however, to be an accomplished comedian, playing Sir Andrew Aguecheek and Sir Joslin Jolly, and was also successful in such parts as Romeo and Orrery's Henry the Fifth. According to the list of his rôles given by Genest (I, pp. 388-389), his first was Alphonso in *The Siege of Rhodes,* 1661, his last Cardinal Beaufort in Crowne's *Henry VI,* 1681.

Sir W. Davenant would not give him, and so he swore he would never act there more, in expectation of being received in the other House; but the King will not suffer it, upon Sir W. Davenant's desire that he would not, for then he might shut up house, and that is true. He tells me that his going is at present a great loss to the House, and that he fears he hath a stipend from the other house privately. He tells me that the fellow grew very proud of late, the King and every body else crying him up so high, and that above Betterton, he being a more ayery man, as he is indeed. But yet Betterton, he says, they all say do act some parts that none but himself can do.

December 10, 1663. Calling at Wotton's, my shoe-maker's, to-day, he tells me . . . that Harris is come to the Duke's house again.

February 3, 1663-64. In Covent Garden tonight, . . . I stopped at the great Coffee-house there, where . . . all the wits of the town, and Harris the player.

July 20, 1664. Very pleasant it was [*Worse and Worse*] and I begin to admire Harris more than ever.

August 13, 1664. Wherein Betterton, Harris, and Ianthe's parts [in *Henry V*] are most incomparably wrote and done.

September 10, 1664. [Gosnell] fell out of the key [in *The Rivals*] . . . and so did Harris[2] also go out of the tune to agree with her.

December 2, 1664. The play [*The Rivals*] not good, nor anything but the good actings of Betterton and his wife and Harris.

[2] His rôle in this play by D'Avenant was Theocles.

January 24, 1666-67.   Harris I first took to my closet; and I find him a very serious and understanding person in all pictures and other things, and a man of fine conversation.

February 20, 1666-67.   When we come to the Duke of York here, I heard discourse how Harris of his play-house is sick, and everybody commends him, and, above all things, for acting the Cardinall.[3]

February 27, 1666-67.   Here I find Harris's picture, done in his habit.

September 4, 1667.   Both Betterton and Harris could not contain from laughing in the midst of a most serious part [in *Mustapha*], from the ridiculous mistake of one of the men upon the stage.

December 11, 1667.   Here [in Westminster Hall] I met . . . Harris, the player, and there we talked of many things, and particularly of "Catiline," which is to be suddenly acted at the King's house; and there all agree that it cannot be well done at that house, there not being good actors enow. . . . Thence home to dinner, and would have had Harris home with me, but it was too late for him to get to the playhouse after it.

January 6, 1667-68.   Did go home to dinner, and there find Mr. Harris, by the like mistake, come to dine with me.   However, we did get a pretty dinner ready for him; and there he and I to discourse of many things, and I do find him a very excellent person, such as in my whole [acquaintance] I do not know another better qualified for converse, whether

[3] Probably Cardinal Wolsey in *Henry VIII*.

in things of his own trade, or of other kinds, a man of great understanding and observation, and very agreeable in the manner of his discourse, and civil as far as is possible. . . . To the Duke's house. . . . Thence, after the play, stayed till Harris was undressed, there being acted "The Tempest," and so he withall, all by coach, home.

February 6, 1667-68. I did hear [Etherege] mightily find fault with the actors, . . . that Harris did do nothing[4] [in *She Would if She Could*], nor could so much as sing a ketch in it.

March 23, 1667-68. We are defeated of Knepp, by her being forced to act to-day, and also of Harris, which did trouble me, they being my chief guests. . . . By and by Mr. Harris.

March 24, 1668. To prick out my song, "It is Decreed," intending to have it ready to give to Mr. Harris on Thursday, when we meet, for him to sing, believing that he will do it more right than a woman that sings better, unless it were Knepp.

March 26, 1668. The epilogue [*The Man's the Master*] little in it but the extraordinariness of it, it being sung by Harris and another in the form of a ballet. Thence to . . . the Blue Balls . . . and anon comes . . . Harris; . . . and mighty merry we were till about eleven or twelve at night.

March 29, 1668. At home to dinner, . . . and by invitation Mr. Harris. . . . Harris do so commend my wife's picture of Mr. Hale's, that I shall have him draw Harris's head.

[4] He played Sir Joslin Jolly.

March 30, 1668. I away with Harris and Hales to the Coffee-house, . . . and there resolve for Hales to begin Harris's head for me, which I will be at the cost of.

April 26, 1668. Thence with Hales to his house, and there did see his beginning of Harris's picture, which I think will be pretty like, and he promises a very good picture.

April 29, 1668. After the play done [*Love in a Tub*], I stepped up to Harris's dressing-room,[5] where I never was, and there I observe much company come to him, and the Witts, to talk, after the play is done, and to assign meetings.

May 11, 1668. Between two acts [of *The Tempest*], I went out to Mr. Harris and got him to repeat to me the words of the Echo, while I writ them down.

May 20, 1668. To Hale's, and there saw the beginnings of Harris's head which he draws for me, which I do not yet like.

May 30, 1668. And here I first understood by their talk the meaning of the company that lately were called Ballers; Harris telling how it was by a meeting of some young blades, where he was among them and my Lady Bennet[6] and her ladies.

June 1, 1668. I met with Harris and Rolt, and carried them to the Rhenish wine-house. . . . Here I did get the words of a song of Harris, that I wanted.

July 19, 1668. Come Mr. Cooper, Hales, Harris,

[5] Harris's part in this play was Sir Frederick Frolic.

[6] A notorious procuress, to whom Wycherley dedicated *The Plain Dealer* (1674).

Mr. Butler, that wrote Hudibras . . . and there we dined.

August 26, 1668. To Mr. Batelier's . . . where I find my wife and Knepp and Harris; . . . and here danced all night long, with a noble supper.

August 29, 1668. Thence carried Harris to his playhouse, where, though four o'clock, so few people there at "The Impertinents," as I went out.

September 5, 1668. To Mr. Hales's new house, . . . and here I find Harris's picture, done in his habit of "Henry the Fifth";[7] mighty like a player, but I do not think the picture near so good as any yet he hath made for me: however it is pretty well.

September 20, 1668. To dinner, staying till past one o'clock for Harris, whom I invited, and to bring Shadwell the poet with him; but they come not.

February 25, 1668-69. A good martial dance of pikemen [in *The Royal Shepherdess*] where Harris and another do handle their pikes in a dance to admiration.

April 16, 1669. Harris, who hath no part in it [*Guzman*], did come to me, and told me in discourse that he was glad of it, it being a play that will not take.

May 7, 1669. He [Silas Taylor] did once offer to show Harris it [his play], but Harris told him he would judge by one Act whether it were good or no, which is indeed a foolish saying.

[7] In the Earl of Orrery's play of that name.

Hart, Charles

August 26, 1667. Sir W. Pen and I had a great deal of discourse with Moll; who tells us that . . . Hart,[1] her [Nell Gwyn's] great admirer, now hates her.

December 7, 1667. But the King's house is at present and hath for some days been silenced upon some difference [between] Hart and Moone.

December 28, 1667. Nell's and Hart's mad parts[2] are most excellently done.

April 7, 1668. She [Knepp] tells me mighty news, that my Lady Castlemayne is mightily in love with Hart of their house, and he is much with her in private, and she goes to him, and do give him many presents.

February 6, 1668-69. Nor another [acting so well] Hart's [part in *Othello*] which was Cassio's.

---

[1] Charles Hart (?-1683), a grand-nephew of Shakespeare, is said to have brought Nell Gwyn, his mistress, on the stage. Before the Civil War, he had acted the Duchess in Shirley's *The Cardinal* with great success. After the Restoration, he played in the King's company such parts as Othello, Brutus, Catiline (in Jonson's *Catiline his Conspiracy*) and Amintor (in *The Maid's Tragedy*). "If he Acted," says Downes (*Roscius Anglicanus,* p. 16), "in any one of these but once in a Fortnight, the House was fill'd as at a New Play. . . . He was no less Inferior in Comedy; as *Mosca* in the Fox; *Don John* in the Chances, *Wildblood* in the Mock Astrologer."

[2] In J. Howard's *All Mistaken, or The Mad Couple;* Hart played Philidor.

Kynaston, Edward

August 18, 1660. [Saw] "The Loyall Subject," where one Kinaston,[1] a boy, acted the Duke's sister,[2] but made the loveliest lady that ever I saw in my life, only her voice not very good.

January 7, 1660-61. Among other things here [in *The Silent Woman*], Kinaston, the boy, had the good turn to appear[3] in three shapes: first, as a poor woman in ordinary clothes, to please Morose; then in fine clothes, as a gallant, and in them was clearly the prettiest woman in the whole house, and lastly, as a man; and then likewise did appear the handsomest man in the house.

February 1, 1668-69. We find no play there; Kinaston that did act a part therein, in abuse to Sir Charles Sedley,[4] being last night exceedingly beaten

---

[1] Edward Kynaston (1640?-1712), originally a member of Rhodes's company at the Cockpit theatre, was one of the most famous of the "boy-actresses" of his time—"a Compleat Female Stage Beauty," asserts Downes (*Roscius Anglicanus,* p. 19), who "perform'd his Parts so well, especially *Arthiope* and *Aglaura* . . . that it has since been Disputable among the Judicious, whether any Woman that succeeded him so sensibly touch'd the Audience as he." By 1662 he had joined the King's company, in which he played such rôles as Leon, in *Rule a Wife and have a Wife,* and Henry IV. His post-Restoration stage career extended from 1659 to 1699.

[2] Olympia. This play was given at the Cockpit, Drury Lane.

[3] As Epicoene.

[4] In *The Heiress* at the King's theatre. Kynaston was said to resemble Sedley—"a similitude," declares the author of the *Memoirs of the Actors and Actresses (An Apology for the Life*

with sticks by two or three that assaulted him, so as he is mightily bruised, and forced to keep his bed.

February 2, 1668-69. They say the King is very angry with Sir Charles Sedley for his being beaten, but he do deny it. But his part is done by Beeston.

February 9, 1668-69. Here [in *The Island Princess*] we find Kinaston to be well enough to act again, which he do very well, after his beating.

Lacy, John

May 21, 1662. Lacy's[1] part [in *The French Danc-*

of Mr. *Colley Cibber*, Lowe ed., II, 341), "of which he was so proud, that he endeavored to display it by the most particular expedients." Then follows a different story in the same vein.

[1] John Lacy (?-1681), who is said to have been taught dancing by John Ogilby, was a member of the King's company. Langbaine (pp. 317-318) gives a glowing account of him: "A Comedian whose Abilities in Acting were sufficiently known to all that frequented the King's Theatre, where he was for many years an Actor, and perform'd all Parts that he undertook to a miracle: in so much that I am apt to believe that as *this* Age never had, so the *next* never will have his *Equal*, at least not his *Superior*. He was so well approv'd of by King *Charles* the Second, an undeniable Judge in Dramatick Arts, that he caus'd his Picture to be drawn, in three several Figures in the same Table, *viz.* that of Teague in the *Committee*, Mr. *Scruple* in *The Cheats*, and Mr. Galliard, in *The Variety:* which piece is still in being in *Windsor Castle:* nor did his Talent wholly ly in Acting, he knew both how to judge and to write Plays." Langbaine then proceeds to discuss Lacy's four plays, of which *The Old Troop, or Monsieur Raggou* is the most notable.

Evelyn refers to Lacy under the date of October 14, 1662,

ing Master], the Dancing Master, the best in the world.

May 22, 1662. The play [*Love in a Maze*] hath little in it, but Lacy's part of a country fellow, which he did to admiration.

May 8, 1663. The play was "The Humerous Lieutenant," a play that hath little good in it, nor much in the very part which,[2] by the King's command, Lacy now acts instead of Clun.

June 10, 1663. The play [*Love in a Maze*] is pretty good, but the life of the play is Lacy's part, the clown, which is most admirable.

June 12, 1663. Saw "The Committee," a merry but indifferent play, only Lacey's part, an Irish footman,[3] is beyond imagination.

June 13, 1663. I am quite out of opinion with any of their actings, but Lacy's [in the King's company] compared with the other house.

April 9, 1667. The best part, "Sawny," [in *Sawney the Scot*] done by Lacy, hath not half its life, by reason of the words, I suppose, not being understood, at least by me.

April 15, 1667. Lacy did act the country-gentleman [in *The Change of Crowns*] come up to Court, who do abuse the Court with all the imaginable wit and plainness about selling of places, and doing every thing for money.

as "the famous Roscius or comedian," and on November 27 records seeing *The Committee*, "where ye mimic Lacy acted the Irish footeman to admiration" (*Diary*, Wheatley ed., II, 155).

[2] The Lieutenant was Clun's part in the original cast.

[3] Teague.

April 16, 1667. Knipp tells me the King was so
angry at the liberty taken by Lacy's part to abuse
him to his face, that he commanded they should act
no more, till Moone [Mohun] went and got leave for
them to act again, but not this play [*The Change of
Crowns*]. The King mighty angry; and it was bitter
indeed, but very true and witty.

April 20, 1667. Here [at the Duke's theatre] met
with Mr. Rolt, who tells me the reason of no play to-
day at the King's house. That Lacy[4] had been committed to the porter's lodge for acting his part in the
late new play [*The Change of Crowns*], and that
being thence released he come to the King's house,
there met with Ned Howard, the poet of the play,
who congratulated his release; upon which Lacy
cursed him as that it was the fault of his nonsensical
play that was the cause of his ill usage. Mr. Howard
did give him some reply; to which Lacy [answered]
him, that he was more a fool than a poet; upon which
Howard did give him a blow on the face with his
glove; on which Lacy having a cane in his hand, did
give him a blow over the pate. Here Rolt and others
that discoursed of it in the pit this afternoon did
wonder that Howard did not run him through, he
being too mean a fellow to fight him. But Howard
did not do anything but complain to the King of it;
so the whole house is silenced, and the gentry seem
to rejoice much at it, the house being become too
insolent.

---

[4] It is said that Lacy was noted for showing his contempt of
courtiers, both on and off the stage.

May 1, 1667. To the King's playhouse, . . . and saw "Love in a Maze": but a sorry play: only Lacy's clowne's part,[5] which he did most admirably indeed; and I am glad to find the rogue at liberty again. Here was but little, and that ordinary, company.

July 13, 1667. Yesterday Sir Thomas Crew told me that Lacy lies a-dying of the pox.

August 13, 1667. Lacy's part [in *The Committee*] is so well performed that it would set off anything.

April 28, 1668. Did see "Love in a Maze" wherein very good mirth of Lacy, the clown.

January 11, 1668-69. Saw "The Joviall Crew"; but ill acted to what it was heretofore, in Clun's time, and when Lacy could dance.

January 19, 1668-69. Lacy hath made a farce of several dances—between each act [of *Horace*] one: but his words are but silly, and invention not extraordinary, as to the dances; only some Dutchmen come out of the mouth and tail of a Hamburgh sow.

Mohun, Michael

November 20, 1660. And here I saw [in *The Beggar's Bush*] the first time one Moone,[1] who is

[5] Johnny Thump.

[1] Michael Mohun (1620?-1691?), whose name is variously spelled by Pepys, was one of the best actors of emotional parts in the King's company; according to Downes, "An Eminent Poet," Nathaniel Lee, is once said to have remarked: *"Oh, Mohun, Mohun! Thou little Man of Mettle, if I should Write a 100 Plays I'd Write a Part for thy Mouth"* (*Roscius Anglicanus,* p. 17).

said to be the best actor in the world, lately come over with the King.

November 22, 1660. I to the new playhouse and saw part of the "Traitor," a very good Tragedy; Mr. Moon did act the Traitor very well.

December 7, 1667. But the King's house is at present and hath for some days been silenced upon some difference [between] Hart and Moone.

February 6, 1668-69. Mohun, which did a little surprise me, not acting Iago's part by much so well as Clun used to do.

Sandford, Samuel

March 26, 1668. To the Duke of York's house, to see the new play, called "The Man is the Master" . . . translated by Sir W. Davenant, . . . the prologue but poor, and the epilogue little in it, but the extraordinariness of it, it being sung by Harris and another[1] in the form in a ballet.

[1] This was Samuel Sandford (?-1704?), who belonged to the Duke's company. He is described by Colley Cibber (*Apology,* Lowe ed., I, pp. 130-131) as "an excellent Actor in disagreeable Characters." "*Sandford* upon the Stage," continues Cibber, "was generally as flagitious as a *Creon,* a *Maligni,* an *Iago,* or a *Machiavil* could make him. . . . But poor *Sandford* was not the Stage-Villain by Choice, but from Necessity; for having a low and crooked Person, such bodily Defects were too strong to be admitted into great or amiable Characters, so that whenever in any new or revived Play there was a hateful or mischievous Person, *Sandford* was sure to have no competition for it."

Smith, William

November 14, 1666. She [Knepp] tells me how Smith,[1] of the Duke's house, hath killed a man upon a quarrel in play; which makes every body sorry, he being a good actor, and, they say, a good man, however this happens. The ladies of the Court do much bemoan him, she says.

October 24, 1667. I hear that Smith do act his [Betterton's] part in "The Villaine," which was then acted as well or better than he, which I do not believe.

February 11, 1667-68. I never saw such good acting of any creature as Smith's part of Zanger.[2]

Wintersell, William

April 28, 1668. Very good mirth of Lacy, the clown, and Wintersell,[1] the country-knight, his master.

[1] William Smith (?-1696?) often played in the same cast with Sandford, to whom he was a great contrast, being tall and handsome. He was the original Sir Fopling Flutter, and the Chamont of Otway's *The Orphan.* Downes (*Roscius Anglicanus,* p. 44) states in connection with Banks's *The Grand Cyrus* (1696) that "Mr. *Smith* having a long part in it, fell Sick upon the Fourth Day and Dy'd."

[2] In the Earl of Orrery's *Mustapha.*

[1] William Wintersell (?-1679) was one of the original actors of the King's company. "Mr. Wintersell," says Downes (*Roscius Anglicanus,* p. 17), "was good in Tragedy, as well as in Comedy, especially in Cokes in 'Bartholomew Fair.'" He played the part of the King in *The Humorous Lieutenant* at

Young, ———

October 16, 1667.   I was vexed to see Young[1] (who is but a bad actor at best) act Macbeth in the room of Betterton.

General References to Actors

February 23, 1660-61.   Besides, I see the gallants do begin to be tyred with the vanity and pride of the theatre actors who are indeed grown very proud and rich.[1]

March 2, 1660-61.   But above all it was strange to see [in *The Queen's Masque* at Salisbury Court] so little a boy as that was to act Cupid, which is one of the greatest parts in it.

the opening performance of the Drury Lane Theatre, May 7 (?), 1663.   The part here referred to is Sir Gervase Simple in *Love in a Maze.*

[1] ——— Young was apparently a lesser member of the Duke's company.

[1] See H. B. Baker's *English Actors from Shakespeare to Macready,* II, Appendix, Note D, for a statement as to the salaries of prominent actors at this time.   Baker gives Hart's salary as £3 a week, and Betterton's and Mrs. Betterton's together as £5.   From Pepys's statement about Harris under July 22, 1663, it appears that there was also an extra bonus for every new play and every old play revived, and we hear occasionally of benefit performances.   But even so, the actor's life was not all beer and skittles.   Pepys refers later to actors who were cruelly beaten, and even slit in the nose, by playgoers whom their acting had disgruntled.

March 23, 1660-61. The actors [at the Red Bull] but common fellows.[2]

December 11, 1667. Here I met . . . Harris, the player, and there we talked of many things, and particularly of "Catiline," which is to be suddenly acted at the King's house; and there all agree that it cannot be well done at that house,[3] there not being good actors enow.

[2] The Duke's and the King's theatres had attracted all the good actors away from the Red Bull where a company had promptly assembled after the issuing of the permit for the opening of the theatres in 1659.

[3] It should be, of course, noted that the speaker belonged to the rival company.

CHAPTER VIII
THE ACTRESSES

CHAPTER VIII

THE ACTRESSES

Betterton, Mary Saunderson ("Ianthe")

April 2, 1662. Though we had seen it [*The Bondman*] so often, yet I never liked it better than to-day, Ianthe[1] acting Cleora's part very well now Roxalana[2] is gone.

September 30, 1662. Saw the "Duchess of Malfy"

[1] "Ianthe" was Mary Saunderson (?-1712), one of the principal actresses of the Duke's company, who married Thomas Betterton in December, 1662. Of her marriage and subsequent career, the author of *The History of the English Stage* (1741) writes as follows: "Mr. *Betterton,* now making, among the *Men,* the Foremost Figure in Sir *William D'Avenant's* Company, he cast his Eyes on Mrs. *Saunderson,* who was no less eminent among the *Women,* and married her. She was bred in the House of the Patentee, improved herself daily in her Profession, and having, by Nature, all the Accomplishments required to make a perfect Actress, she added to them the distinguishing Characteristick of a virtuous Life" (p. 9). In the same vein, the *Biographia Dramatica* (1812 ed.) comments: "Both as an actress and as a woman [Mrs. Betterton] was everything that human perfection was capable of arriving at" (Vol. I, Part II, p. 37). The appeal of her impersonations of Shakespeare's heroines from Juliet to Lady Macbeth is said to have been due in part to her remarkably clear and graceful reading of the lines.

[2] Mrs. Davenport.

well performed, but Betterton and Ianthe[3] to admiration.

October 22, 1662. Benier, . . . being acquainted with all the players, do tell me that Betterton is not married to Ianthe, as they say.

December 1, 1662. There being no pleasure in it [*The Cid*], though done by Betterton and by Ianthe.

February 1, 1663-64. Her [Anne Marshall's] voice not so sweet as Ianthe's.

July 28, 1664. But Betterton and my poor Ianthe outdo all the world [in *The Bondman*].

April 13, 1664. Betterton, Harris, and Ianthe's parts[4] [in Orrery's *Henry V*] are most incomparably wrote and done.

December 2, 1664. The play [*The Rivals*] not good, nor anything but the good actings of Betterton and his wife and Harris.[5]

April 3, 1665. To a play . . . called "Mustapha," which being not good, made Betterton's part and Ianthe's but ordinary too.[6]

Coleman, Mrs.

October 31, 1665. Anon comes Mrs. Coleman with her husband . . . But, for singing, among other

[3] Mrs. Saunderson played the Duchess.

[4] Betterton played Owen Tudor; Harris, King Henry; and Mrs. Betterton, Princess Katherine.

[5] Betterton was Philander; and Harris, Theocles. Mrs. Betterton's name does not appear in the cast. (Cf. Genest, I, 54.)

[6] Betterton's part was Solyman; Mrs. Betterton's, Roxalana.

things, we got Mrs. Coleman[1] to sing part of the
Opera, though she won't owne that ever she did
get any of it without book in order to the stage; but,
above all, her counterfeiting of Captain Cooke's part,
in his reproaching his man with cowardice—"Base
slave," etc.—she do it most excellently.

Corey, Mrs. ("Doll Common")

December 27, 1666. To the King's playhouse, and
meeting Creed took him up, and there saw "The
Scornfull Lady" well acted; Doll Common[1] doing
Abigail most excellently.

January 15, 1668-69. It [the stir at Court] is
about my Lady Harvy's being offended at Doll
Comman's acting of Sempronia [in *Catiline*] to
imitate her; for which she got my Lord Chamberlain,
her kinsman, to imprison Doll: when my Lady Castlemayne made the King to release her, and to order her
to act it again, worse than ever, the other day, where
the King himself was: and since it was acted again,

---

[1] The wife of Edward Coleman, the musician. It has been
said that in 1656 Mrs. Coleman played Ianthe in the first part
of D'Avenant's *Siege of Rhodes,* in which she spoke in recita-
tive. If, as Pepys seems to think, she did take part in the play,
this was probably her only appearance on the stage.

[1] Mrs. Corey "the mimic," so called from the part of Doll
Common in Jonson's *The Alchemist,* which she acted, was one
of the chief actresses of the King's company, remaining in it,
according to Downes (*Roscius Anglicanus,* p. 39), as late as
1682.

and my Lady Harvy provided people to hiss her and fling oranges at her: but it seems the heat is come to a great height, and real troubles at Court about it.

Davenport, Francis

April 7, 1668. The eldest Davenport[1] is, it seems, gone from this house, to be kept by somebody; which I am glad of, she being a very bad actor.

Davis, Mary

April 17, 1666. This day I am told that Moll Davis,[1] the pretty girle that sang and danced so well at the Duke's house, is dead.

March 7, 1666-67. Only little Mis. Davis did dance a jig after the end of the play [*The English Princess*] and there telling the next day's play; so that it come in by force only to please the company to

---

[1] Not to be confused with her younger sister, Elizabeth Davenport, the famous "Roxalana." Francis seems to have been a minor member of the King's company.

[1] Mary Davis, a popular actress of the Duke's company. Downes (*Roscius Anglicanus,* pp. 23-24) says that she was very pleasing in the part of "Celia" in D'Avenant's *The Rivals*— "especially in Singing several Wild and Mad Songs *My Lodging it is on the Cold Ground,* &c. She perform'd so Charmingly that not long after, it Rais'd her from her Bed on the Cold Ground, to a Bed Royal." Soon afterward she was "by force of Love" "erept the Stage."

see her dance in boy's clothes; and, the truth is, there is no comparison between Nell's dancing the other day at the King's house[2] in boy's clothes and this, this being infinitely beyond the other.

January 11, 1667-68. Knepp come and sat by us, and her talk pleased me a little, she telling me how Mis Davis is for certain going away from the Duke's house, the King being in love with her.

January 14, 1667-68. She did sit near the players of the Duke's house [at *The Indian Emperor* at Court]; among the rest Mis Davis, who is the most impertinent slut, she says, in the world; and the more, now the King do show her countenance; and is reckoned his mistress, even to the scorne of the whole world; the King gazing on her, and my Lady Castlemaine being melancholy and out of humour, all the play, not smiling once. The King, it seems, hath given her a ring of £700, which she shews to every body, and owns that the King did give it her; and he hath furnished a house for her in Suffolke Street most richly, which is a most infinite shame. It seems she is a bastard of Colonell Howard, my Lord Berkshire;[3] . . . Pierce says that she is a most homely jade as ever she saw, though she dances beyond any thing in the world.

April 7, 1668. She [Knepp] tells me mighty news that my Lady Castlemayne is mightily in love with

[2] In *The Maiden Queen* on March 2, in which Nell Gwyn played Florimel.

[3] Another story was that she was the daughter of a Wiltshire blacksmith. The truth of the matter is not known.

Hart of their house: . . . and by this means she is even with the King's love to Mrs. Davis.

May 31, 1668. I hear that Mrs. Davis is quite gone from the Duke of York's house. . . . At the play at Court the other night, Mrs. Davis was there; and when she was come to dance her jigg,[4] the Queene would not stay to see it, which people do think it was out of displeasure at her being the King's whore.

December 21, 1668. It vexed me to see Moll Davis, in a box[5] over the King's and my Lady Castlemayne's head, look down upon the King and he up to her, and so did my Lady Castlemayne once, to see who it was, but when she saw, she looked fire.

January 21, 1668-69. Saw "The Tempest," but it is but ill done by Gosnell, in lieu of Moll Davis.[6]

February 15, 1668-69. Here in Suffolk Street lives Moll Davis; and we did see her coach come for her, a mighty pretty fine coach.

Gosnell, Mrs.

May 28, 1663. Who should we see come upon the stage [in *Hamlet*] but Gosnell,[1] my wife's maid? but

[4] Perhaps as Celania in *The Rivals*.

[5] At the Duke's theatre, where *Macbeth* was being given.

[6] Probably in the part of Miranda—the cast is not given by Downes.

[1] Under the date of December 5, 1662, Pepys writes: "I find Gosnell come, who, my wife tells me, is likely to prove a pretty companion, . . . and who sings exceedingly well." She stayed, however, only a few days in the Diarist's household. From

MRS ELLEN GWYNN.

P. Lely Eques Pinx.t   R. H. Cook Sculp.t

neither spoke, danced nor sung; which I was sorry for. But she becomes the stage very well.

May 29, 1663. To the Duke's house, and there saw "The Slighted Mayde," wherein Gosnell acted Pyramena, a great part, and did it very well, and I believe will do it better and better, and prove a good actor.

September 10, 1664. Gosnell comes and sings and dances finely [in *The Rivals*] but, for all that, fell out of the key.

May 31, 1668. I hear that Mrs. Davis is quite gone from the Duke of York's house, and Gosnell comes in her room which I am glad of.

July 28, 1668. To the Duke of York's playhouse, and there saw "The Slighted Maid." . . . Here we saw Gosnell, who is become very homely, and sings meanly, I think, to what I thought she did.

January 21, 1668-69. Saw "The Tempest"; but it is but ill done by Gosnell, in lieu of Moll Davis.

Gwyn, "Nell"

April 3, 1665. All the pleasure of the play [*Mustapha*] was, the King and my Lady Castlemayne were there; and pretty witty Nell,[1] at the

Pepys's later accounts, "Gosnell" would seem to have become one of the important actresses at the Duke's house, in fact, a successor to Moll Davis. Wheatley says: "There does not appear to be any record of Mrs. Gosnell as an actress outside the Diary" (Pepys's *Diary*, III, 139n).

[1] Ellen, or Eleanor, Gwyn (1650-51 to 1687), a much praised comedienne of the King's company, and the most popular of

King's house, and the younger Marshall sat next us; which pleased me mightily.

December 8, 1666. And the women do very well [in *The English Monsieur*]; but, above all, little Nelly.[2]

January 23, 1666-67. Knipp took us all in, and brought us to Nelly, a most pretty woman, who acted the part of Cœlia [in *The Humourous Lieutenant*] to-day very fine, and did it pretty well: I kissed her, and so did my wife; and a mighty pretty soul she is.

March 2, 1666-67. To the King's house to see "The Mayden Queene," a new play of Dryden's . . . and, the truth is, there is a comical part done by Nell, which is Florimell, that I never can hope ever to see the like done again, by man or woman. The King and Duke of York were at the play. But so great a performance of a comical part was never, I believe in the world before as Nell do this, both as a mad girle, then most and best of all when she comes in like a young gallant; and hath the motions and carriage of a spark the most that ever I saw any man have. It makes me, I confess, admire her.

March 7, 1666-67. The truth is, there is no comparison between Nell's dancing the other day at the King's house in boy's clothes and this,[3] this being infinitely beyond the other.

Charles the Second's mistresses, made her first appearance on the stage at about this time in the part of Cydaria in Dryden's *The Indian Emperor.*

[2] She played Lady Wealthy, the principal woman's part.

[3] That is, between Nell Gwyn's dancing in *The Maiden Queen* and Moll Davis's in *The English Princess.*

March 25, 1667. So done by Nell, her merry part [Florimell], as cannot be better done in nature I think.

May 1, 1667. Saw pretty Nelly standing at her lodgings' door in Drury-lane in her smock sleeves and bodice, looking upon one: she seemed a mighty pretty creature.

May 24, 1667. Saw "The Mayden Queene," which, . . . yet pleases me infinitely, it being impossible, I think, ever to have the Queen's part, which is very good and passionate, and Florimel's part, which is the most comicall that ever was made for woman, ever done better than they two are by young Marshall and Nelly.

July 13, 1667. [Mr. Pierce] tells us what troubles me, that my Lord Buckhurst hath got Nell away from the King's house, lies with her, and gives her £100 a year, so as she hath sent her parts to the house, and will act no more.

July 14, 1667. To the King's Head [Epsom], . . . and hear that my Lord Buckhurst and Nelly are lodged at the next house and Sir Charles Sidly with them: and keep a merry house. Poor girl! I pity her; but more the loss of her at the King's house.

August 1, 1667. [Knepp] told us the story how Nell is gone from the King's house and is kept by my Lord Buckhurst.

August 22, 1667. To the King's playhouse, and there saw "The Indian Emperour"; where I find Nell come again, which I am glad of; but was most infinitely displeased with her being put to act the Emperour's daughter; which is a great and serious part which she do most basely.[4]

August 26, 1667. Sir W. Pen and I had a great deal of discourse with Moll;[5] who tells us that Nell is already left by my Lord Buckhurst, and that he makes sport of her; swears she hath had all she could get of him; and Hart, her great admirer, now hates her; and that she is very poor, and hath lost my Lady Castlemayne, who was her great friend also: but she is come to the House, but is neglected by them all.

October 5, 1667. To the women's shift, where Nell was dressing herself, and was all unready, and is very pretty, prettier than I thought. . . . But to see how Nell[6] cursed, for having so few people in the pit, was pretty.

October 26, 1667. Mrs. Pierce tells me . . . that Nelly and Beck Marshall, falling out the other day, the latter called the other my Lord Buckhurst's whore. Nell answered then, "I was but one man's whore, though I was brought up in a bawdy-house

---

[4] Successful as she was in light comedy, it seems to be the general opinion—in which Nell herself shared—that she was a failure in "serious parts"; witness the lines in the epilogue to *The Duke of Lerma,* which she spoke,

> . . . "I know you in your hearts,
> Hate serious plays,—as I hate serious parts";

and also the following from the epilogue to Dryden's *Tyrannic Love,*

> " . . . I die
> Out of my calling in a tragedy."

[5] "Orange Moll," head orange-woman at the King's theatre.

[6] She had acted Flora in *Flora's Vagaries.*

to fill strong waters to the guests; and you are a whore to three or four, though a Presbyter's praying daughter!" which was very pretty.

November 11, 1667. Above all things Nell's ill speaking of a great part [in *The Indian Emperor*] made me mad.

December 26, 1667. The actors not pleasing me [in *The Surprisal*]; and especially Nell's acting of a serious part,[7] which she spoils.

December 28, 1667. Nell's and Hart's mad parts[8] [in *The Mad Couple*] are most excellently done, but especially her's: which makes it a miracle to me to think how ill she do any serious part, as, the other day, just like a fool or changeling; and, in a mad part, do beyond all imitation almost.

January 11, 1667-68. [Knepp says] that the King did send several times for Nelly, and she was with him, but what he did she knows not; this was a good while ago . . . and I am sorry for it, and can hope for no good to the State from having a Prince so devoted to his pleasure.

February 20, 1667-68. Knepp and Nell spoke the prologue [in *The Duke of Lerma*] most excellently.

May 7, 1668. I did see . . . Nell, in her boy's clothes, mighty pretty. But Lord! their confidence! and how many men do hover about them as soon as they come off the stage, and how confident they are in their talk![9]

[7] Samira.

[8] Mirida was Nell's "mad part."

[9] This was in the greenroom of the King's theatre, after a performance of *The Man's Master*.

January 7, 1668-69. We sat in an upper box [at
The Island Princess], and the jade Nell[10] come and
sat in the next box; a bold merry slut, who lay laughing there upon people; and with a comrade of hers
of the Duke's house, that come in to see the play.

Knepp, Mrs.

December 6, 1665. Here the best company for
musique I ever was in, in my life, . . . Mrs. Pierce,
and my wife and Knipp,[1] who is pretty enough; but
the most excellent mad-humoured thing, and sings the
noblest that ever I heard in my life.

December 8, 1665. By water down to Greenwich,
and there found all my company come; that is, Mrs.
Knipp, and an ill, melancholy, jealous-looking fellow, her husband, that spoke not a word to us all the
night. . . . Most excellent musique we had in abund-
ance, and a good supper, dancing, and a pleasant
scene of Mrs. Knipp's rising sicke from table, but
whispered me it was for some hard word or other her
husband gave her just now when she laughed and
was more merry than ordinary. But we got her in

[10] Nell left the stage soon after this, in 1670, her last part
being Almahide in Dryden's *The Conquest of Granada*. Her
son Charles, afterward made Duke of St. Albans, was born in
May of this year.

[1] Mrs. Knepp (or Knipp) "probably made her début on the
stage of the Theatre Royal as Epicene in Ben Jonson's 'Silent
Woman' on 1 June, 1664" (*Dictionary of National Biography*,
XXXI, 273). She disappears from the stage in 1678, and nothing is known of her subsequent history.

humour again, and mighty merry; spending the night, till two in the morning, with most complete content as ever in my life.[2]

February 23, 1665-66. She [Knepp] also entertained me with repeating many of her own and others' parts of the play-house, which she do most excellently; and tells me the whole practices of the playhouse and players.

December 27, 1666. Saw "The Scornfull Lady" well acted; [Knipp] doing . . . the widow very well, and will be an excellent actor, I think.

January 2, 1666-67. Saw "The Custome of the Country" . . . wherein Knipp does the Widow well; . . . sings a little song admirably.

January 15, 1666-67. To a play . . . where Knipp acts Mrs. Weaver's great part in "The Indian Emperour," and he [Lord Brouncker] says is coming on to be a great actor.

January 23, 1666-67. Saw "The Humerous Lieutenant": . . . and then Knipp's singing did please us.

January 24, 1666-67. Comes Mr. Harris of the Duke's playhouse, and brings Mrs. Pierce with him and also one dressed like a country mayde with a straw hat on; which, at first, I could not tell who it was, though I expected Knipp: but it was she coming off the stage just as she acted this day in "The Goblins"; a merry jade.

February 5, 1666-67. A good play [*The Chances*]

---

[2] The *Diary* abounds in accounts of similar social gatherings, to which Mrs. Knepp was party, and also in brief references to her private life, which will not be quoted except where they bear upon stage history.

I find it, and the actors most good in it; and pretty to hear Knipp sing in the play very properly, "All night I weepe"; and sung it admirably.

February 12, 1666-67.   [T. Killigrew] says that Knipp is like to make the best actor that ever come upon the stage, she understanding so well: that they are going to give her £30 a year more.

May 22, 1667.   Saw the last two acts of "The Goblins," . . . but here[3] Knipp spied me out of the tiring-room, and come to the pit door.

August 1, 1667.   To see "The Custome of the Country." . . . After the play, we went into the house and spoke with Knepp.

August 17, 1667.   I was pleased to see Knipp dance [in *Queen Elizabeth's Troubles*] among the milkmaids and to hear her sing a song to Queen Elizabeth; and to see her come out in her night-gowne with no lockes on, but her bare face and hair only tied up in a knot behind.

August 22, 1667.   Saw "The Indian Emperour." . . . Knipp sent by Moll to desire to speak to me after the play; and she beckoned to me at the end of the play.

September 9, 1667.   [T. Killigrew] says that Knepp wont take pains enough, but that she understands her part so well upon the stage that no man or woman in the house do the like.

September 14, 1667.   Knipp acted in it [*The Northern Castle*], and did her part very extraordinary well.

---

[3] At the King's theatre.

October 5, 1667. Met with Knepp and she took us up into the tireing-rooms [at the King's theatre]: . . . here I read the questions to Knepp, while she answered me, through all her part[4] of "Flora's Figarys" which was acted to-day. . . . But, Lord! to see how they were both painted.[5]

February 20, 1667-68. Knepp and Nell spoke the prologue most excellently, especially Knepp [in *The Duke of Lerma*] who spoke beyond any creature I ever heard.

March 25, 1668. Knepp did act her part of grief[6] very well.

April 7, 1668. Saw "The English Monsieur"; . . . the play done, I down to Knipp, and did stay her undressing.

April 17, 1668. Saw "The Surprizall," where base singing, only Knepp, who come, after her song in the clouds, to me in the pit.

May 6, 1668. Saw "The Virgin Martyr," . . . and intended to have seen Knepp, but I let her alone.

May 16, 1668. Saw the best of "The Sea Voyage," where Knepp I see do act her part of sorrow very well.

June 3, 1668. Saw good part of "The Scornfull Lady," and that done, would have taken Knepp out, but she was engaged.

September 18, 1668. Saw a piece of "Henry the Fourth"; at the end of the play, thinking to have gone

[4] Otrante.
[5] Mrs. Knepp and Nell Gwyn.
[6] Aminta in *The Storm*.

abroad with Knepp, but it was too late, and she to get
her part against to-morrow, in "The Silent Woman."[7]

September 19, 1668. Saw "The Silent Woman."
. . . Knepp did her part mighty well.

January 1, 1668-69. Saw "The Mayden Queene."
Knepp[8] looked upon us.

February 2, 1668-69. "The Heyresse" . . . is
acted. . . . But that, that pleased me most in the
play is, the first song that Knepp sings, she singing
three or four; and, indeed, it was very finely sung, so
as to make the whole house clap her.

Marshall, Anne

February 12, 1660-61. To the Theatre and there
saw "The Scornfull Lady,"[1] now done by a woman,
which makes the play appear much better than ever
it did to me.

February 1, 1663-64. The eldest Marshall[2] did do

[7] Epicoene.

[8] In this play Mrs. Knepp played the part of Asteria.

[1] Downes (*Roscius Anglicanus*, p. 6) mentions in the cast for
this play a "Mrs. Marshal" as having acted "the Lady"; this
may have been for a later performance.

[2] Anne Marshall was, according to Genest (I, 379), "for many
years the principal actress in the King's company," and was
probably the more gifted of the two sisters, generally reported
to have been the daughters of Stephen Marshall, an eminent
Presbyterian minister. In regard to this story, Wheatley says
(Pepys's *Diary*, IV, 28 n.): "Colonel Chester proved conclu-
sively that this was not the case." Anne Marshall's part in this
play was Zemboalla, the Queen. Downes does not usually dis-

her part [in *The Indian Queen*] most excellently well
as I ever heard woman in my life; but her voice not
so sweet as Ianthe's.

October 26, 1667. Mrs. Pierce tells me that the
two Marshalls at the King's house are Stephen Marshall's, the great Presbyterian's daughters.

June 27, 1668. To the King's playhouse, and saw
"The Indian Queene," but do not doat upon Nan
Marshall's acting therein, as the world talks of her
excellence therein.

Marshall, Rebecca

April 3, 1665. Pretty witty Nell, at the King's
house, and the younger Marshall[1] sat next us; which
pleased me mightily.

December 7, 1666. Saw the remainder of "The
Maid's Tragedy"; a good play, and well acted especially by the younger Marshall,[2] who is become a
pretty good actor.

May 24, 1667. Saw "The Mayden Queene," which,
though I have often seen yet pleases me infinitely, it

tinguish between the two sisters, and it is evident from Pepys
that several of the rôles ascribed by Genest (I, pp. 379-380) to
the elder were created by the younger Marshall.

[1] Rebecca Marshall, younger sister of Anne, wrongly said to
have been the daughter of Stephen Marshall, the Presbyterian
minister; she was one of the most popular actresses of the King's
company. This was at a performance of *Mustapha* at the Duke's
theatre.

[2] In the part of Evadne.

being impossible, I think, ever to have the Queen's part which is very good and passionate, and Florimel's part, which is the most comicall that ever was made for woman, ever done better than they two are by young Marshall and Nelly.

August 24, 1667.   Saw "The Cardinall" at the King's house, wherewith I am mightily pleased; but, above all, with Becke Marshall.[3]

September 11, 1667.   Sat by Becke Marshall [at the Duke's theatre], who is very handsome near hand.

October 26, 1667.   Mrs. Pierce tells me that the two Marshalls at the King's house are Stephen Marshall's, the great Presbyterian's daughters:[4] and that Nelly and Beck Marshall, falling out the other day, the latter called the other my Lord Buckhurst's whore.   Nell answered then, "I was but one man's whore, though I was brought up in a bawdy-house to fill strong waters to the guests; and you are a whore to three or four, though a Presbyter's praying daughter!"

January 24, 1667-68.   [*The Maiden Queen*] is certainly the best acted of anything ever the House did, and particularly Becke Marshall,[5] to admiration.

February 27, 1667-68.   It [*The Virgin Martyr*] is finely acted by Becke Marshall.[6]

[3] Probably as the Duchess Rosaura.

[4] See p. 252, n. 2.

[5] As the Queen of Sicily.

[6] Genest (I, 80) says: "No doubt she acted the Virgin Martyr" —that is, St. Dorothea.

Norton, Mrs.

December 1, 1662. To the Cockpitt, with much crowding and waiting where I saw "The Valiant Cidd," . . . there being no pleasure in it though done by Betterton and Ianthe, and another fine wench that is come in the room of Roxalana.[1]

December 27, 1662. To the Duke's Theatre, and saw the second part of "Rhodes," done with the new Roxalana; which do it rather better in all respects for person, voice, and judgment, than the first Roxalana.

July 2, 1666. Called by Pegg Pen to her house, where . . . Mrs. Norton, the second Roxalana, a fine woman, indifferent handsome, good body and hand, and good mine, and pretends to sing, but do it not excellently.

"Roxalana" (Elizabeth Davenport)

February 18, 1661-62. A good play and well performed [*The Law against Lovers*], especially the little girl's (whom I never saw before) dancing and singing; and were it not for her the loss of Roxalana[1] would spoil the house.

[1] Mrs. Norton was probably one of the lesser actresses of the Duke's company; her name rarely appears in Downes's casts.

[1] Elizabeth Davenport (1642-?) one of the principal actresses of the Duke's company, was so called from the part she created in *The Siege of Rhodes*.

April 2, 1662. Saw "The Bondman" most excellently acted; and though we had seen it so often, yet I never liked it better than to-day, Ianthe[2] acting Cleora's part very well now Roxalana is gone.

May 20, 1662. Saw the 2nd part of "The Siege of Rhodes," but it is not so well done as when Roxalana was there, who it is said, is now owned by my Lord of Oxford.[3]

December 1, 1662. Saw "The Valiant Cidd," . . . done by Betterton and Ianthe, and another fine wench that is come in the room of Roxalana.

December 27, 1662. Saw the second part of "Rhodes," done with the new Roxalana; which do it rather better in all respects for person, voice, and judgment, than the first Roxalana.

January 1, 1662-63. Here [at the Duke's theatre] we saw the old Roxalana in the chief box, in a velvet gown, as the fashion is, and very handsome, at which I was glad.

[2] Mrs. Betterton.

[3] The story is told in the *Memoirs of the Count de Gramont* (Vizetelly ed., II, 101). Evelyn refers to it in the following entry for January 9, 1661-62: "I saw acted 'The Third [*sic*] Part of the Siege of Rhodes.' In this acted ye faire and famous comedian call'd Roxalana from ye part she perform'd, and I think it was the last, she being taken to be the Earle of Oxford's *Misse* (as at this time they began to call lewd women)" (*Diary,* Wheatley ed., II, 141). This actress, whom Gramont called "very virtuous and very modest," left the stage soon afterwards —as Pepys's reference of February 18, 1661-62, attests—to be enticed into a mock marriage with Aubrey de Vere, Earl of Oxford.

Weaver, Mrs.

January 15, 1666-67. My Lord Bruncker would have made me promise to go with him to a play this afternoon, where Knipp acts Mrs. Weaver's[1] great part in "The Indian Emperour."

January 11, 1667-68. She [Knepp] says that the King first spoiled Mrs. Weaver, which is very mean, methinks, in a prince, and I am sorry for it.

General References to Women on the Stage

January 3, 1660-61. Here the first time that ever I saw women come upon the stage.[1]

January 8, 1660-61. To . . . "The Widdow" an indifferent good play, but wronged by the women being to seek in their parts.

[1] Mrs. Weaver was evidently one of the lesser actresses of the King's company.

[1] In *The Beggar's Bush* at the King's theatre, Vere Street. This was not the first time that actresses had appeared on the English stage. In 1629 a French company in which there were women (denounced as "monsters" by Prynne in his *Histrio-mastrix,* 1633), played at Blackfriars, the Red Bull, and the Fortune theatres; and before the Restoration a few English women are mentioned as having acted. Lady Strangelove in R. Brome's *Court Beggar* (1632), Act V, Sc. 2, says: "Women-Actors now grow in request." In 1656 Mrs. Coleman, wife of Edward Coleman, was Ianthe in D'Avenant's *Siege of Rhodes;* and on November 5, 1660, in his Articles of Agreement with the actors of his company, D'Avenant had definitely arranged for the maintenance of actresses at his theatre. But Killigrew seems to have anticipated him in bringing professional actresses on the stage. The woman who played the part of Desdemona with Killigrew's company, December 8, 1660, has been called,

February 12, 1660-61.   Saw "The Scornfull Lady" now done by a woman which makes the play appear much better than ever it did to me.[2]

October 28, 1661.   To the Theatre . . . where a woman[3] acted Parthenia, and came afterwards on the stage in men's clothes, and had the best legs that ever I saw.

October 4, 1664.   To-morrow they told us should be acted, or the day after, a new play, called "The Parson's Dreame" acted all by women.[4]

October 11, 1664.   He [Luellin] tells me what a bawdy loose play this "Parson's Wedding" is, that is acted by nothing but women at the King's house, and I am glad of it.

the "first English actress."   Her name remains unknown, though the quaint "Prologue to introduce the first woman that came to act on the stage" has been preserved.   The speaker thus prepares the audience:

> "I come unknown to any of the rest,
> To tell you news; I saw the lady drest;
> The woman plays to-day: mistake me not
> No man in gown, or page in petticoat. . . . "

(Cf. Malone's *Shakspeare,* 1821 ed., III, 128.)

It was therefore only about a month after their formal introduction that Pepys records seeing women on the stage.

[2] Downes states (*Roscius Anglicanus,* p. 6) that the following women appeared in this play, probably at a later date: Mrs. [Anne] Marshall ("The Lady"), Mrs. Rutter ("Martha"), and Mrs. Corey ("Abigail").   This performance was at the Salisbury Court theatre.

[3] It is not known what women acted in *Argalus and Parthenia.*

[4] This was, of course, done to heighten the effect of grossness and obscenity, which in this comedy certainly needed no emphasis.   The practice of having plays entirely acted by women is

October 5, 1667. To the King's house, and there, going in, met with Knepp, and she took us up into the tireing-rooms:[5] and to the women's shift, where Nell was dressing herself. . . . And so walked all up and down the house above, and then below into the scene-room, and there sat down, and she gave us fruit. . . . But, Lord! to see how they were both painted would make a man mad, and did make me loath them; and what base company of men comes among them, and how lewdly they talk! . . . But to see how Nell cursed, for having so few people in the pit, was pretty; the other house carrying away all the people at the new play [*The Coffee House*] and is said now-a-days, to have generally most company, as being better players. By and by into the pit.

September 28, 1668. Knepp's maid comes to me, to tell me that the women's day at the playhouse is to-day. . . . There saw "The City Match."

thus defended in an epilogue to Dryden's *Secret Love, or The Maiden Queen,* spoken by "Mrs. Reeve in man's clothes":

> "What think you, sirs, was't not all well enough?
> Will you not grant that we can strutt and huff?
> Why should not then we women act alone?
> Or whence are men so necessary grown?"

(Cf. *The Works of John Dryden,* Scott-Saintsbury ed., II, 510.)

[5] In April, 1667, as a result of a quarrel between Rebecca Marshall and Sir Hugh Middleton described by Dr. Doran in his *Annals of the English Stage* (Lowe's ed., I, 262-263), "A royal decree was issued," which prohibited gentlemen from entering the "tiring rooms of the ladies of the King's theatre"— to what avail may be judged from this entry for October of the same year!

CHAPTER IX
THE PLAYWRIGHTS

CHAPTER IX

THE PLAYWRIGHTS

Brome, Alexander

April 10, 1663. To the Royall Oak Tavern in Lumbard Street, where Alexander Broome[1] the poet was, a merry and witty man, I believe if he be not a little conceited.

July 3, 1666. Alexander Broome, the great song-maker is lately dead.

Cowley, Abraham

November 18, 1663. Walked home again reading of a little book of new poems of Cowley's,[1] given me by his brother. Abraham do lie, it seems, very sicke still, but like to recover.

August 10, 1667. Cowley, he [Herringman] tells me, is dead,[2] who, it seems, was a mighty civil, serious man; which I did not know before.

[1] Alexander Brome (1620-1666) was the author of one play, *The Cunning Lovers* (1639), besides many songs and epigrams.

[1] Abraham Cowley (1618-1667), the poet, was the author of *Cutter of Coleman Street,* and several minor plays.

[2] Compare Evelyn's entry for August 1, 1667: "I receiv'd the sad newes of Abraham Cowley's death, that incomparable poet

August 12, 1667.   Do hear Mr. Cowley mightily lamented his death, by Dr. Ward, the Bishop of Winchester, and Dr. Bates, who were standing there [at Herringman's] as the best poet of our nation, and as a good man.

D'Avenant, Sir William

July 22, 1663.   At Wotton's, the shoemaker's, who tells me the reason of Harris's going from Sir Wm. Davenant's[1] house, that he grew very proud and demanded £20 for himself extraordinary, . . . upon every new play and £10 upon every revive; which with other things Sir W. Davenant would not give him, and so he swore he would never act there more, in expectation of being received at the other House; but the King will not suffer it, upon Sir W. Davenant's desire that he would not, for then he might shut up house, and that is true.

and virtuous man, my very deare friend, and was greately deplored" (*Diary*, Wheatley ed., II, 222). Evelyn further records that on August 3, he "went to Mr. Cowley's funerall, whose corps lay at Wallingford House, and was there conveyed to Westminster Abbey in a hearse with 6 horses and all funeral decency, neere an hundred coaches of noblemen and persons of qualitie following; among these all the witts of the towne, divers bishops and cleargymen. He was interr'd next Geoffry Chaucer and neere to Spenser" (*Ibid.*).

[1] Sir William D'Avenant (1605-1668), poet, dramatist, and patentee of the Duke of York's company after 1660, had paved the way for the reinstatement of the theatre towards the close of the Interregnum by operatic productions as early as 1656.

February 13, 1666-67. Captain Cooke,[2] had the arrogance to say that he was fain to direct Sir W. Davenant in the breaking of his verses into such and such lengths, according as would be fit for musick, and how he used to swear at Davenant, and command him that way, when W. Davenant would be angry, and find fault with this or that note—but a vain coxcomb I perceive he is.

April 7, 1668. Here I hear that Sir W. Davenant is just now dead;[3] and so who will succeed him in the mastership of the house is not yet known.

April 9, 1668. Up and down to the Duke of York's playhouse,[4] there to see, which I did, Sir W. Davenant's corpse carried out towards Westminster, there to be buried.

Dryden, John

February 3, 1663-64. In Covent Garden to-night, . . . I stopped at the great Coffee-house[1] there,

[2] Henry Cooke, a well-known musician and composer, made Master of the Children of the Chapel Royal. He probably refers to D'Avenant's "opera," *The Siege of Rhodes.*

[3] Sir William D'Avenant was "Bury'd," according to Downes (*Roscius Anglicanus,* p. 30), "in *Westminster-Abbey,* near Mr. *Chaucer's* Monument, Our whole Company attending his Funeral." Pepys heard the news at the King's theatre, where *The English Monsieur* had been played.

[4] D'Avenant's house adjoined the theatre.

[1] "The Rose," afterwards "Will's" at the corner of Bow and Russell streets.

where I never was before; where Dryden[2] the poet (I knew at Cambridge), and all the wits of the town, . . . there, I perceive, is very witty and pleasant discourse.

February 2, 1666-67. I am very well pleased this night with reading a poem[3] I brought home with me last night from Westminster Hall, of Dryden's upon the present war; a very good poem.

July 29, 1667. Tom Porter went out, and meeting Dryden the poet, told him of the business,[4] . . . and desired Dryden to let him have his boy to bring him notice which way Sir H. Bellasses goes.

September 20, 1668. Having since church heard the boy read over Dryden's Reply to Sir R. Howard's Answer,[5] about his Essay of Poesy, and a letter[6] in answer to that; the last whereof is mighty silly, in behalf of Howard.

[2] John Dryden (1631-1700), poet and critic and dramatist, took his B. A. degree at Trinity College, Cambridge, in 1654.

[3] *Annus Mirabilis; the Year of Wonders, 1666, an Historical Poem.*

[4] His impending duel with H. Bellasses.

[5] Dryden's reply to "Sir R. Howard's Answer" (the preface to *The Duke of Lerma*) was a *Defence of an Essay of Dramatic Poesy* (1668).

[6] For a discussion of the letter probably referred to here, printed by Thomas Newcomb, 1668, and signed R. F. (Richard Flecknoe (?)), see an article by Peter Cunningham in *The Gentleman's Magazine* for December, 1850, Vol. XXXIV, pp. 597-599.

Howard, Edward

April 20, 1667. [Mr. Rolt tells me] that Lacy had been committed to the porter's lodge for his acting his part in the late new play, and that being thence released he come to the King's house, there met with Ned Howard,[1] the poet of the play,[2] who congratulated his release; upon which Lacy cursed him as that it was the fault of his nonsensical play that was the cause of his ill usage. Mr. Howard did give him some reply; to which Lacy [answered] him, that he was more a fool than a poet, upon which Howard did give him a blow on the face with his glove; on which Lacy, having a cane in his hand, did give him a blow over the pate. Here Rolt and others that discoursed of it in the pit this afternoon did wonder that Howard did not run him through, he being too mean a fellow to fight with. But Howard did not do anything but complain to the King of it; so the whole house is silenced, and the gentry seem to rejoice much at it, the house being become too insolent.

[1] Edward Howard (1624?-1669?), brother of Sir Robert Howard, was the author of several plays. "Lacy's opinion of his abilities was shared by many of his contemporaries," says Wheatley (Pepys's *Diary,* Vl, 258 n).

[2] *The Change of Crowns.*

Howard, Sir Robert

December 8, 1666.   Sir Robert Howard,[1] who is one of the King's servants, at least hath a great office, and hath got, they say, £20,000 since the King come in.

May 5, 1668.   By Sir Positive At-all, I understand, is meant Sir Robert Howard.[2]

May 8, 1668.   But, Lord! to see how this play of Sir Positive At-all in abuse of Sir Robert Howard, do take, all the Duke's and every body's talk being of that, and telling more stories of him, of the like nature, that it is now the town and country talk, and, they say, is most exactly true.   The Duke of York himself said that of his playing at trap-ball is true, and told several other stories of him.

September 20, 1668.   Heard the boy read over Dryden's Reply to Sir R. Howard's Answer,[3] about his Essay of Poesy, and a letter in answer to that; the last whereof is mighty silly, in behalf of Howard.

[1] Sir Robert Howard (1626-1698) was prominent both as a politician and a playwright at Charles II's court.   He was Auditor of the Exchequer.

[2] Evelyn has this entry for February 16, 1685: "I din'd at Sr Robt Howard's, Auditor of the Exchequer, a gentleman pretending to all manner of arts and sciences, for which he had ben the subject of comedy, under the name of Sir Positive; not ill-natur'd, but insufferably boasting" (*Diary*, Wheatley ed., II, 450).   Sir Positive At-all is a character in Shadwell's *The Sullen Lovers, or The Impertinents.*

[3] In his preface to *The Duke of Lerma,* 1668.   "Dryden's Reply" was a *Defense of an Essay of Dramatic Poesy* (1668).

Killigrew, Thomas

May 24, 1660. Walking upon the decks,[1] where persons of honour all the afternoon, among others, Thomas Killigrew[2] (a merry droll, but a gentleman of great esteem with the King), who told us many merry stories.

October 30, 1662. Thos. Killigrew's way of getting to see plays when he was a boy. He would go to the Red Bull, and when the man cried to the boys, "Who will go and be a devil, and he shall see the play for nothing?" then would he go in, and be a devil upon the stage, and so get to see plays.

February 12, 1666-67. Here [at Lord Brouncker's house] we met Tom Killigrew. . . . T. Killigrew and I to talk: and he tells me how the audience at his house is not above half so much as it used to be before the late fire. . . . That the stage is now by his pains a thousand times better and more glorious than ever heretofore. . . . He tells me that he hath gone several times, eight or ten times, he tells me, hence to Rome to hear good musique; so much he loves it, though he never did sing or play a note.

September 9, 1667. I fell in talk with Tom Killigrew about musick.

February 13, 1667-68. Tom Killigrew hath a fee

[1] Of *The Naseby*, later *The Charles*, on its return voyage from Holland, on which it was bringing over the King.

[2] Thomas Killigrew (1612-1683), dramatist and, as Pepys attests, court fool to Charles II, had followed the fortune of his royal patron in exile; he became in 1660 patentee of the King's theatre.

out of the Wardrobe for cap and bells, under the title
of the King's Foole or Jester; and may with privilege
revile or jeere any body, the greatest person, without
offence, by the privilege of his place.

July 6, 1668.   Hear many pretty stories of . . .
Tom Killigrew, in his being bred in Ram Ally.

January 24, 1668-69.   I to talk with Tom Killigrew, who told me and others, talking about the playhouse, that he is fain to keep a woman on purpose at
20*s.* a week to satisfy 8 or 10 of the young men of
his house.

March 6, 1668-69.   He [Sir W. Coventry] told
me the matter of the play that was intended for his
abuse.[3] . . . But that, that he is offended with, is his
being made so contemptible, as that any should dare
to make a gentleman a subject for the mirth of the
world: and that therefore he had told Tom Killigrew
that he should tell his actors, whoever they were, that
did offer at anything like representing him that he
would not complain to my Lord Chamberlain, which
was too weak, nor get him beaten, as Sir Charles Sedley is said to have done; but that he would cause his
nose to be cut.

---

[3] Wheatley says (Pepys's *Diary,* IX, pp. 164-165): "He was
informed that the Duke of Buckingham and Sir R. Howard were
contemplating a caricature of him on the stage, so he at once
sent a challenge to the duke, with the result that he found himself
in the Tower."

Sedley, Sir Charles

October 4, 1664. I happened to sit near to Sir Charles Sidly;[1] who I find a very witty man, and he did at every line take notice of the dullness of the poet and badness of the action, that most pertinently; which I was mightily taken with; and among others where by Altemire's command Clarimont, the Generall, is commanded to rescue his Rivall, whom she loved, Lucidor, he, after a great deal of demurre, broke out, "Well, I'll save my Rivall and make her confess, that I deserve, while he do but possesse." "Why, what, pox," says Sir Charles Sydly, "would he have him have more, or what is there more to be had of a woman than the possessing her?"

February 18, 1666-67. To the King's house, to "The Mayd's Tragedy"; but vexed all the while with two talking ladies and Sir Charles Sedley; yet pleased to hear their discourse he being a stranger. And one of the ladies would, and did sit with her mask on, all the play. . . . He was mighty witty. . . . But by that means lost the pleasure of the play wholly, to which now and then Sir Charles Sedley's exceptions against both words and pronouncing were very pretty.

July 14, 1667. Hear that my Lord Buckhurst and

---

[1] Sir Charles Sedley (1639?-1701) enjoyed a threefold reputation in his own day as wit, rake, and playwright. This account of his conversation at a performance of *The Generall* at the King's theatre is typical of the man, and also of the attitude of his contemporaries towards him.

Nelly [Gwyn] are lodged at the next house,[2] and Sir Charles Sidly with them: and keep a merry house.

February 6, 1667-68.   There[3] I found him [the Duke of Buckingham] with my Lord Buckhurst, and Sidly, and Etherige, the poet.

February 1, 1668-69.   To the King's playhouse, thinking to have seen "The Heyresse," first acted on Saturday last; but when we come thither, we find no play there; Kinaston[4] that did act a part therein, in abuse to Sir Charles Sedley, being last night exceedingly beaten with sticks, by two or three that assaulted him.

February 9, 1668-69.   We find Kinaston to be well enough to act again, . . . after his beating by Sir Charles Sedley's appointment.

Shadwell, Thomas

September 19, 1668.   To the King's playhouse, and there saw "The Silent Woman"; . . . and sitting by Shadwell the poet,[1] he was big with admiration of it.

---

[2] This was at Epsom, where Pepys was staying at the King's Head inn.

[3] In the pit at the Duke's theatre for the *première* of *She Would if She Could.*

[4] Edward Kynaston.

[1] Thomas Shadwell (1642?-1692), the poet, was also the author of comedies of contemporary life; among them is *A True Widow* (1679), the fourth act of which is laid in a theatre and gives a lively picture of the inside of a Restoration playhouse.

April 16, 1669. But here I did meet with Shadwell, the poet, who, to my great wonder, do tell me that my Lord of [Orrery] did write this play.[2] . . . This do trouble me, for it is a mean thing, and so he says.

[2] Guzman.

CHAPTER X

THE AUDIENCES

CHAPTER X

THE AUDIENCES

Dress

May 8, 1663. The play[1] being done, we home by water, having been a little ashamed that my wife and woman were in such a pickle, all the ladies being finer and better dressed in the pitt than they used, I think, to be.

June 12, 1663. Here[2] I saw my Lord Falconbridge, and his Lady, my Lady Mary Cromwell, who looks as well as I have known her, and well clad; but when the House began to fill she put on her vizard,[3] and so kept it on all the play; which of late is become a great fashion among the ladies, which hides their whole face. So to the Exchange, to buy things with my wife; among others, a vizard for herself.

[1] *The Humourous Lieutenant* at the new Theatre Royal in Drury Lane.

[2] At the King's theatre.

[3] This fashion had unfortunate consequences; witness the following reference in James Wright's *Historia Histrionica,* 1699, (in Dodsley's *Old English Plays,* Hazlitt ed., XV, 409): "Whereas of late the Play-houses are so extreamely pestered with Vizard-masks and their Trade (occasioning continual Quarrels and Abuses) that many . . . shun the Theater as they would a House of Scandal.

February 18, 1666-67. And one of the ladies would and did sit with her mask on, all the play, and, being exceedingly witty as ever I heard a woman, did talk most pleasantly with him [Sir Charles Sedley].

December 12, 1667. To the Duke of York's house, and saw "The Tempest." . . . Here I saw a French lady in the pit, with a tunique, just like one of ours, only a handkercher about her neck; but this fashion for a woman did not look decent.

Prominent Spectators

April 20, 1661. To the Cockpitt [Whitehall], and there by the favour of one Mr. Bowman, he and I got in and there saw the King and the Duke of York and his Duchess (which is a plain woman, and like her mother, my Lady Chancellor). And so saw "The Humersome Lieutenant" acted before the King, but not very well done. But my pleasure was great to see the manner of it, and so many great beauties, but above all Mrs. Palmer,[1] with whom the King do discover a great deal of familiarity.

August 17, 1661. The Queen of Bohemia[2] was here brought by my Lord Craven.

[1] Barbara Villiers (1640-1709), who married Roger Palmer in 1659. The latter was created Earl of Castlemaine in 1661. His wife, mistress of Charles II, later bore the titles of Baroness Nonsuch, Countess of Southampton, and Duchess of Cleveland.

[2] At the Duke's playhouse. She was Elizabeth, daughter of James I, widow of Frederic, Elector Palatine.

November 17, 1662. At Whitehall by appointment, Mr. Creed carried my wife and I to the Cockpitt, and we had excellent places, and saw the King, Queen,[3] Duke of Monmouth,[4] his son, and my Lady Castlemaine, and all the fine ladies.

February 12, 1666-67. This done, T. Killigrew and I to talk, and he tells me how the audience at his house is not above half so much as it used to be before the late fire.[5] . . . Then, the Queen seldom and the King never would come; now, not the King only for state, but all civil people do think they may come as well as any . . . He tells me plainly that the City audience was as good as the Court, but now they are most gone.

July 22, 1667. Creed tells me of the fray between the Duke of Buckingham at the Duke's playhouse the last Saturday . . . and Henry Killigrew, whom the Duke of Buckingham did soundly beat and take away his sword, and make a fool of, till the fellow prayed him to spare his life.

August 12, 1667. Here[6] was many fine ladies— among others, the German Baron, with his lady, who is envoyé from the Emperour, and their fine daughter.

February 6, 1667-68. I to the Duke of York's playhouse; where a new play of Etherige's, called

[3] Katherine of Braganza (1638-1705), who had married Charles II, May 21, 1662.

[4] James Crofts (1649-1685), son of Charles II by Lucy Waters, created Duke of Monmouth February 4, 1662-1663, and Duke of Buccleuch in 1673.

[5] The great fire of 1666.

[6] At the King's theatre where *Brennoralt* was being given.

"She Would if She Could." . . . The King was there. . . . And among the rest, here was the Duke of Buckingham to-day openly sat in the pit; and there I found him[7] with my Lord Buckhurst, and Sidly, and Etherige, the poet.

December 21, 1668. Thence to the Duke's play-house, and saw "Macbeth." The King and Court there; and we sat just under them and my Lady Castlemayne, and close to the woman that comes into the pit a kind of loose gossip, that pretends to be like her, and is so, something. . . . The King and Duke of York minded me, and smiled upon me, at the handsome woman near me: but it vexed me to see Moll Davis,[8] in the box over the King's and my Lady Castlemayne's head, look down upon the King, and he up to her; and so did my lady Castlemayne once, to see who it was, but when she saw her, she looked fire.

Manners

January 28, 1660-61.   And here[1] I sitting behind in a dark place, a lady spit backward upon me by a

[7] George Villiers, Duke of Buckingham—who had been recently accused of high treason—Charles Sackville (Lord Buckhurst) Sir Charles Sedley, and Sir George Etherege, the dramatist.

[8] Mary Davis, the actress who had left the Duke's company to become mistress to the King.

[1] At the King's theatre during a performance of *The Lost Lady.*

mistake,[2] not seeing me, but after seeing her to be a very pretty lady, I was not troubled at it at all.

October 2, 1662.   Into one of the boxes next the King's,[3] but so as I could not see the King or Queene, but many of the fine ladies, who yet are really not so handsome generally as I used to take them to be, but that they are finely dressed. . . . The company that came in with me into the box, were all Frenchmen that could speak no English, but Lord! what sport they made to ask a pretty lady that they got among them that understood both French and English to make her tell them what the actors said.

January 5, 1662-63.   To the Cockpitt [Whitehall], where we saw "Claracilla." . . . (Neither the King nor Queen were there, but only the Duke and Duchess, who did show some impertinent and, methought, unnatural dalliances there, before the whole world, such as kissing, and leaning upon one another.)

February 18, 1666-67.   To the King's house to "The Mayd's Tragedy"; but vexed all the while with two talking ladies and Sir Charles Sedley, yet pleased to hear their discourse, he being a stranger.   And one of the ladies would and did sit with her mask on, all the play, and, being exceedingly witty as ever I heard woman, did talk most pleasantly with him; but was,

[2] For further information on the manners and customs in the Restoration theatre, see Doran's *Annals of the English Stage,* Lowe ed., Vol. I, Chapter XII (*Audiences of the Seventeenth Century*).

[3] At *The Cardinal* at the Cockpit.

I believe, a virtuous woman, and of quality. He
would fain know who she was, but she would not tell;
yet did give him many pleasant hints of her knowledge of him, by that means setting his brains at work
to find out who she was, and did give him leave to
use all means to find out who she was but pulling
off her mask. He was mighty witty, and she also
making sport of him very inoffensively, that a more
pleasant recontre I never heard. By that means lost
the pleasure of the play wholly, to which now and
then Sir Charles Sedley's exceptions against both
words and pronouncing were very pretty.

August 12, 1667. All alone to the King's playhouse, and there did happen to sit just before Mrs.
Pierce, and Mrs. Knepp, who pulled me by the hair;
and so I addressed myself to them, and talked to them
all the intervals of the play, and did give them fruit.

February 6, 1667-68. I to the Duke of York's
playhouse; where a new play of Etherige's called
"She Would if she Could," and though I was there
by two o'clock, there was 1000 people put back that
could not have room in the pit. . . . The play being
done, I into the pit to look [for] my wife, and it being
dark and raining, I to look my wife out but could not
find her; and so staid going between the two doors
and through the pit an hour and a half, I think, after
the play was done; the people staying there till the
rain was over, and to talk with one another.

Refreshments

March 26, 1668.   And there[1] I sat it costing me
8*s.* upon them in oranges at 6*d.*[2] a-piece.

April 15, 1668.   Saw "The Maid's Tragedy,"[3] a
good play . . . play and oranges 2*s.*6*d.*

April 14, 1668.   To a play, "Love's Cruelty." . . .
Play part 2*s.* Oranges 1*s.*

April 17, 1668.   Knepp . . . come after her song
in the clouds[4] to me in the pit, and there oranges 2*s.*

May 11, 1668.   But there[5] happened one thing
which vexed me, which is, that the orange-woman did
come in the pit, and challenge me for twelve oranges,
which she delivered by my order at a late play, at
night, to give to some ladies in a box, which was
wholly untrue, but yet she swore it to be true. But,
however, I did deny it, and did not pay her; but for
quiet did buy 4*s.* worth of oranges of her, at 6*d.*
a-piece.

[1] At the King's theatre.

[2] This was the usual price of oranges as instanced in this line
from the prologue to Aphra Behn's *Young King* (1698):

"Half-Crown my Play, Sixpence my Orange Cost."

[3] At the King's theatre.

[4] In *The Surprisal.*

[5] At the Duke's theatre. The following statement is cited by
P. Cunningham (*The Story of Nell Gwyn,* Wheatley ed., pp. 22-
23) from *The Young Gallant's Academy* (1674): "The next
step is to give a turn to the China orange wench, and give her
her own rate for her oranges (for 'tis below a gentleman to stand
haggling like a citizen's wife), and then to present the fairest
to the next vizard-mask."

Orange Moll

August 29, 1666. Found Sir W. Pen talking to Orange Moll,[1] of the King's house, who, to our great comfort, told us that they begun to act on the 18th of this month.

August 22, 1667. Knipp sent by Moll to desire to speak to me after the play.

August 26, 1667. Sir W. Pen and I had a great deal of discourse with Moll; who tells us that Nell [Gwyn] is already left by my Lord Buckhurst.

November 2, 1667. A gentleman of good habit, sitting just before us, eating of some fruit in the midst of the play, did drop down as dead, being choked; but with much ado Orange Moll did thrust her finger down his throat, and brought him to life again.

December 30, 1667. In the first act ["Love's Cruelty"] Orange Moll[2] come to me, with one of our porters by my house, to tell me that Mrs. Pierce and Knepp did dine at my house to-day, and that I was desired to come home. So I went out presently, and by coach home, and they were just gone away; so . . . to the King's playhouse again, and come in in the

---

[1] The head "orange-woman" was generally so-called. The orange-women stood during the play in the front of the pit with their backs to stage; before the play and between the acts they went about crying "Oranges! will you have any oranges?"— (Shadwell's *A True Widow*, 1679, Act IV, Sc. I) and selling their wares at sixpence apiece. The men about town "broke jests" and gossiped with them in Restoration fashion, and used them as messengers.

[2] This was perhaps the head orange-woman of the rival theatre, the Duke's house. "Orange Moll" belonged to the King's theatre.

fourth act. . . . But the jest is, that here telling Moll how I lost my journey, she told me that Mrs. Knepp was in the house, and so shews her to me, and I went to her and sat out the play.

PART THREE

CHAPTER XI
THE THEATRES

CHAPTER XI

THE THEATRES

Blackfriars

January 29, 1660-61. Went to Blackfryers[1] (the first time I was ever there since plays begun), and there . . . I saw three acts of "The Mayd in ye Mill" acted to my great content.

October 19, 1668. To the Duke of York's playhouse; and there saw, the first time acted "The Queene of Arragon," an old Blackfriar's play.[2]

[1] Probably to a theatre in what was known as Cobham House, which stood in Water Lane, Blackfriars, on the site of Apothecaries' Hall before the Great Fire. Downes (*Roscius Anglicanus,* p. 20) states that D'Avenant's company acted for a time at Apothecaries' Hall before moving into the new "Opera" in Lincoln's Inn Fields in 1662. It has, however, been pointed out by Joseph Knight in his edition of *Roscius Anglicanus* (Preface, pp. XXIV-XXV) that Apothecaries' Hall was not built until after the Fire—until 1670, in fact. Its site had been occupied up to that time by Cobham House. "To this," he concludes, "which seems to have been devoted to the same purposes as the present building, Downes assumably refers." Knight's statement would, of course, apply to this entry of Pepys, who, however, gives us to understand that D'Avenant moved into his new "Opera" as early as June, 1661.

[2] This play by William Habington had been staged at the old Blackfriars theatre of Elizabethan fame, pulled down on August 5, 1655, according to Wheatley's *London Past and Present* (I, 201).

"Chyrurgeons' Hall"

February 27, 1662-63. I walked to Chyrurgeon's Hall,[1] we being all invited thither, and promised to dine there, where we were led into the theatre.

August 29, 1668. To Chyrurgeon's-hall, where they are building it new, very fine; and there to see their theatre, which stood all the fire.

The Cockpit, Drury Lane

February 20, 1659-60. I heard Mr. Harrington, and my Lord Dorset and another Lord, talking of getting another place as the Cockpit,[1] and they did believe it would come to something.

[1] Barber-Surgeons' Hall, Monkwell Street. In *London Past and Present* (I, p. 102), Wheatley says of it: "The Theatre, 1636-1637, called by Walpole, 'one of the best of Inigo's works,' was pulled down in 1783." Pepys attended a lecture on this occasion.

[1] The Cockpit in Drury Lane had been used as a theatre as early as 1617-18. In 1658 Sir William D'Avenant's so-called "opera," *The Cruelty of the Spaniards in Peru,* was brought out here. Later a company of actors assembled at the Cockpit, at one time under the management of John Rhodes, to whom Sir Henry Herbert sent a warrant dated October 8, 1660, demanding his authority for "Erecting of said House, Into a Playhouse." (Cf. *A Collection of Ancient Documents respecting the Office of Master of the Revels,* compiled by J. O. Halliwell-Phillips, p. 26.) H. B. Baker, in *A History of the London Stage and its Famous Players* (p. IX), gives 1661 as the probable date of its destruction.

There has been great confusion between this public theatre in Drury Lane and the royal private theatre of the same name

August 18, 1660. To the Cockpitt play, the first that I have had time to see since my coming from sea, "The Loyall Subject," where one Kinaston, a boy, acted the Duke's sister.

October 11, 1660. To the Cockpit to see "The Moore of Venice," which was well done. Burt[2] acted the Moore.

October 16, 1660. To the Cockpit, where, understanding that "Wit without money" was acted, I would not stay.

October 30, 1660. In the afternoon . . . to the Cockpit all alone, and there saw . . . "The Tamer Tamed."

The Cockpit, Whitehall Palace

November 20, 1660. I found my Lord [Sandwich] in bed late, he having been with the King, Queen, and Princesse, at the Cockpit[1] all night, where . . . a play, where the King did put a great affront upon Singleton's musique.

adjoining Whitehall Palace. These four entries would seem to refer to the Drury Lane playhouse. References in the *Diary* to "the Cockpit" after November 15, 1660, appear from the context to point definitely to the Whitehall theatre.

[2] Nicholas Burt, who had been one of the prominent actors of this company as early as August 14, 1660, when his name appears in an agreement with Sir Henry Herbert, was drafted into the King's company.

[1] This was evidently the royal private theatre adjoining Whitehall Palace, as the plays at the Cockpit in Drury Lane and all other public theatres were acted in the afternoon,—the companies being therefore free to perform before the King in the

April 20, 1661. Then with my Lady [Sandwich] . . . to Whitehall. . . . That being done . . . I carried my Lady back . . . So back to the Cockpitt, and there by the favour of one Mr. Bowman, he and I got in . . . and so saw "The Humersome Lieutenant" acted before the King, but not very well done. . . . The play being done went to Mrs. Harper's and there sat and drank, it being about twelve at night.

October 2, 1662. At night by coach towards Whitehall . . . hearing that there was a play at the Cockpit . . . I do go thither, and by very great fortune, did follow four or five gentlemen who were carried to a little private door in the wall, and so crept through a narrow place and come into one of the boxes next the King's, but so as I could not see the King or Queene, but many fine ladies. . . . Here we saw "The Cardinall."

November 17, 1662. At Whitehall by appointment, Mr. Creed carried my wife and I to the Cockpitt, and . . . saw . . . "The Scornfull Lady" well performed. They had done by eleven o'clock.

December 1, 1662. To the Cockpit . . . I saw "The Valiant Cidd" . . . done by Betterton and Ianthe.

January 5, 1662-63. To the Cockpitt, where we saw "Claracilla," a poor play, done by the King's house.

evening. "The site is now occupied by the Privy Council Office." (Cf. Edgar Sheppard, *The Old Royal Palace of Whitehall*, p. 67, and also Fisher's plan at end of the volume, showing the exact location of Cockpit.)

The Court Theatre, Whitehall Palace

February 23, 1662-63. To Court, and there got good places, and saw "The Wilde Gallant," performed by the King's house, but it was ill acted. . . . But it being . . . the last play that is likely to be acted at Court before Easter, because of the Lent coming in, I was the easier content to fling away so much money.[1]

October 17, 1664. Went early home to bed, my wife not being come home from my Lady Jemimah, with whom she hath been at a play at Court to-day.

April 20, 1665. This night I am told the first play is played in White Hall noon-hall, which is now turned to a house of playing. I had a great mind, but could not go to see it.

October 29, 1666. To White Hall and into the new play-house[2] there, the first time I ever was there, and the first play I have seen since before the great plague . . . the play being "Love in a Tub," a silly play. . . . Besides, the House, though very fine, yet bad for the voice, for hearing.

December 28, 1666. To White Hall, and got my Lord Bellasses to get me into the playhouse; and

[1] "The Court theatre was so far public that persons could get in by payment" (Pepys's *Diary,* Wheatley ed., III, 48).

[2] "Charles built a new playhouse at Whitehall, to which Pepys went" (Wheatley, *London Past and Present,* III, 512). Sheppard in his *The Old Royal Palace of Whitehall* mentions no theatre there except the Cockpit, and states that the location of the "noon-hall" referred to is not known. There is a warrant appointing Henry Glover "Keeper of the Royal Theatre at Whitehall, with scenes, engines, etc." dated November 21, 1666. (Cf. *Calendar of State Papers,* 1666-67, p. 278.)

there . . . saw "Henry the Fifth" well done by the Duke's people, and in most excellent habits, all new vests, being put on but this night. But I sat so high and far off, that I missed most of the words, and sat with a wind coming into my back and neck, which did much trouble me.

November 16, 1667. To White Hall; and there got into the theater-room, and there heard both the vocall and instrumentall musick.

January 14, 1667-68. Thence by coach to Mrs. Pierce's, where my wife and Deb. is; and there they fell to discourse of the last night's work at Court, where the ladies and Duke of Monmouth and others acted "The Indian Emperour."

February 15, 1668-69. To White Hall; and there, by means of Mr. Cooling, did get into the play, the only one we have seen this winter: it was "The Five Hours' Adventure"; but I sat so far that I could not hear well, nor was there any pretty woman that I did see, but my wife, who sat in Lady Fox's pew with her.

February 22, 1668-69. To White Hall, and there did without much trouble get [the ladies] into the playhouse, there in a good place among the Ladies of Honour, and myself also sat in the pit, and there by and by come the King and Queen, and they begun "Bartholomew Fayre." But I like no play here so well as at the common playhouse; besides that, my eyes being very ill since last Sunday and this day se'n-night, with the light of the candles, I was in mighty pain to defend myself now from the light of the candles.

The Duke's Playhouse ("The Opera"), Lincoln's Inn Fields

July 2, 1661. To Sir William Davenant's Opera; this being the fourth day that it hath begun,[1] and the first that I have seen it. . . . And by the breaking of a board over our heads, we had a great deal of dust fell into the ladies' necks and the men's hair, which made good sport. The King being come, the scene opened; which indeed is very fine and magnificent.

August 15, 1661. To the Opera which begins again to-day with "The Witts" never yet acted with

---

[1] In spite of the fact that Downes (*Roscius Anglicanus*, p. 20) gives the spring of 1662 as the date of the opening of D'Avenant's theatre in Lincoln's Inn Fields, and that Maidment and Logan (*The Dramatic Works of Sir William D'Avenant*, III, 245) state that this performance of *The Siege of Rhodes* "appears from Pepys" to have taken place at Salisbury Court, this evidence to the contrary would seem to be weighty, if not final. It will be noted that Pepys refers again on November 4, 1661, to the removal of the Duke's company from Salisbury Court. In the "Articles of Agreement" between D'Avenant and his company, headed by Betterton and Harris, dated November 5, 1660 (in J. O. Halliwell-Phillipps's *A Collection of Ancient Documents respecting the Office of the Master of the Revels*, pp. 27-31), several interesting stipulations with regard to the new theatre are made: D'Avenant is to nominate "a Consort of Musiciens" "not exceeding the rate of 30s. the day"; provision is made for the "making of frames for Scenes," as well as for scenes, properties, and costumes; seven of the fifteen shares of the "receipts" are to go to D'Avenant "to mainteine all the Women"; and admission is to be by "Ballatine or tickettes."

scenes; . . . a most excellent play and admirable scenes.

October 21, 1661. To the Opera which is now newly begun to act again, after some alteracion of their scene,[2] which do make it very much worse; but the play "Love and Honour" . . . well done.

November 4, 1661. To the Opera, where we saw "The Bondman," which of old we both did so doat on, and do still; though to both our thinking not so well acted here . . . as formerly at Salisbury-Court.

July 22, 1663. [Wotton] tells me the reason of Harris's going from Sir Wm. Davenant's house, that he grew very proud and demanded £20 for himself extraordinary, more than Betterton or any body else, upon every new play, and £10 upon every revive; which with other things Sir W. Davenant would not give him.

October 24, 1663. By the Duke of York's persuasion Harris is come again to Sir W. Davenant upon his terms that he demanded.

October 25, 1666. Mrs. Williams says, the Duke's house will now be much the better of the two, because of their women; which I was glad to hear.

March 21, 1666-67. Unexpectedly I come to see only the young men and women of the house act; they having liberty to act for their own profit on Wednesdays and Fridays this Lent, and the play [*The Marriage Night*] they did yesterday, being

[2] Downes does not mention this "alteration of their scene," but describes (*Roscius Anglicanus*, pp. 21-22) the costumes worn by the various actors in this play, which was "Richly C[l]oath'd."

Wednesday, was so well taken, that they thought fit to venture it publickly to-day.

July 22, 1667. Creed tells me of the fray between the Duke of Buckingham at the Duke's playhouse the last Saturday (and it is the first day I have heard that they have acted at either the King's or Duke's houses this month or six weeks) and Henry Killigrew.

The King's Theatre, Vere Street, Clare Market

November 20, 1660. Mr. Shepley and I to the new Play-house[1] near Lincoln's-Inn-Fields (which was formerly Gibbon's tennis-court), where the play of "Beggar's Bush" was newly begun; . . . and indeed it is the finest play-house, I believe, that ever was in England.

March 11, 1660-61. After dinner I went to the Theatre, and there saw "Love's Mistress" done by them, which I do not like in some things as well as their acting[2] in Salsbury Court

July 4, 1661. But strange to see this house, that used to be so thronged, now empty since the Opera begun; and so will continue for a while, I believe.

June 1, 1663. Walked to the New Theatre, which, since the King's players are gone to the Royal one

[1] This was the theatre, in Vere Street, occupied by the King's company, managed by Thomas Killigrew, from November 8, 1660, until May 7 (?), 1663.

[2] The Duke's company.

is this day begun to be employed by the fencers to play prizes at.[3]

April 23, 1669. My wife . . . at the New Nursery, which is set up at the house in Lincoln's Inn Fields which was formerly the King's house.

The King's Theatre, Drury Lane

September 24, 1662. Thence to Mr. Wotton, the shoemaker's, . . . and he told me . . . that the new theatre of all[1] will be ready against term.

February 6, 1662-63. Thence to Lincoln's Inn Fields, and it being too soon to go to dinner, I walked up and down, and looked upon the outside of the new theatre, now a-building in Covent Garden, which will be very fine.

May 7, 1663. This day the new Theatre Royal[2]

---

[3] According to Pepys, the King's company had removed to the theatre in Drury Lane on May 7 of this year. A similar fate overtook the Red Bull Playhouse.

[1] Evidently the theatre being built, at a cost of £1,500, for the King's company in Drury Lane.

[2] April 8, 1663, is the date generally given for the opening performance at this Drury Lane theatre on the authority of Downes (*Roscius Anglicanus,* p. 3), and an alleged playbill bearing this date reproduced in facsimile in H. B. Baker's *English Actors* (I, 37). Pepys's statement may, however, still stand. He not only asserts definitely twice that the theatre was opened on May 7, but on April 22 he saw at the "King's Theatre" *Wit without Money,* and did not comment on the playhouse as he surely would have done had it been the new one in Drury Lane. R. W. Lowe (*Thomas Betterton,* 1891 ed., pp. 100-101) calls

begins to act with scenes the Humourous Lieutenant, but I have not time to see it.

May 8, 1663. Thence to the new playhouse, but could not get in to see it. . . . Thence to my brother's, and there took up my wife and Ashwell to the Theatre Royall, being the second dáy of its being opened. The house is made with extraordinary good contrivance,[3] and yet hath some faults, as the narrowness of the passages in and out of the pitt, and the distance from the stage to the boxes, which I am confident cannot hear, but for all other things it is well, only, above all, the musique being below,[4] and most of it sounding under the very stage, there is no hearing of the bases at all, nor very well of the trebles, which sure must be mended. The play was "The Humerous Lieutenant."

attention to inconsistencies in Downes's statement that the opening was on Thursday of Easter week in 1663, April 8 not being "Thursday in Easter week" and not Thursday at all but Wednesday. He regards the playbill as a "not very astute forgery." All authorities are agreed that the play given at the opening performance was Fletcher's *The Humourous Lieutenant.*

[3] H. B. Baker, in *A History of the London Stage and its Famous Players,* p. 46, quotes the following account of the theatre written by the French traveler, Balthasar de Monconys, who visited it about two weeks later, on May 22, 1663: "Le théâtre est le plus propre et le plus bien que j'ai jamais vu, tout tapissé par le bas de bayette verte; aussi bien que toutes les loges qui en sont tapissés avec des bandes de cuir doré. Tous les bancs du parterre, où toutes les personnes de condition se mettent aussi, sont ranger en amphitheatre les uns plus hauts que les autres. Les changements de théâtre, et les machines sont fort ingenieusement inventées et executées."

[4] Up to this time the musicians had occupied a gallery.

March 19, 1665-66. After dinner we walked to the King's play-house, all in dirt, they being altering of the stage to make it wider. But God knows when they will begin to act again; but my business here was to see the inside of the stage and all the tiring-rooms and machines; and, indeed, it was a sight worthy seeing.

December 11, 1667. All agree that it [*Catiline*] cannot be well done at that house, there not being good actors enow. . . . The King gives them £500 for robes, there being, as they say, to be sixteen scarlett robes.

January 11, 1667-68. Catelin . . . for want of clothes which the King promised them, will not be acted for a good while.

May 1, 1668. To the King's playhouse, and . . . a disorder in the pit by its raining in, from the cupola at top, it being a very foul day.

September 28, 1668. Knepp's maid comes to me, to tell me that the women's day at the playhouse is to-day.[5]

The Red Bull

August 3, 1660. I could not do as I had intended, that is to return to them and go to the Red Bull Playhouse.[1]

[5] The women's benefit.

[1] The Red Bull Playhouse, in St. John's Street, was one of the pre-Restoration theatres of the poorer class. Here a company

Changling

Simpleton

S^r I Falstafe

Hostes

Clause

STAGE OF THE SO-CALLED RED BULL THEATRE

March 23, 1660-61. Then out to the Red Bull (where I had not been since plays come up again), but coming too soon I went out again. . . . At last came back again and went in, where I was led by a seaman that knew me, but is here as a servant, up to the tireing-room, where strange the confusion and disorder that there is among them in fitting themselves, especially here, where the clothes are very poor, and the actors but common fellows. At last into the pitt, where, I think there was not above ten more than myself, and not one hundred in the whole house. And the play, which is called "All's lost by Lust," poorly done; and with so much disorder, among others, that in the musique-room the boy that was to sing a song, not singing it right, his master fell about his ears and beat him so, that it put the whole house in an uprore.

October 30, 1662. Thos. Killigrew's way of getting to see plays when he was a boy. He would go to the Red Bull, and when the man cried to the boys, "Who will go and be a devil, and he shall see the play for nothing?" then he would go in and be a devil upon the stage.

May 26, 1662. To the Redd Bull, where we saw Dr. Faustus wretchedly and poorly done.

April 25, 1664. To the Red Bull, and there saw the latter part of a rude prize fought.[2]

of "old actors" was assembled as soon as Monck declared for the King in 1659; before March 23, 1660-61, when Pepys went there, the best actors had gone over to Killigrew. (Cf. H. B. Baker, *A History of the London Stage* . . . , p. 36.)

[2] That the Red Bull still further degenerated is shown by an

The Salisbury Court Theatre, Whitefriars

February 9, 1660-61.   Creed and I to Whitefriars[1] to the Play-house and saw "The Mad Lover."

February 12, 1660-61.   By water to Salsbury Court play-house, where not liking to sit, we went out again.

February 23, 1660-61.   Then by water to Whitefriars to the Play-house and there saw "The Changeling."

March 1, 1660-61.   To Whitefryars and saw "The Bondman" acted. . . . But above all that ever I saw, Betterton do the Bondman best.

March 2, 1660-61.   To Salsbury Court, where the house as full as could be; and it seems it was a new play "The Queene's Maske."

allusion in D'Avenant's *The Playhouse to be Let* (1663?).   The Player says (Act I):

> "Tell 'em the Red Bull stands empty for fencers:
> There are no tenants in it but old spiders.
> Go, bid the men of wrath allay their heat
> With prizes 'there."

[1] It is usually understood that here and elsewhere the term "Whitefriars" is used to designate the quarter so-called (between Fleet Street and the Thames, east of the Temple), in which stood the Salisbury Court theatre, rebuilt in 1660, and not to designate the old Whitefriars theatre of the pre-Restoration period.   It will be noted from a comparison of the entries for March 19 and March 26 that Pepys used the terms "Whitefriars" and "Salisbury Court" interchangeably.   D'Avenant's company, to which Betterton belonged, probably played here from November, 1660, to the time the Lincoln's Inn Fields house was

March 16, 1660-61. To Whitefriars and saw "The Spanish Curate."

March 19, 1660-61. To White-Fryars, where we saw "The Bondman" acted most excellently.

March 25, 1661. To Salisbury Court by water, and saw part of the "Queene's Maske."

March 26, 1661. To Salisbury Court, . . . and saw "The Bondman" done to admiration.

April 1, 1661. To White-Fryars and there saw part of "Rule a wife and have a wife."

April 2, 1661. To White-fryars and saw "The Little Thiefe."

April 6, 1661. To Salisbury Court and there saw "Love's Quarrell."

September 9, 1661. To Salisbury Court play house where was acted the first time " 'Tis pity Shee's a Whore," a simple play and ill acted.

The Projected Nursery for Actors, Moorfields

August 2, 1664. Thence to the King's play-house, and there saw "Bartholomew Fayre." . . . I chanced to sit by Tom Killigrew who tells me that he is setting up a Nursery;[1] that is, is going to build a house

opened, June, 1661, except for rehearsals, and performances in January, at Apothecaries' Hall (?), Blackfriars.

[1] This reference is either to the proposed "Nursery" which William Legg was granted a license to build in March of this year "For breeding players in London or Westminster under the oversight and approbation of Sir William Davenant and Thos. Killigrew" (Cf. *Calendar of State Papers,* Domestic,

in Moorefields, wherein he will have common plays acted. But four operas it shall have in the year, to act six weeks at a time; where we shall have the best scenes and machines, the best musique, and every thing as magnificent as is in Christendome; and to that end hath sent for voices and painters and other persons from Italy.

February 12, 1666-67. He [Killigrew] do intend to have some times of the year these operas to be performed at the two present theatres, since he is defeated in what he intended in Moorefields on purpose for it.

"The Nursery"

January 7, 1667-68. To the Nursery,[1] where I never was yet, and there to meet my wife, . . . but the house did not act to-day.

1663-64, p. 539), or to one planned by Killigrew for the sole benefit of the King's company in Moorfields, but, as Pepys attests, never built. It is probable that Killigrew afterwards made use of a Nursery in Hatton Garden, and later, of the old "King's theatre" in Lincoln's Inn Fields for similar purposes. The location of the various "Nurseries" is one of the still vexed questions of Restoration stage history.

[1] Either the one in Golden Lane, Barbican, ridiculed by Dryden in his *McFlecknoe*—

> "Near there a Nursery erects its head
> Where queens are formed, and future heroes bred,"

as H. B. Baker asserts (*A History of the London Stage and its Famous Players*, pp. 39-40); or the Nursery in Hatton Garden built by Captain Bedford, probably managed by Killigrew.

February 24, 1667-68. To the Nursery, where none of us ever were before; where the house is better and the musique better than we looked for, and the acting not much worse, because I expected as bad as could be: and I was not much mistaken, for it was so. However, I was pleased well to see it once. . . . Their play was a bad one, called "Jeronimo is Mad Again,"[2] a tragedy. Here was some good company by us, who did make mighty sport at the folly of their acting.

February 25, 1667-68. I took my wife and Deb. up, and to the Nursery, where I was yesterday, and there saw them act a comedy, a pastorall, "The Faythful Shepherd,"[3] having curiosity to see whether they did a comedy better than a tragedy; but they do it both alike, in the meanest manner, that I was sick of it, but only for to satisfy myself once in seeing the manner of it, but I shall see them no more, I believe.

March 7, 1667-68. One Hanes,[4] only lately come thither from the Nursery.

March 27, 1668. So up and down to the Nursery, where they did not act.

[2] Kyd's *The Spanish Tragedy, or Hieronymo is Mad Again.*

[3] A translation of Guarini's *Il Pastor Fido.*

[4] Joseph Haines, who had just joined the King's company. The author of *The Life of the Famous Comedian, Jo. Haynes, containing his Comical Exploits and Adventures both at Home and Abroad,* asserts that he had acted under Captain Bedford "whilst the playhouse in Hatton Garden lasted." "This," says Wheatley, "would seem to be the Nursery alluded to by Pepys" (Pepys's *Diary,* VII, 33 n.). And Pepys's entry for April 23, 1669, seems rather to confirm than to contradict this.

The Nursery, Lincoln's Inn Fields

April 23, 1669. [My wife] seeing a play at the New Nursery,[1] which is set up at the house in Lincoln's Inn Fields, which was formerly the King's house.

Details of the Buildings

July 2, 1661. By the breaking of a board above our heads[1] we had a great deal of dust fell into the ladies' necks and the men's hair which made good sport.

February 6, 1662-63. Thence to Lincoln's Inn Fields; . . . I walked up and down, and looked upon the outside of the new theatre,[2] now a-building, in Covent Garden.

May 8, 1663. To the Theatre Royall[3] being the second day of its being opened. The house is made

---

[1] Probably used by Killigrew after the Nursery in Hatton Garden, which gave Haines to his company, was closed or destroyed. At least, the theatre in Lincoln's Inn Fields would naturally have been used by Killigrew, as his company had previously played there.

[1] At Sir William D'Avenant's "opera," otherwise known as the Duke of York's theatre, on "the fourth day" after it had been opened.

[2] The "new Theatre in Drury Lane" was opened, according to Downes (*Roscius Anglicanus,* p. 3), on *"Thursday in Easter* Week, being the 8*th,* Day of *April* 1663, With the Humorous Lieutenant"; according to Pepys, on May 7, 1663.

[3] *The Silent Woman* at the Theatre Royal.

with extraordinary good contrivance, and yet hath some faults, as the narrowness of the passages in and out of the pitt, and the distance from the stage to the boxes, which I am confident cannot hear; but for all other things it is well, only, above all, the musique being below, and most of it sounding under the very stage, there is no hearing of the bases at all, nor very well of the trebles, which sure must be mended.

June 1, 1664. Before the play was done, it fell such a storm of hayle, that we in the middle of the pit were fain to rise; and all the house in a disorder, and so . . . out.

March 19, 1665-66. Walked to the King's play-house, all in dirt, they being altering of the stage to make it wider. But God knows when they will begin to act again;[4] but my business here was to see the inside of the stage and all the tiring-rooms and machines. . . . The machines are fine, and the paintings very pretty.

February 12, 1666-67. [T. Killigrew tells me] that the stage is now by his pains a thousand times better and more glorious than ever heretofore. Now, wax candles[5] and many of them; then, not above 3 lbs. of tallow: now all things civil, no rudeness anywhere; then, as in a bear-garden: then two or three fiddlers; now, nine or ten of the best; then, nothing

---

[4] After the plague. It was the following November before the theatres were regularly open.

[5] "At this time the stage was lighted from above, by branches or loops of candles suspended from the ceiling" (R. W. Lowe, *Thomas Betterton,* 1891 ed., p. 54).

but rushes upon the ground, and every thing else mean; and now, all otherwise.

May 1, 1668. To the King's playhouse, and there saw "The Surprizall": and a disorder in the pit by its raining in, from the cupola at top, it being a very foul day.

The Seats

January 19, 1660-61. Here[1] I was troubled to be seen by four of our office clerks, which sat in the half-crown box and I in the 1*s.* 6*d.*[2]

[1] At the King's theatre.

[2] The prices of seats in the theatre in Pepys's day, as we learn from the *Diary*, were as follows: seats in *boxes* (just above the pit), four shillings; *pit*, two shillings, six pence; *middle gallery*, eighteen pence; *upper gallery*, one shilling. Pepys often sat in the middle gallery during the earlier years of his theatre-going. It appears from this statement and also from the comment about Moll Davis (December 21, 1668), who sat "in a box over the King's and my lady Castlemayne's head," that there were boxes in the middle gallery as well as just above the pit. These upper boxes were probably situated at the centre of the middle gallery. From the Articles of Agreement, dated November 5, 1660, drawn up between Sir William D'Avenant and the members of his company headed by Betterton and Harris (in J. O. Halliwell-Phillipps, *A Collection of Ancient Documents respecting the Office of Master of the Revels,* pp. 27-31), we learn that admission to the projected theatre, later called the Duke's house, was to be "by Ballatine or tickettes soulled for all doores and boxes." D'Avenant was to appoint "three persons to receive money for said Tickettes in a room adjoining to said Theatre," while the actors had the privilege

January 31, 1660-61. To the Theatre, and there sat in the pit among the company of fine ladys, etc.; and the house was exceeding full, to see Argalus and Parthenia.

November 29, 1661. To the Theatre, but it was so full that we could hardly get any room, so he went up to one of the boxes, and I into the 18*d.* places, and there saw "Love at first sight."

December 16, 1661. To the Opera[3] . . . and it being the first time, the pay was doubled, and so to save money my wife and I went up into the gallery, and there sat and saw very well.

April 22, 1663. It[4] costing me four half-crowns for myself and company.

October 19, 1667. We were forced to go into one of the upper boxes, at 4*s.* a piece, which is the first time I ever sat in a box in my life. And in the same box come, by and by, behind me, my Lord Barkeley [of Stratton] and his lady.

December 30, 1667. Sir Philip Carteret would fain have given me my going into a play, but yet, when he come to the door, he had no money to pay for himself, I having refused to accept of it for myself, but was

of appointing two or three "watchers" of the money-taking. D'Avenant reserved to himself the nomination of "half the number of the doore keepers necessary for the receipt of the said Tickettes for doores and Boxes, the Wardrobe Keeper, barber" etc.; and he also stipulated that the theatre should maintain a private box for Thomas Killigrew, the rival manager, "sufficient to conteine six persons" who were to use it free of charge.

[3] *Cutter of Coleman Street* was being played there.

[4] *Wit without Money* at the King's theatre. There were four in the "company."

fain; and I perceive he is known there, and do run upon the score for plays,[5] which is a shame.

January 1, 1667-68.   Here[6] a mighty company of citizens, 'prentices, and others; and it makes me observe, that when I begun first to be able to bestow a play on myself, I do not remember that I saw so many by half of the ordinary 'prentices and mean people in the pit at 2*s*.6*d*. a-piece as now; I going for several years no higher than the 12*d*. and then the 18*d*. places, though I strained hard to go in them when I did: so much the vanity and prodigality of the age is to be observed in this particular.

January 6, 1667-68.   The house[7] being full, was

---

[5] There is a passage in Shadwell's *A True Widow* (1679), Act II, Sc. I, which shows how this and other customs complicated the duties of the playhouse door-keeper.   Several ladies are entering the theatre accompanied by men:

"*Door-keeper:* Pray, Sir, pay me; my Masters will make me pay it.

3 Man: Impertinent Rascal! do you ask me for money?   Take that, Sirrah!

Door-Keeper: Will you pay me, Sir?

4 Man: No I don't intend to stay.

Door-Keeper: So you say every Day, and see two or three Acts for nothing.

4 Man: I'll break your Head, you Rascal!

Door-keeper: Pray, Sir, pay me!

3 Man: Set it down; I have no silver about me; or bid my man pay you.

Theodosia: What, do Gentlemen run on Tick for Plays?

Carlos: As familiarly as with their Taylors."

[6] At *Sir Martin Mar-all* at the Duke's playhouse.

[7] The Duke's for a performance of *The Tempest*.

forced to carry them to a box, which did cost me 20*s.,* besides oranges.

January 7, 1667-68. To look for them and there by this means, for nothing, see an act in "The Schoole of Compliments" at the Duke of York's house.

March 26, 1667-68. To the Duke of York's house, to see the new play, called "The Man is the Master." . . . By and by the King come; and we sat just under him,[8] so that I durst not turn my back all the play.

May 2, 1668. To the Duke of York's playhouse, at a little past twelve, to get a good place in the pit, against the new play, and there setting a poor man to keep my place,[9] I out . . . and so back again, where I find the house quite full.

May 18, 1668. To the King's playhouse, where the doors were not then open; but presently they did open; and we in, and find many people already come in, by private ways into the pit.

February 15, 1668-69. To White Hall;—and . . . did get into the play, . . . "The Five Hours' Adventure"; but I sat so far I could not hear well, nor was there any pretty woman that I did see, but my wife, who sat in my Lady Fox's pew[10] with her.

[8] That is, in the pit, just below the King's box.

[9] It became soon after this a common custom among people of fashion to send their servants to do this office for them.

[10] Evidently a current name for a seat or box in this theatre.

CHAPTER XII
STAGE PRODUCTIONS

CHAPTER XII

STAGE PRODUCTIONS

Scenery

July 2, 1661. The scene[1] opened; which is indeed very fine and magnificent.

[1] In *The Siege of Rhodes* at the Duke's house. The scenes were designed and executed by John Webb. Of this production Downes (*Roscius Anglicanus*, p. 20) says there were "New Scenes and Decorations, being the first that e're were Introduc'd in *England*." It is interesting to compare with Pepys's statements the following comment by Richard Flecknoe in *A Short Discourse of the English Drama and Stage* (1660?), attached to *Love's Kingdom, A Pastoral Comedy* (1664): "Now for the difference betwixt our Theatres and those of former times, they were but plain and simple, with no other scenes, nor Decorations of the Stage, but onely old Tapestry, and had as good or rather better than any we have now . . . Of this curious Art [stage decoration] the Italians (this latter age) are the greatest masters, the French good proficients, and we in England only Schollars and Learners yet, having proceded no further than to bare painting, and not having arrived to the stage strewd with Rushes (with their Habits accordingly) whereas ours now for cost and ornament are arrived at the height of Magnificence. . . . For Scenes and Machines, they are no new invention, our Masks and some of our Playes in former times (though not so ordinary) having stupendious wonders of your great Ingeniers, especially not knowing yet how to place our Lights, for the more advantage and illuminating of

August 15, 1661. To . . . "The Witts," never acted yet with scenes.[2]

August 24, 1661. To the Opera, and there saw "Hamlet, Prince of Denmark," done with scenes very well.

June 13, 1663. To the Royall Theatre. . . . Here we saw "The Faithful Sheepheardesse," a most simple thing, and yet much thronged after, and often shown, but it is only for the scene's sake, which is very fine indeed and worth seeing.

March 19, 1665-66. To the King's play-house, all in dirt, they being altering of the stage. . . . The machines are, fine, and the paintings very pretty.

October 19, 1667. At the King's house, . . . forced to go into one of the upper boxes; . . . from this place the scenes do appear very fine indeed, and much better than in the pit.

December 19, 1668. A fine scene of the Senate,[3] and of a fight that ever I saw in my life.

January 7, 1668-69. To the King's playhouse and there saw "The Island Princesse," . . . and a good scene of a town on fire.

the Scenes" (Richard Flecknoe's *A Short Discourse of the English Drama and Stage* (*circa* 1660) reprinted in *The English Drama and Stage under the Tudor and Stuart Princes 1543-1664* in the *Roxburghe Library,* pp. 280-281).

[2] This was D'Avenant's second production at the "Opera."

[3] In *Catiline* at the King's theatre.

Costumes

March 23, 1660-61. To the Red Bull . . . up to the tireing-room, where strange the confusion and disorder that there is among them in fitting themselves, especially here, where the clothes are very poor.

March 8, 1663-64. The garments like Romans[1] very well. . . . But at the beginning, at the drawing up of the curtaine, there was the finest scene of the Emperor and his people about him, standing in their fixed and different postures in their Roman habitts, above all that ever I yet saw at any of the theatres.

March 19, 1665-66. But to see their clothes,[2] and the various sorts, and what a mixture of things there was; here a wooden-leg, there a ruff, here a hobbyhorse, there a crown, would make a man split himself to see with laughing; and particularly Lacy's wardrobe, and Shotrell's. But then, again, to think

---

[1] In D'Avenant's production of *Heraclius* at the Duke's house. Downes frequently praises the costuming of plays here, particularly of *The Adventures of Five Hours, The Impertinents, or The Sullen Lovers, Macbeth, Love and Honour* and *Henry V* [*Orrery's*]; for the last two he says that the King and Duke of York loaned the actors their Coronation suits. In the "Articles of Agreement" between himself and his company, D'Avenant stipulates that he shall not be obliged to provide out of the share of receipts allowed to him for the costumes "eyther Hattes, feathers, Gloves, ribbons, sworde beltes, bandes, stockinge, or shoes for any of the men Actors" (J. O. Halliwell-Phillipps, *A Collection of Ancient Documents respecting the Office of Master of the Revels*, p. 31).

[2] In the "tiring room" at the King's theatre.

how fine they show on the stage by candlelight and how poor things they are to look now too near hand, is not pleasant at all.

August 17, 1667. "Queen Elizabeth's Troubles" . . . is merely a shew, only shews the true garbe of the Queen in those days just as we see Queen Mary and Queen Elizabeth painted.

December 11, 1667. The King gives them £500 for robes,[3] there being, as they say, to be sixteen scarlett robes.

May 11, 1668. Had the pleasure to see the actors[4] in their several dresses, especially the seamen and monster which were very droll.

December 19, 1668. The least diverting[5] that ever I saw any, though most in fine clothes.

Music   MACBETH

April 19, 1667. It is one of the best plays for a stage, and variety of dancing and musique,[1] that ever I saw.

[3] For *Catiline* at the King's theatre.

[4] In *The Tempest* at the Duke's.

[5] *Catiline.*

[1] Downes states (*Roscius Anglicanus*, p. 33) that the music for D'Avenant's version of *Macbeth*, to which Pepys is here presumably referring, was written by Lock. Maidment and Logan note (*The Dramatic Works of Sir William D'Avenant*, III, 237-238) that "the music in Macbeth, of which the rude and wild excellence cannot be surpassed, has been attributed by some to Henry Purcell and not to Matthew Lock, whose productions

Music   THE TEMPEST

November 7, 1667. The most innocent play that
I ever saw; and a curious piece of musique[2] in an echo
of half sentences, the echo repeating the former half,
while the man goes on to the latter; which is mighty
pretty.

Music   THE SIEGE OF RHODES

June 28, 1660. Among other things I was pleased
that I could find out a man by his voice, whom I had
never seen before, to be one that sang behind the
curtaine formerly at Sir W. Davenant's opera.[1]

December 6, 1665. I spent the afternoon upon a
song[2] of Solyman's words to Roxalana that I have
set.

January 22, 1666-67. There come to me Darnell
the fiddler, one of the Duke's house, and brought me
a set of lessons. . . . I did give him a crowne for

otherwise are far inferior, while to Purcell's peculiar style it
bears a closer resemblance"—though the fact that Purcell was
born in 1658 would seem to conflict with this even if D'Avenant's
Macbeth should be assigned to a date as late as 1672.

[2] Evidently Ferdinand's song in Act III, Sc. 4, of the version
by Dryden and D'Avenant,—the one Pepys saw,—the music
for which was written by John Bannister.

[1] This "opera" might be either *The Siege of Rhodes* (1656) or
The Cruelty of the Spaniards in Peru (1658).

[2] The song beginning "Beauty retire," in *The Siege of Rhodes,*
Part II, Act IV, Sc. 2.

them, and did enquire after the musique[3] of "The Siege of Rhodes," which, he tells me, he can get me, which I am mighty glad of.

February 13, 1666-67. Discoursed most about plays and the Opera, where, among other vanities, Captain Cooke,[4] had the arrogance to say that he was fain to direct Sir W. Davenant in the breaking of his verses into such and such lengths, according as would be fit for musick, and how he used to swear at Davenant, and command him that way, when W. Davenant would be angry, and find fault with this or that note—but a vain coxcomb I perceive he is, though he sings and composes so well. . . . I do think, and he [Dr. Clerke] confesses, "The Siege of Rhodes" as good as ever was writ.

Music   THE VIRGIN MARTYR

February 27, 1667-68. But that which did please me beyond any thing in the whole world was the wind-musique when the angel comes down,[1] which is so

[3] The music for *The Siege of Rhodes,* in which Lock, Lawes, Cooke, and Coleman each had a hand, has unfortunately disappeared.

[4] Henry Cooke, who had been a captain in the Royal army, became prominent in music after the Restoration, and was made Master of the Children of the Chapel Royal.

[1] The reference is apparently to Sc. 1, Act V, of this play by Massinger and Dekker. Sir Frederick Bridge states that the instrument here used was evidently the flageolet. (Cf. *Samuel Pepys, Lover of Musique,* pp. 7-8.)

sweet that it ravished me, and indeed, in a word, did wrap up my soul so that it made me really sick, just as I have formerly been when in love with my wife; that neither then, nor all the evening going home, and at home, I was able to think of any thing, but remained all night transported, so as I could not believe that ever any musick hath that real command over the soul of a man as this did upon me; and makes me resolve to practice wind-musique, and to make my wife do the like.

March 2, 1667-68. To the King's house to see the "Virgin Martyr" again, which do mightily please me, but above all the musique at the coming down of the angel, which at this hearing the second time, do still commend me as nothing ever did, and the other musique is nothing to it.

Music   GENERAL REFERENCES

November 20, 1660. I found my Lord [Sandwich] in bed late, he having been with the King, Queen, and Princesse at the Cockpit all night, where . . . the King did put a great affront upon Singleton's musique,[1] he bidding them stop and bade the French musique play, which, my Lord says, do much outdo all ours.

May 8, 1663. Above all, the musique being below,[2]

[1] John Singleton (?-1686), performer on the sackbut, violin, and flute.

[2] At the recently opened Theatre Royal in Drury Lane.

and most of it sounding under the very stage, there is no hearing of the bases at all, nor very well of the trebles, which sure must be mended.

February 12, 1666-67. He[3] tells me that he hath gone several times, eight or ten times, . . . hence to Rome to hear good musique; so much he loves it, though he never did sing or play a note. That he hath endeavoured in the late King's time, and in this, to introduce good musique, but he never could do it, there never having been any musique here better than ballads. Nay, says "Hermitt poore" and "Chevy Chese"[4] was all the musique we had; and yet no ordinary fiddlers get so much money as ours do here, which speaks our rudenesse still. That he hath gathered our Italians from several Courts in Christendome, to come to make a concert for the King.

February 26, 1668-69. The emptiness of the house[5] took away our pleasure a great deal, though I liked it the better, for that I plainly discern the musick is the better by how much the house the emptier.

---

[3] Thomas Killigrew, manager of the King's theatre.

[4] The ballads referred to are—*Like hermit poor in pensive place obscure* (before 1593), music for which was written by Alfonso Ferrabosco, the younger, and published in his *Ayres* (1609); and *Chevy Chase* (1500?), printed in 1719 by Thomas Hearne in an edition of William of Newbury's *Chronicle*.

[5] The King's theatre, at which Fletcher's *The Faithful Shepherdess* was being given. Cf. p. 86 for Pepys's praise of the performance of a "French Eunuch," one of Killigrew's imported musicians in this play. Pepys also commends the singing of Gosnell, Mrs. Knepp, and Henry Harris in various plays.

Advertising

March 24, 1662. I went to see if any play was acted, and I found none upon the post,[1] it being Passion week.

July 28, 1664. Seeing "The Bondman" upon the posts, . . . I went thither.

December 25, 1666. Walked alone on foot to the Temple . . . thinking to have seen a play all alone; but there missing of any bills, concluded there was none.

March 7, 1666-67. Little Mis. Davis did dance a jig after the end of the play,[2] and there telling the next day's play.

April 20, 1667. To King's house, but there found the bill torn down and no play acted.

Theatres and Fasts

February 23, 1662-63. To Court . . . and saw "The Wilde Gallant" . . . the last play that is likely to be acted at Court before Easter because of the Lent coming in.

[1] At this time performances at the theatres were advertised in playbills displayed on the outside of the theatres and on the posts in the streets. A facsimile of the playbill for the performance of *The Mourning Bride*, February 27, 1700, is given in R. W. Lowe's *Thomas Betterton*, 1891 ed., p. 14.

[2] *The English Princess* at the Duke's house. It was customary to announce the second performance—of a play which had succeeded—at the end of the first day's performance.

March 24, 1662-63. I went to see if any play was acted, and I found none upon the post, it being Passion week.[1]

October 15, 1666. She [Lady Carteret] cries out of the vices of the Court, and how they are going to set up plays already; and how the next day after the late great fast, the Duchesse of York did give the King and the Queene a play. Nay, she told me that they have heretofore had plays at Court the very nights before the fast for the death of the late King.

March 1, 1666-67. That it were not Friday (on which in Lent there are no plays) I had carried her to a play.

March 21, 1666-67. To the Duke of York's playhouse where unexpectedly I come to see only the young men and women of the house act; they having liberty to act for their own profit on Wednesdays and Fridays this Lent.[2]

---

[1] In a letter to Lord Cornebery, from London, February 9, 1664-65, Evelyn deplores "The frequency of our theatrical pastimes during that indiction [Lent] . . . so as the ladys & the gallants come reaking from the play late on Saturday night to their Sonday devotions" (*Diary,* Wheatley ed., II, pp. 301-302).

[2] Evidently in spite of the custom, noted above, of having no plays on Fridays in Lent. Genest (I, 152) comments: "It appears from Pepys . . . that the young actors of the Duke's Company were allowed to act for their own advantage on Wednesdays and Fridays in Lent—and from the Epilogue to the Rival Kings that the young performers of the King's Theatre had a similar privilege."

BIBLIOGRAPHY

BIBLIOGRAPHY

I

THE CHIEF BRITISH PERIODICALS CONTAINING REVIEWS COMMENTING ON THE THEATRICAL MATERIAL IN LORD BRAYBROOKE'S EDITION (1825) OF *THE MEMOIRS OF SAMUEL PEPYS, ESQ.*

The Eclectic Review (July, 1825), Vol. XXIV, pp. 75-88.

The Edinburgh Review (November, 1825), Vol. XLIII, pp. 23-54. Review by Francis Jeffrey.

The Gentleman's Magazine (September, 1825), Vol. XCV, pp. 233-240.

The Ladies Magazine, or Mirror of the Belles-Lettres (July, 1825), Vol. VI, pp. 394-397.

The London Literary Gazette (June 18-August 13, 1825), Nos. 439-447.

The London Magazine (December, 1825), New Series, Vol. III, pp. 536-540.

The Monthly Repository of Theology and General Literature (August, 1825), Vol. XX, pp. 449-454.

The Museum of Foreign Literature and Science (July-December, 1825), Vol. VII, pp. 247-262 (from *The Monthly Review*); (March, 1826), New Series, Vol. I, pp. 231-242 (from *The British Critic*).

The New Monthly Magazine and Literary Journal (Part II, 1825), Vol. XIV, pp. 97-110.

The Quarterly Review (March, 1826), Vol. XXXIII, pp. 281-314.   Review by Sir Walter Scott.

The Westminster Review (October, 1825), Vol. IV, pp. 408-456.

II

EDITIONS OF PEPYS'S *DIARY*

Memoirs of Samuel Pepys, Esq., F.R.S., Secretary to the Admiralty in the Reigns of Charles II and James II, comprising his Diary from 1659 to 1669 deciphered by the Rev. John Smith, A.B., from the Original Short-hand MS. in the Pepysian Library, and a Selection from his private Correspondence.   Edited by Richard, Lord Braybrooke.   2 vols.   1825.   2d ed.   5 vols.   1828.[1] 3d ed., with additions and corrections, 5 vols.   1848-49. 4th ed., with considerable additions, 4 vols.   1853.   5th ed.   4 vols.   1854.   6th ed., with additions and improvements (*Bohn's Historical Library*), 4 vols.   1858. An illustrated reproduction of Lord Braybrooke's edition by Charles Curtis Bigelow, 4 vols.   Philadelphia. 1906.   Lord Braybrooke's edition, with a note by Richard Garnett (*Everyman's Library*), 2 vols.   London and New York.   1906.   (Several re-issues.)

Diary and Correspondence of Samuel Pepys, Esq., F.R.S. from his MS. cypher in the Pepysian Library, with a Life and Notes by Richard, Lord Braybrooke.   Deciphered with additional notes by Rev. Mynors Bright, M.A.   6 vols.   1875-79.   Limited ed.   10 vols.   New York.   1884.

---

[1] If not otherwise stated, the place of publication is London.

The Diary of Samuel Pepys, M.A., F.R.S., Transcribed from the Shorthand MS. in the Pepysian Library, Magdalene College, Cambridge, by Rev. Mynors Bright, with Lord Braybrooke's Notes. Edited with additions by Henry B. Wheatley. 8 vols. 1893-96. Vol. IX, Index. 1899. Supplementary volume, *Pepysiana or Additional Notes on the Particulars of Pepys's Life and on Some Passages in the Diary, with Appendixes.* 1899. Smaller edition in 8 vols., 1904-05 (without *Pepysiana*).

A Bicentenary (*St. Olave*) edition, a reproduction of the above, with an introduction by H. B. Wheatley. 18 vols. New York. 1903.

III

WORKS RELATING TO PEPYS AS A DRAMATIC HISTORIAN

Anonymous. *Pepys at the Play.* In *The Theatre,* April 1, 1884, Vol. III, pp. 201-206.

Bridge, Sir Frederick. *Samuel Pepys, Lover of Musique.* 1903.

Hadden, J. Cuthbert. *Samuel Pepys.* In *The Fortnightly Review,* May 1, 1903, Vol. LXXIII, pp. 911-917.

Hueffer, Francis. *Mr. Pepys the Musician.* In *Italian and Other Studies.* 1883.

Hunt, Leigh. *Dramatic Essays.* Ed. with notes and an introduction by William Archer and Robert W. Lowe. 1894.

Johnson, Charles F. *Shakespeare and his Critics.* Boston. 1909.

Lee, Sidney. *Pepys and Shakespeare.* In *Shakespeare and the Modern Stage, with other Essays.* New York. 1906.

Lounsbury, Thomas R. *Shakespeare as a Dramatic Artist.* New York and London. 1901.

Moorhouse, E. Hallam. *Samuel Pepys, Administrator, Observer, Gossip.* 1909.

Palmer, John. *The Comedy of Manners.* 1913.

Stevenson, Robert Louis. *Samuel Pepys.* In *Familiar Studies of Men and Books.* 1882.

Wheatley, Henry B. *Evelyn and Pepys.* In *The Cambridge History of English Literature*, Vol. VIII. Cambridge. 1912.

Wheatley, Henry B. *Samuel Pepys and the World he Lived In.* 1880. Several re-issues.

IV

WORKS DEALING WITH THE STAGE IN THE DECADE COVERED BY PEPYS'S *DIARY*

Adams, W. Davenport. *A Dictionary of the Drama* . . . Vol. I, A-G. 1904.

Adams, W. H. Davenport. *The Merry Monarch, or England under Charles II: Its Art, Literature, and Society.* 2 vols. 1885.

Albright, Victor E. *The Shaksperian Stage* [Chapter IV, *Some Principles of Restoration Staging*]. New York. 1909.

Arber, E. *The Term Catalogues, 1668-1709.* . . . *A Contemporary Bibliography of English Literature in the reigns of Charles II, James II, William and Mary, and Anne.* Ed., E. Arber. 3 vols. 1903-06.

Baker, H. Barton. *History of the London Stage and its Famous Players (1576-1903).* London and New York. 1904.

Beljame, Alexandre. *Le Public et les Hommes de Lettres en Angleterre au dix-huitième Siècle, 1660-1744.* 2d ed. Paris. 1897.

Besant, Sir Walter. *London in the Time of the Stuarts.* 1903.

Betterton, Thomas. *The History of the English Stage from the Restauration to the Present Time, including the Lives, Characters and Amours of the most Eminent Actors and Actresses.* 1741.

Biographia Dramatica; or, A Companion to the Playhouse. . . . Originally compiled, to the year 1764, by David Erskine Baker. . . . Continued thence to 1782, by Isaac Reed, F.A.S. And brought down to the End of November 1811 . . . by Stephen Jones. 3 vols. 1812.

Boulton, William B. *The Amusements of Old London.* 2 vols. 1901.

Brooke, C. F. Tucker. *The Tudor Drama.* Boston. 1911.

The Cambridge History of English Literature. Ed., A. W. Ward and A. R. Waller. Vol. VIII [Chapters V, VI, and VII by F. E. Schelling, Charles Whibley, and A. T. Bartholomew, respectively]. Cambridge. 1912.

Canfield, Dorothea Frances. *Corneille and Racine in England: a Study of the English Translations of the two Corneilles and Racine, with especial reference to their Presentation on the English Stage.* New York and London. 1904.

Charlanne, L. *L'Influence Française en Angleterre au dix-septième Siècle.* Paris. 1906.

Chase, L. N. *The English Heroic Play.* New York. 1903.

[Chetwood, William Rufus.] *The British Theatre, containing the Lives of the English Dramatic Poets, with an*

Account of all their Plays, together with the Lives of most of the Principal Actors, as well as Poets. To which is prefixed a Short View of the Rise and Progress of the English Stage. Dublin. 1750.

Cibber, Colley. *An Apology for the Life of Mr. Colley Cibber.* A new edition, with notes and supplement by Robert W. Lowe. 2 vols. 1889.

[Collier, John Payne.] *Punch and Judy,* accompanied by . . . an Account of its Origin, and of Puppet Plays in England. 6th ed. 1873.

Cunningham, Peter. *The Story of Nell Gwyn and the Sayings of Charles the Second.* . . . With introduction, additional notes, and a life of the author, by Henry B. Wheatley. 1903.

D'Avenant, Sir William. *The Dramatic Works of Sir William D'Avenant,* with prefatory memoir and notes [by James Maidment and W. H. Logan]. 5 vols. Edinburgh and London. 1872-74.

Davies, Thomas. *Dramatic Miscellanies: Consisting of Critical Observations on several Plays of Shakspeare . . . with Anecdotes of Dramatic Poets, Actors, &c.* 3 vols. 1784. [Vol. II dated 1783.]

Dibdin, C. *A Complete History of the English Stage.* 5 vols. 1800.

Dictionary of National Biography. Ed., Leslie Stephen and Sidney Lee. Revised ed. 22 vols. London and New York. 1908-09.

Dobson, Austin. *Miscellanies* [Chapter VIII, *Old Whitehall*]. New York. 1899.

Doran, Dr. *"Their Majesties' Servants." Annals of the English Stage from Thomas Betterton to Edmund Kean.* Edited and revised by Robert W. Lowe. 3 vols. 1888.

[Downes, John.] *Roscius Anglicanus, or, An Historical Review of the Stage, from 1660 to 1706. A Facsimile Reprint of the Rare Original of 1708.* With an historical preface by Joseph Knight. 1886.

Dryden, John. *The Works of John Dryden, illustrated with Notes, historical, critical, and explanatory, and a Life of the Author,* by Sir Walter Scott, Bart. Revised and corrected by George Saintsbury. 18 vols. Edinburgh [Vols. XV-XVIII, London]. 1882-93.

Evelyn, John. *Diary of John Evelyn, Esq., F.R.S.* . . . Edited from the original MSS. by William Bray, F.S.A. Ed., Henry B. Wheatley. 4 vols. 1906.

Fitzgerald, Percy. *A New History of the English Stage from the Restoration to the Liberty of the Theatres in Connection with the Patent Houses.* 2 vols. 1882.

Fleay, Frederick Gard. *A Biographical Chronicle of the English Drama, 1559-1642.* 2 vols. 1891.

Galt, John. *The Lives of the Players.* 2 vols. 1831.

[Genest, John.] *Some Account of the English Stage, from the Restoration in 1660 to 1830.* 10 vols. Bath. 1832.

[Halliwell-Phillipps, J. O.] *A Collection of Ancient Documents respecting the Office of the Master of the Revels, and other Papers relating to early English Theatres.* 1870.

Halliwell [-Phillipps], J. O. *A Dictionary of Old English Plays, existing either in Print or in Manuscript, from the earliest Times to the Close of the Seventeenth Century; including also Notices of Latin Plays written by English Authors during the same Period.* 1860.

Hamilton, Count Anthony. *Memoirs of the Count de Gramont, containing the Amorous History of the English Court under the Reign of Charles II.* Ed., Henry Vizetelly. 2 vols. 1889.

Hazlitt, W. C. *Collections and Notes.* 1876.

[Hazlitt, W. C.] *The English Drama and Stage under the Tudor and Stuart Princes, 1543-1664, illustrated by a Series of Documents, Treatises, and Poems.* The Roxburghe Library. 1869.

Hazlitt, W. C. *A Manual for the Collector and Amateur of Old English Plays.* Edited from the material formed by Kirkman, Langbaine, Downes, Oldys, and Halliwell-Phillipps, with extensive additions and corrections. 1892.

Ingleby, C. M. *Shakespeare's Centurie of Prayse, being Materials for a History of Opinion on Shakespeare and his Works, Culled from Writers of the first Century after his Rise.* 1874.

Kilbourne, Frederick W. *Alterations and Adaptations of Shakespeare.* Boston. 1906.

Langbaine, Gerard. *An Account of the English Dramatick Poets, or, some Observations and Remarks on the Lives and Writings, of all Those that have publish'd either Comedies, Tragedies, Tragi-Comedies, Pastorals, Masques, Interludes, Farces, or Opera's in the English tongue.* Oxford. 1691.

Langbaine, Gerard. *The Lives and Characters of the English Dramatick Poets. . . .* Improved and continued . . . by a careful hand [Charles Gildon]. [1699.]

Lowe, Robert W. *Thomas Betterton.* 2d ed. 1891. [Vol. II of *Eminent Actors* series.]

Lowe, Robert W. *A Bibliographical Account of English Theatrical Literature from the earliest Times to the present Day.* 1888.

Magnin, Charles. *Histoire des Marionettes en Europe depuis L'Antiquité jusqu'à nos Jours.* [*Livre Sixième, Les Marionettes en Angleterre.*] 2d ed. Paris. 1862.

Malone, Edmond. *Historical Account of the Rise and Progress of the English Stage and the Economy and Usages of our Ancient Theatres*. In Malone's edition of *The Plays and Poems of William Shakspeare*, Vol. I, Part II. 1790.

Mantzius, Karl. *A History of Theatrical Art, in Ancient and Modern Times*. With an introduction by William Archer. Authorized translation by Louise von Cossel. Vol. V [pp. 306-337, *The Betterton Period*]. 1909.

Molloy, J. F. *Famous Plays, with a Discourse by Way of Prologue on the Playhouses of the Restoration*. 1886.

Nettleton, George Henry. *English Drama of the Restoration and Eighteenth Century (1642-1780)*. New York. 1914.

de Neuville, Lemercier. *Histoire Anecdotique des Marionettes Modernes*. Avec une préface de Jules Claretie. Paris. 1892.

Oliver, D. E. *The English Stage: its Origins and Modern Developments: A Critical and Historical Study*. 2d ed. 1912.

Parry, C. Hubert H. *The Music of the Seventeenth Century*. In *The Oxford History of Music*, Vol. III. Oxford. 1902.

Schelling, Felix E. *Elizabethan Drama, 1558-1642*. 2 vols. Boston. 1908.

Schelling, Felix E. *English Drama*. New York. 1914. [In *The Channels of English Literature* series.]

Shadwell, T. *Works*. With a prefatory memoir by his son. 4 vols. 1720.

Sharp, R. Farquharson. *A Short History of the English Stage from its Beginnings to the Summer of the Year 1908*. London and New York. 1909.

Sheppard, Edgar. *The Old Royal Palace of Whitehall*. 1902.

Thorndike, Ashley H. *Tragedy*. Boston. 1908. [In *The Types of English Literature* series.]

Ward, Adolphus William. *A History of English Dramatic Literature to the Death of Queen Anne*. New and revised ed. 3 vols. London and New York. 1899.

Wheatley, Henry B. *London Past and Present*. 3 vols. 1891.

Wilkes, [Saul Derrick]. *A General View of the Stage*. 1759.

[Wright, James.] *Historia Histrionica: An Historical Account of the English Stage, shewing the Ancient Uses, Improvement, and Perfection of Dramatic Representations, in this Nation. In a Dialogue of Plays and Players*. 1699. Reprinted in Dodsley's *A Select Collection of Old English Plays*, ed., W. C. Hazlitt, vol. XV. 1876.

INDEX

INDEX OF NAMES AND TITLES